t :
:ns and

A Mythic Land Apart

A Mythic Land Apart

Reassessing Southerners and Their History

Edited by
John David Smith and
Thomas H. Appleton, Jr.

Contributions in American History,
Number 173

Greenwood Press
Westport, Connecticut • London

Library of Congress Cataloging-in-Publication Data

A mythic land apart : reassessing Southerners and their history / John
    David Smith and Thomas H. Appleton, Jr., editors.
        p.   cm.—(Contributions in American history, ISSN 0084–9219
 ; no. 173)
    Includes bibliographical references (p.) and index.
    ISBN 0–313–29304–X (alk. paper)
    1. Southern States—History. I. Smith, John David, 1949– .
II. Appleton, Thomas H., 1950– . III. Series.
F209.5H64 1997
975—dc20   96–27389

British Library Cataloguing in Publication Data is available.

Library of Congress Catalog Card Number: 96–27389
ISBN: 0–313–29304–X
ISSN: 0084–9219

First published in 1997

Greenwood Press, 88 Post Road West, Westport, CT 06881
An imprint of Greenwood Publishing Group, Inc.

Printed in the United States of America

The paper used in this book complies with the
Permanent Paper Standard issued by the National
Information Standards Organization (Z39.48–1984).

10 9 8 7 6 5 4 3 2 1

To
Charles Pierce Roland
and
Allie Lee Aycock Roland

Contents

Introduction

The South is "A Mythic Land Apart." More than a region, it is an idea, an abstraction, and to some—an obsession. Since the colonial period, the South has been both connected to and distanced from the rest of North America. Its settlement pattern, its crops, and, most significant, its commitment to racial slavery have earmarked the South as different and distinctive. As historian C. Vann Woodward has noted, its defeat in the Civil War and experiences during Reconstruction left an indelible blot on the South. Yet in the post-Vietnam world, the South seems very much "American"—increasingly like the rest of the country.

Dating back as far as the 1880s, historians and critics have defined and redefined southern history in innumerable ways. The "Nationalist" historians, the "Dunning School," the "Agrarians," the "Revisionists," the "Post-Revisionists," the Marxists, and, today, all manner of deconstructionists have tried to squeeze some contemporary meaning from the history of the South. Writers regularly interpret the region's history and culture in such varied journals and magazines as the *Journal of Southern History, Southern Review, Southern Humanities Review, Southern Living, Southern Exposure, Southern Studies,* and *Southern Cultures.* In 1979 the *Encyclopedia of Southern History* appeared, followed ten years later by the *Encyclopedia of Southern Culture.* Both within and beyond the region, there seems to be an insatiable appetite for information on the South and its people.[1]

In fact, no region in America, including New England and the West, has received as much in-depth analysis and reflection as has the American South. Insiders (native southerners) and outsiders (non-southerners, including an unusually large number of northern and European specialists on the South) agree that the Southland has a particular *Weltanschauung*, one loaded with irony, pathos, paradox, and racial and class conflict. In some universities, southern history long has reigned as a major research field. They confer doctorates in the field. Many academic publishers consider "southern studies" a veritable cottage industry. Associations and institutions sponsor regular symposia and conferences regionally, nationally, and internationally on the South's past.

A generation ago, when the South ranked as "the nation's No. 1 economic problem," sociologists dissected the region's pathologies, especially its historic race problem and poverty. Today, social scientists marvel at the "Sun Belt"—its thriving and alluring prosperity built atop longstanding anti-union sentiment, its daunting skyscrapers, its rapid transit systems, its social and racial progress. Atlanta, the region's bourgeois mecca, has numerous lesser rivals throughout the former Confederacy—Dallas, New Orleans, Miami, Nashville, Charlotte, Raleigh/Durham, and Richmond. Cable television, chain restaurants, New York department stores, malls and their accompanying outlet shops—even the *New York Times* "national edition" (printed in Georgia and flown to chain bookstores throughout the South!)—dot the southern landscape like the proverbial cotton plants of old.

Grits may remain on southern breakfast menus, but franchise bagel shops and gourmet coffeehouses, pizza parlors, and hoagie restaurants have found a welcome home in the modern South. There seems to be no limit to the adaptability of southern palates. Though scholars debate endlessly on this point, the South has become culturally homogenized—for better or worse—just like the rest of the nation. Is the once distinctive South vanishing?

For four decades Professor Charles Pierce Roland, a distinguished professor of southern history, first at Tulane University and then at the University of Kentucky, has wrestled with this question. Since his days as a graduate student at Louisiana State University under the tutelage of legendary historian Francis Butler Simkins, Roland has chronicled the ebb and flow of his native region's history and culture. No other student of the South has been more attuned to the myths, contradictions, subtleties, and nuances of the region's past than Roland. In his many books, articles, and reviews (listed in the back of this book), he has underscored continuity and distinctiveness—often accompanied by tumultuous social and economic change in the southern past. Roland's influential writings—covering the entire span of the South's history—have emphasized the role of place, localism, ecology, religion, and, especially, the power of history in constructing the idea of "the South."

Southerners of all classes and races remember, insisted Roland in an influential essay published in 1970. Like the Bourbons of the 1880s, southerners rarely forget. They maintain an uncanny historical consciousness unique among Americans. But, also like the Bourbons, Roland argued, southerners suffered from a common human failing—"historical amnesia." In their discourse, southerners frequently mention their personal or local history. It empowers them, to be sure, but it also serves to entrap them.[2]

This collection of articles on the South has been inspired by Professor Roland's careful intellectual nurturing; his insistence on exhaustive research; his unrelenting demand for clear, concise, and graceful prose; and his love of irony and dry wit. Two of the authors of this volume studied with Dr. Roland at Tulane and seven worked with him at Kentucky. Each shares his belief in southern distinctiveness. The subjects of the articles reflect Roland's broad interests in the South's often contradictory, enigmatic, ambivalent, and improbable history and culture. The articles soar widely and dig deeply into the South's historic patterns of homogeneity and heterogeneity; tolerance and intolerance; reform and extravagance; scientific innovation and educational and economic backwardness; gentility/military prowess and gratuitous violence; racial repression and racial uplift; longstanding public service and scandal; and the vital nexus between the South's myths and its realities.

Jason H. Silverman places Philip Mazzei, an Italian immigrant, into his rightful place among leading intellectuals and agriculturists of the colonial South. Though always a minority, immigrants nonetheless have added much to the warp and woof of the South's cultural fabric. Regrettably, they have received surprisingly little attention in the region's historiography. A confidant of Thomas Jefferson and other notable Founding Fathers, Mazzei advanced "conservation, expanded education . . . women's rights . . . and," according to Silverman, "arguably . . . may be considered the first historian of the new United States of America."

Thomas H. Appleton, Jr., studies the evolution of alcohol reform along Kentucky's antebellum frontier. Alcohol was a mainstay of rural life, Appleton explains. Its opponents, however, marshaled an impressive barrage of arguments to eliminate what they considered to be alcohol's across-the-board direful effects on pioneer society. Though unsuccessful during the pre-Civil War years, "temperance reformers never abandoned their faith that the evils they perceived could be eradicated." In subsequent decades they fought on and on for a "dry" Kentucky, a commonwealth known nationally, regionally, and internationally for its distinctive bourbon whiskey.

Dwayne Cox looks carefully at nineteenth-century medical education in Louisville, Kentucky, and revises previous interpretations of the significance of the city's leading medical schools. Louisville Medical Institute, Kentucky School of Medicine, Louisville Medical College, and the Hospital College of Medicine provided competent training, Cox insists, but their progress was stymied by personal, professional, and intrastate rivalries. Unwilling to judge early medical training by modern standards, Cox celebrates medical education in the "Falls City" and concludes that "southern medical education resembled the national model more than it differed from it."

Melba Porter Hay unravels the famous 1838 duel between Congressmen William J. Graves and Jonathan Cilley and its impact on Senator Henry Clay's bid for the presidency in 1844. After meticulously sorting out the key players in this incident, and pondering the influence of southern "honor," Hay concludes that Clay played no role in promoting the duel. On the other hand, the Great Compromiser did little to prevent it. She interprets the duel as symptomatic of "the increasing stridency in political debate, the loss of civility in speech and conduct" that came to dominate politics in the pre-Civil War decades.

As the war approached, sectional tension and racial violence became acute below the Mason and Dixon Line. In his essay, Donald E. Reynolds makes the important distinction between slave *insurrections* (noticeably rare) and insurrection *panics* (that erupted on occasion before and during the conflict). Reynolds looks closely at vigilante racial "justice" in Texas directed at white Republicans, abolitionists, northern Methodists, and blacks in 1859, during the 1860 presidential election, and the ensuing secession crisis. During the 1860 "slave panic," the South's "fire eaters" employed the fear of slave revolt for partisan political purposes. Reynolds emphasizes, however, "it is entirely possible that they [secessionists] had deluded themselves into believing their own propaganda." Years of proslavery, antinorthern rhetoric had left white southerners on edge—at fever pitch. They stood ready to terrorize, even lynch, blacks and white Republicans in an environment that historian Steven A. Channing has termed a "crisis of fear."

Carol Reardon frames one of Professor Roland's early articles within contemporary historiographical, tactical, and logistical perspective and explains its relevancy within the context of the cold war. In "The Generalship of Robert E. Lee" (1964), Roland argued that Lee's military legacy was complex yet timely. Looking back to two world wars (one in which he was a highly decorated combat officer), Roland remarked: "Armies of the future must be composed of semi-independent, self-contained units . . . capable of operating over great distances on a fluid battlefield, and with a minimum of control from higher headquarters."[3] Unknowingly, to be sure, Roland prefigured the military tactics of the victorious North Vietnamese. Reardon notes prudently that, viewed from the perspective of modern military history, "we can see that Roland had been correct when he asserted that the great Southern leader's [Lee's] career still held relevant lessons for modern soldiers."

John David Smith's essay on the 1900 Montgomery, Alabama, Race Conference examines themes that Roland discussed in his many books, articles, and reviews. Smith comments on the limitations of the "conference idea," common during the Progressive Era, and illumines the hypocrisy, intellectual dishonesty, and racism of southern white reformers who professed to favor improvements in race relations during the age of Jim Crow. Smith judges the highly publicized Montgomery Race Conference "a disaster." By excluding blacks as equal participants with whites in the meeting, the Race Conference quite predictably accomplished little more than to codify white supremacy—specifically, disfranchisement. "Blacks," he explains, "never were seriously considered active participants in the discourse." Relegated to second-class seating in the Jim Crow gallery, blacks, including Booker T. Washington, remained outcasts, on the periphery of the dialogue of racial change.

Richard C. Smoot's article reminds readers of Professor Roland's own fascination with, and deep understanding of, the South's politicians and its political culture. Smoot's overview of the career and influence of Kentucky Senator John Sherman Cooper reveals success, ambiguity, and paradox. In many ways Cooper symbolized the trials, triumphs, and tragedies of the modern South. According to Smoot, Cooper "was a Republican in a state where Democrats dominated two to one. He was an open-minded progressive who could become, at times, quite partisan." Many years later Cooper, a veteran of World War II and a liberator of Nazi concentration camps, "emerged as a leading dove in the U.S. Senate debate surrounding the Vietnam War." Smoot uses Cooper's life to illustrate many of the themes— public service, nationalism, internationalism, conservatism, and liberalism—that Roland employed to interpret the South since the 1950s.

Finally, Roger A. Fischer assesses the South as a distinctive region through the genre of modern film. Like his mentor, Fischer interprets the South as overcoming—in fact, triumphing over—the forces of homogenization. Much as Roland explained in his 1981 address, "The Ever-Vanishing South," Fischer argues that "the modern South has demonstrated an ability to absorb innovation without sacrificing its core identity." This, Fischer insists, is no mean achievement. His analysis of "the image of the South" in Hollywood, 1988–1991, is timely and insightful. Looking critically at "stock southern stereotypes," Fischer challenges simplistic renderings of the region in such films as Allen Parker's *Mississippi Burning* (1988). According to Fischer, this "is a fundamentally dishonest film reminiscent of the most tawdry exploitation movies inspired by the civil rights conflicts of the 1960s. . . ." Though willing to concede the accuracy of the film's renderings of Ku Klux Klan violence and intimidation, Fischer nevertheless complains that "their compression into a timespan of a few weeks in a single Mississippi community constitutes manipulative sensationalism at best." Original, interpretive, and iconoclastic, Fischer's essay faults Hollywood's writers and producers for their willingness to succumb to familiar, gratuitous stereotypes of the South and southerners. In his opinion, "It seems clear that Hollywood remains receptive to excess and eccentricity in its southerns, that in theatres if not in reality the South is destined for years to come to live on as a mythic land apart."[4]

Whether dealing, then, in representations of the South in fact or in fiction, the authors of these essays collectively owe an immense intellectual debt to their mentor, their *Doktorfater*, Professor Charles Pierce Roland. We dedicate *A Mythic Land Apart* both to him and his wife, Allie Lee Aycock Roland. She, too, has befriended all of us. On more than one occasion Mrs. Roland has succored us through the intricacies of doctoral training and postdoctoral life. The authors hope that the Rolands will see in these essays both glimpses of Professor Roland's influence upon them and their intellectual maturation. Like their professor, the authors observe in the South a certain inherent tension—"a land becoming and not a land become—a garden spot that beckons only to recede like a mirage when approached. It is America's will-o'-the-wisp Eden."[5]

The editors wish to thank several people who assisted in the preparation of this collection of essays to honor the Rolands. Allie Lee Aycock Roland and Dorothy A. Leathers provided lists of Dr. Roland's Tulane and Kentucky doctoral graduates and helped keep this book a secret. Cynthia R. Levine, Daniel J. Salemson, and Yvette M. Stillwell of North Carolina State University and Rebecca L. Lubas of Louisiana State University aided with the compilation of Dr. Roland's publications. Mary Lou Madigan and James Russell Harris of the Kentucky Historical Society and Norene Miller of North Carolina State University provided vital and most appreciated staff support. Finally, Cynthia Harris, our editor at the Greenwood Publishing Group, waited patiently for the manuscript—always with confidence, professionalism, kindness, and good cheer.

NOTES

1. There are seemingly as many assessments of the South's distinctiveness as there are southern historians. For a summary of current interpretations, see Larry J. Griffin and Don H. Doyle, eds., *The South as an American Problem* (Athens, GA, 1995).

2. Patrick Gerster and Nicholas Cords, *Myth and Southern History*, 2 vols. (Chicago, 1974), 2:183–84.

3. Roland, "The Generalship of Robert E. Lee," in Grady McWhiney, ed., *Grant, Lee, Lincoln and the Radicals: Essays on Civil War Leadership* (Evanston, IL, 1964), 68.

4. See Roland, "The Ever-Vanishing South," *Journal of Southern History*, 48 (1982): 1-20.

5. Charles P. Roland, "The South, America's Will-o'-the-Wisp Eden," *Louisiana History*, 11 (1970): 119.

1

The Immigrant Influence in the Colonial South: The Case of Philip Mazzei

Jason H. Silverman

Think of the Founding Fathers and certain names immediately leap to mind: Washington, Jefferson, Madison, Adams, Franklin, and the like. Think of prominent colonial southerners and some of the same names come to mind, as well as names such as Henry, Mason, and Lee. For most people the name Philip Mazzei is an unknown one; for a few others the name is familiar only as a footnote to the illustrious career of Thomas Jefferson. Yet Mazzei was a compelling figure of the Enlightenment and the early South, albeit a neglected one. Born in Poggio a Caiano, near Florence, Italy, on December 25, 1730, Mazzei traveled on three continents, lived in ten countries, and participated in such momentous events as the American and French revolutions, and the Polish constitutional reform of 1791.

Mazzei was a surgeon in Italy, a merchant and teacher in London, an agriculturalist and vehement Whig in Virginia, an author and diplomat in Paris, and a royal chamberlain and privy councillor in Warsaw. Beyond this, Mazzei greatly influenced the Founding Fathers on matters of political ideology, befriended and collaborated with the Virginia leaders during the Revolution, and defended their cause abroad. Despite these accomplishments he has never been accorded a prominent place in American or southern history textbooks. The story of Philip Mazzei, then, is an important and untold one in the early history of both the American republic and the colonial South.[1]

It was at the University of Florence where Mazzei studied medicine, but he left the university without ever obtaining his degree (one step ahead of the Inquisition, in fact!). Nevertheless, for a time he practiced medicine in Smyrna, Turkey. In 1755 he relocated to London as the personal agent of

Grand Duke Leopold I of Tuscany. While in London, Mazzei opened a small retail store specializing in imported foods and, as fate would have it, made the acquaintance of Benjamin Franklin. It was Franklin who introduced Mazzei to other Americans, and the Italian quickly became particularly fond of Thomas Adams, a Virginia friend of Thomas Jefferson.

It was in this friendship that Mazzei's American and southern adventure would begin. In 1771 he devised a plan to create an agricultural company dedicated to the introduction of the various European cultures to the American colonies. His plan having met with the approval of Thomas Adams and a group of other influential Virginians, Mazzei prepared to leave for the colonies with great anticipation. "I hope you will believe that I speake from my hart [sic]," he wrote Adams. "Know then, my dear Friend, that I want no courage, that I want nothing else but to be in Virginia."[2]

Handpicking experienced farmers well versed in the culture of vines and olive trees, as well as in the production of silk, Mazzei and his group set sail for America on September 2, 1773. It did not take Mazzei long to become respected in America. Indeed, through the good offices of Thomas Adams, he was offered some five thousand acres of land by the Virginia Assembly that he gratefully declined. Preferring to go beyond the mountains to find his land, Mazzei made the acquaintance of another Virginia gentleman with whom the Italian immigrant instantly became friends: Thomas Jefferson. Involved in his own farming experiments, Jefferson found Mazzei knowledgeable, articulate, and fascinating in his plans to alter the Virginia agricultural landscape.

During a tour of Monticello, Mazzei learned that an adjoining four hundred acres were virtually unused. Excited at the prospect of collaborating with Mazzei, Jefferson invited him to stay and, to persuade further, offered an additional two thousand acres. Over the next few months the land was cleared and Jefferson himself supervised the construction of the main house for Mazzei. In short order, Mazzei's estate, called Colle (or hill), rose within the shadow of Jefferson's Monticello.

The financial arrangement worked out between Jefferson and Mazzei was an elaborate plan that created a "Company or Partnership for the Purpose of raising and making Wine, Oil, agruminious Plants, and Silk." In essence, what Mazzei had unknowingly organized was the first wine company in American history and one whose descendants are very much alive and well today in the Old Dominion countryside. Supporting Mazzei's new venture were some prominent and influential Virginians, among them Lord Dunmore, George Washington, and Thomas Jefferson, each of whom invested fifty pounds sterling per share in the company. "The time is already approaching," Benjamin Latrobe would later write Mazzei, "when our vines & our Olives will spread your name & our gratitude over the great portion of our country."[3]

Indeed, the response to Mazzei's early accomplishments in the Virginia countryside was nothing short of overwhelming. Colle was put into operation in spring 1774 and soon planters from all over came to observe the Italian farmers at work. In his *Memoirs*, Mazzei noted that within eight months of his arrival in the Old Dominion he was naturalized under Virginia law as an English subject and was elected to a Committee of Twelve in Albemarle County. This committee advised the central government, was responsible for the preservation of law and order, and kept in touch with the Committees of Correspondence in other colonies. Mazzei also soon became a vestryman of St. Ann's Parish and actively immersed himself in the politics of his new home.[4]

As the colonial break with England approached, Mazzei wasted no time espousing the cause of the colonies and sounding quite like his fellow Virginians. His agricultural pursuits soon became subordinated to the exciting military and political events unfolding before him. With Jefferson, Mazzei shared his political ideas and soon the two agreed to publish "through the gazettes a periodic paper aiming to show the people how things really stood and how necessary it was to be prepared in order not to be caught by surprise in case of an attack." Mazzei's articles in this venture appeared under the pseudonym "Furioso"; others he penned under the name "Citizen of the World."[5]

Mazzei's political fortunes continued to flourish. Late in 1774 he was elected to the Virginia Committee of Correspondence, an incredible accomplishment for such a recent arrival. Writing to the *Virginia Gazette*, Mazzei implored that "All men are by nature equally free and independent. Their equality is necessary in order to set up a free government. Every man must be the equal of any other in natural rights. Class distinction has always been and will always be an effective obstacle and for a very plain reason." Furthermore, "a true republican government cannot endure except where men, from the richest to the poorest, are perfectly equal in their natural rights." The effect that Mazzei's words and ideas had upon Jefferson and the Declaration of Independence is clearly evident in this one passage alone.[6]

Not sharing the reluctance of other Americans to sever all ties with Great Britain, Mazzei performed his greatest service to the cause of American independence as a propagandist. On June 10, 1775 (before Thomas Paine's immortal words in *Common Sense*), Mazzei wrote an essay for the *Gazetta Universale*. The colonies are "united and are now so tightly bound together," wrote Mazzei, "that the whole world cannot disunite them, and if but one is touched, all of them will react." For both the Virginia and Italian gazettes Mazzei was soon writing essays that conjoined investigative journalism with the acerbic pen of the editorialist.[7]

Yet Mazzei was no mere spectator of the action. When hostilities broke out he and Jefferson quickly joined an "independent company" of militia being raised in Albemarle County to protect Hampton, Virginia, from a rumored attack by the British navy. The volunteers marched gallantly toward Hampton, but when no such attack materialized the company disbanded. Still, Hampton figured prominently in the Italian's activities. When Royal Governor Lord Dunmore sought refuge on a British man-of-war offshore, the Virginia Assembly requested that the munitions and arms which were left in place be removed to the public magazine. After Lord Dunmore refused to comply, on June 24, 1775, a group of twenty-four Virginians, including Philip Mazzei, successfully stole the arms. Indeed, Mazzei personally helped finance the clandestine operation.

Concurrent with his burgeoning political philosophy, Mazzei turned his attention to religion, joining Jefferson in working for the dismantling of the Church of England in Virginia. A religious man by nature and a Roman Catholic by birth, Mazzei remembered well being a near-victim of the Inquisition. While he maintained an affection for the Anglican Church—it being sufficiently Catholic for him to admire—it was Mazzei's experience of having lived his entire life in places where there was an established religion (Tuscany, Turkey, England, and Virginia) that motivated his desire to make all Virginia Christians equal. Affixing his name to numerous documents and petitions calling for universal religious freedom for Christians in Virginia, Mazzei joined others in describing himself as a "dissenter from the Church of England." He even took an oath revoking his allegiance to King George III as both the "temporal ruler and head of the Church of England."[8]

But it was in the realm of politics that Mazzei remained most active. By 1776 he was a formidable presence in Virginia and the South. His letters to such fellow Virginians as Patrick Henry clearly indicate his empathy with the colonial cause. Wanting very much to participate in the drafting of a constitution for the new state of Virginia, Mazzei in May 1776 penned one of his most influential pieces, titled "Instructions of the Freeholders of Albemarle County to their Delegates in Convention." "With rapture of joy," wrote Mazzei prophetically, "we see so near the happy period, when the most spirited men, now labouring under the oppression of Tyranny in other Countries, will fly to free this Land [America] to partake with us & our Posterity all those blessings, that must be the ensuing consequence of a Government founded upon such principles, as to be admired by all just & good men, & true Philosophers of all Nations and Religions." The importance of Mazzei's document was recognized almost forty years ago when Julian Boyd, editor of *The Papers of Thomas Jefferson*, commented that Jefferson's "own draft-constitution of 1783 was influenced by [the] views of the Albemarle inhabitants," though at that time it was unknown that Mazzei was the author of the "Instructions."[9]

It might have taken forty years for modern-day scholars to recognize the identity of Philip Mazzei, but to his contemporaries, Mazzei quickly established his reputation. When Virginia sought funds and supplies from abroad, Governor Patrick Henry, Jefferson, and other prominent Virginians agreed to send Mazzei as Virginia's agent to the Grand Duke of Tuscany. "[Mazzei] possesses first rate ability," wrote Jefferson to John Hancock in 1778, "[he] is pretty well acquainted with the European courts . . . is a native of Tuscany with good connections and I have seen certain proofs of the Grand Duke's personal regard for him. He has been a zealous whig from the beginning and I think he may be relied on perfectly in point of integrity." Thus, Jefferson and his Virginia colleagues considered Mazzei's knowledge of the European sovereigns and their ways as indispensable to the colonial cause.[10]

But Mazzei's mission to Europe was doomed from the start. When he arrived in Paris in November 1779, Benjamin Franklin, the minister pleni-potentiary of the Continental Congress in France, sabotaged Mazzei's efforts. While Franklin greeted Mazzei cordially, the elder statesman of Pennsylvania personally disapproved of fund-seeking missions by the separate states. Indeed, to Franklin, only Congress should enter into foreign debts since any debt contracted by an individual state would serve only to weaken the potential of creating an acceptable federal government in the colonies. Consequently, Franklin withheld Mazzei's diplomatic credentials.

While he waited for another set of papers, Mazzei championed the American cause and longed to return to the South. His letters and articles written during this time include "Why The American States Cannot Be Accused of Having Rebelled," "The Importance of Securing Trade With Virginia," and "The Justice of the American Cause." Mazzei indeed had plenty of time to write. His second set of official papers took some two years to arrive. He was convinced that Franklin was responsible for the delay since the Pennsylvanian had been entrusted to forward Mazzei's mail to him. By then, it was far too late. Failing to persuade the Grand Duke, his old friend, to offer any financial assistance, Mazzei traveled to Florence where he remained until December 1782, when he received a letter of recall from Virginia's Governor Benjamin Harrison.[11]

But Mazzei never lost faith in the nobility or the success of the American cause. In a lengthy farewell letter to Grand Duke Leopold, Mazzei wrote: "The ill-considered assertions that England will never recognize American independence, no matter what the cost, come from minds stirred up by passion or paltry politics, for it can easily be seen that such a step, however hard it may be, is equally inevitable."[12]

Writing in the third person, Mazzei described his activities as Virginia's agent overseas in a pamphlet entitled *A Representation of Mr. Mazzei's Conduct, from the time of his appointment to be Agent of the State in Europe until his return to Virginia* (1784). "He made it a point to confute with his tongue, and still more with his pen, as long as the war continued," Mazzei wrote of his own experiences, "the assertions of the Enemy, which might in any way prejudice, directly or indirectly, the American Cause."[13] In addition to writing "constantly" for newspapers in Holland and Italy, he lobbied influential persons throughout Europe on behalf of the "justice" of the American cause.[14]

Mazzei's vehement defense of the American cause did not go unnoticed. Writing to Thomas Jefferson in 1780, John Adams commented that Mazzei was "a zealous defender of our Affairs. His Variety of Languages, and his Knowledge of American affairs, gave him advantages which he did not neglect." Three years later, in a letter to Patrick Henry, Adams's enthusiasm for Mazzei had not waned. "Mr. Mazzei has uniformly discovered in Europe," wrote Adams, "an attachment and zeal for the American Honor and Interest, which would have become any Native of our Country. I wish upon his return he may find an agreeable Reception."[15]

When he returned to Virginia, Mazzei found that his business and property had suffered enormously in his absence. The vineyard was gone, and the plants, the land, and the houses were all deteriorating. Perhaps to mitigate the disappointment of his failed mission to Europe and the pain of seeing the condition of Colle, Mazzei again turned his attention to politics. In 1784 he became the primary catalyst in the creation of the Constitutional Society. Founded to encourage discussion of the significant issues before the legislature, the society could boast a membership of thirty-four, including the likes of Patrick Henry, James Madison, James Monroe, and John Marshall. The Constitutional Society became a manifestation of Mazzei's belief in the importance of ideas and the power of the written word. By their own definition, the members agreed that "The Society being persuaded, that the liberty of a people is most secure when the extent of their rights, and the measures of government concerning them are known, do declare that the purpose of this institution is to communicate by fit publications such facts and sentiments, as tend to unfold and explain the one or the other." Although the society met but a few times, its formation demonstrated the esteem in which Mazzei was held by Virginia's Founding Fathers and the degree to which he was involved in the political ferment of the postrevolutionary years.[16]

Mazzei's sojourn in Virginia, however, was short lived. By 1785, he was back in Paris, attracted perhaps by the presence of Thomas Jefferson, the new minister plenipotentiary of the United States. While it was Mazzei's hope that Jefferson could secure for him some diplomatic post or mission, he was unaware that Jefferson adamantly opposed non-natives representing the United States. Still, leaving America was not easy for Mazzei. "I am leaving," he wrote Madison, "but my heart remains [in Virginia]." Poignantly he continues,

America is my Jupiter, Virginia my Venus. When I think over what I felt on when I crossed the Potomac, I am ashamed of my weakness. I do not know what will happen when I shall lose sight of Sandy-Hook. I know well that wherever I shall be and under any circumstances I will never relent my efforts toward the welfare of my adopted country.[17]

Once in Europe, Mazzei found that he almost daily felt the need to clarify and explain the American Revolution to those Europeans suffering from what he considered to be myriad fabrications, inaccuracies, and canards. Convinced that only a complete work of his own would provide the needed information and history of the American colonies and the new American nation, Mazzei undertook the writing of his four-volume *Historical and Political Enquiries on the United States of North America* (Paris, 1788). After reviewing the founding and development of the thirteen colonies, Mazzei included chapters on law and government, the right to vote and to be a representative, and the true cause of the Revolution. The second volume consisted primarily of a discussion on the nature of government, the character of the people of the United States, administration and education, and freedom of the press and religion. The third volume included narrative on the Quakers and on the climate of the United States. The final volume contained a series of essays on the political, financial, and social conditions present in the American colonies, including emigration, slavery, Indians, and the Society of Cincinnati.

"Such have been my reflections on the influence of the American Revolution," concluded Mazzei in the fourth volume. "I do not think I have exaggerated its importance, nor that I have been carried away by the enthusiasm inspired by the noble and impressive contributions this new nation makes to the world." The manuscript, written in Italian, was translated and published in French. In 1789 it appeared in German. Interestingly, however, Mazzei's work never appeared either in Italian or English.[18]

Still, Mazzei received good reviews for his efforts. A two-part review in the February and March 1788 issues of the *Mercure de France* commented that "it is easy to recognize through the veil that shrouds the Author, an illustrious philosopher, worthy for his genius and the elevation of his character, to enlighten men, to defend their rights, and destined through the power of his thought to exert influence on the happiness of his century and posterity." In the preface to the German edition the publisher writes of Mazzei's history that "his work is distinguished in more than one favorable aspect from many others which have been published on the remarkable revolt of the Thirteen States against Great Britain. I find in it more method, more thoroughness, less empty declamation, and many more severe expressions notwithstanding more moderation, than in many other champions of the American Revolution."[19]

Having just authored a well-received history of one revolution, Mazzei soon witnessed another. Primarily an observer and reporter of the French Revolution, Mazzei, always eager to form clubs for the discussion of significant social and political issues, joined with Lafayette, Mirabeau, and La Rochefoucauld to found "The Club of 1789." Quickly, Mazzei was elected the club's secretary of foreign correspondence.

But Mazzei's reputation had spread far and wide. After reading Mazzei's history of the American Revolution, King Stanislaus of Poland invited the Italian to be his employee. Consequently, Mazzei first functioned as an unofficial agent of Poland and then became the Polish chargé d'affaires in Paris. In December 1791 Mazzei was summoned to Warsaw by the king to help improve the financial conditions of Poland. While there Mazzei authored *Reflections on the Nature of Money and Exchange*, a treatise advising the king against issuing paper money. Stanislaus was so impressed with Mazzei's reasoning he had fourteen thousand copies printed and distributed immediately. Later, the pamphlet was translated into French and ultimately an Italian version would be printed as well.[20]

Mazzei remained in Poland until the summer of 1792 when, at the age of sixty-one, he returned to Italy and established residency in Pisa. By no means, however, did he retire. Despite assuming the simple life (his friends called him Pippo Il Giardinere—Phil the Gardener), he maintained his correspondence with old friends like Jefferson, always discussing politics, commerce, treaties, and the like, and also spent time reflecting on his remarkable life by penning his *Memoirs*. Jefferson even sought Mazzei's assistance in the hiring of Italian sculptors to work on the new national capitol in Washington. To accommodate his former Virginia neighbor, Mazzei traveled to Florence and Rome and hired Giovanni Andrei and Giuseppe Franzoni to bring their Italian artistic talents to the United States. "I think myself honored by the commission you are pleased to give me, and am much obliged to the President and to you," Mazzei wrote Benjamin Latrobe, "for having procured me the opportunity of imploying [*sic*] myself in the service of my dear adopted Country, where I have never lost the hope of ending my old days."[21]

Mazzei's remaining years, though, were spent in Pisa devoted to his wife Antonia and daughter Elisabetta. When he died on March 19, 1816, at the age of eighty-six, the event did not go unnoticed in America. Newspapers in New York, Pennsylvania, and Virginia printed lengthy and complimentary obituaries. Even though he had not returned to the United States in over thirty years, Mazzei was praised and remembered. "Mazzei was a distinguished politician," wrote one Pennsylvania newspaper. "In principles he was a republican, and a confessed enemy to tyrants, both of church and state. His work on America furnishes ample proof of his adherence to the best principles in politics." A Virginia newspaper commented that Mazzei "was possessed of a great ingeniousness of character and simplicity of manners. His knowledge of mankind was extensive; and he was a profound adept in the science of human nature. Towards the United States his affections were entirely devoted; and his principal consolation in the decline of life was derived from seeing that country flourish, of which he was proud to consider himself an adopted citizen."[22]

An almost prophetic memorial came from his old friend Thomas Jefferson. "He was of solid worth," Jefferson wrote, "honest, able, zealous in sound principles moral & political, constant in friendship, and punctual in all his undertakings." The former president continued, "he was greatly esteemed in this country, and some one has inserted in our papers an account of his death, with a handsome and just eulogy of him, and a proposition to publish his life in one volume. I have no doubt but that what he has written of himself during the portion of the revolutionary period he passed with us, would furnish some good materials for our history, of which there is already a wonderful scarcity. But where this undertaker of his history is to get his materials, I know not, nor who he is."[23]

"Posterity is my child," wrote Mazzei on many occasions. And so it was. That Philip Mazzei, an Italian immigrant, could obtain the respect and acceptance into eighteenth-century Virginia society that he did was surely a tribute to his intellect and many accomplishments. His faith in, and enthusiasm toward, the American cause endeared him to many a patriot in the colonies. Disseminator of European ideas in America and transmitter of American ideas across the Atlantic, Mazzei served as a fascinating example of the transatlantic nature of the Enlightenment. Furthermore, his career is testimony to the often overlooked but nevertheless significant presence of immigrants in southern history. He either came into direct contact or corresponded with almost all of the prominent historical figures of his day, both in Europe and in America. Extremely modernist and internationally minded in his thought, Mazzei was an accomplished agriculturalist while still foreseeing the success and industrialization of America. In his many writings he advocated such progressive notions as conservation, expanded education including special education for the blind, and women's rights; he railed against the dangers of monetary inflation, and arguably he may be considered the first historian of the new United States of America. To his death he remained a close and trusted friend of America's Founding Fathers.

And yet Mazzei remains a relatively obscure figure in American history and an invisible figure in the history of the South. If he is mentioned at all in American history textbooks it is probably in reference to what has now been termed the famous "Mazzei Letter": a letter to Mazzei from Thomas Jefferson dated April 24, 1796, in which Jefferson criticized some eminent American politicians. In an unwitting breach of confidence, Mazzei translated the pertinent paragraphs and circulated it among his friends. From Italian the letter was translated into French and published in France, then retranslated into English and published in the United States. Since the United States was caught in the middle of the war between England and France at that time, Jefferson's letter, which decried what he perceived as a raging Anglomania, was used by the Federalists to attack him and his supporters for their French sympathies. Although the letter did indeed embarrass Jefferson, it did not do irrevocable damage to his friendship with, or respect for, Mazzei.[24]

Nonetheless, a significant figure in early American and southern history has basically been relegated to a footnote. In this day of renewed homage to the diverse threads in the American social fabric, we are well served to pause and remember the role and contributions to American history of an Italian immigrant to Virginia whose friends simply called him "Phil the Gardener."

NOTES

The author wishes to thank the Winthrop University Research Council for a generous grant that enabled him to purchase microform materials essential to this study.

1. Philip Mazzei has been the subject of only one English-language biographical study. None utilizes Mazzei's recently assembled papers. See Richard C. Garlick, *Philip Mazzei—Friend of Jefferson. His Life and Letters* (Baltimore, 1933).

2. Margherita Marchione, *Philip Mazzei: World Citizen (Jefferson's "Zealous Whig")* (Lanham, Md., 1994), 37. Dr. Marchione, a pioneer in the collection and publication of Mazzei's works, is also the editor of *The Comprehensive Microform Edition of Philip Mazzei's Papers, 1730–1816* (New York, 1982) (hereafter *Comprehensive Edition*). See also her collection titled *Philip Mazzei: Selected Writings and Correspondence, 1765–1816*, 3 vols. (Prato, Italy, 1983) (hereafter *Selected Writings*). Also useful is Glenn Weaver, *The Italian Presence in Colonial Virginia* (New York, 1988).

3. Marchione, *Philip Mazzei: World Citizen*, 44. See also Donald Jackson and Dorothy Twohig, eds., *The Diaries of George Washington, vol. 4: 1784–June 1786* (Charlottesville, 1978).

4. Philip Mazzei, *My Life and Wanderings*, translated by S. Eugene Scalia and edited by Margherita Marchione (Morristown, NJ, 1980), 207–8.

5. Ibid., 207.

6. *Selected Writings*, 1:68–69.

7. Marchione, *Philip Mazzei: World Citizen*, 47. See also Renato Galliani, "A Friend of the American Revolution: Philip Mazzei," *Italian Americana*, 2 (1976): 213–27.

8. Mazzei, *My Life and Wanderings*, 215–23.

9. Marchione, *Philip Mazzei: World Citizen*, 54-55. The Boyd quote is from Julian P. Boyd, ed., *The Papers of Thomas Jefferson* (Princeton, 1952), 6:284–90.

10. Boyd, *The Papers of Thomas Jefferson*, 2:225.

11. Mazzei, *My Life and Wanderings*, 246–47.

12. *Selected Writings*, 1:375–76.

13. Ibid., 414–15.

14. Philip Mazzei, *Researches on the United States*, trans. and ed. Constance D. Sherman (Charlottesville, 1976), xiii.

15. Boyd, *The Papers of Thomas Jefferson*, 3:470. See also Margherita Marchione, trans. and ed., *Philip Mazzei: Jefferson's "Zealous Whig"* (New York, 1975), 22. This latter source is a translation of volume one of Mazzei's four-volume *Historical and Political Enquiries Concerning the United States of North America*.

16. *Selected Writings*, 1:447.

17. Marchione, *Philip Mazzei: World Citizen*, 62.

18. Marchione, ed., *Mazzei: Jefferson's "Zealous Whig,"* 28.

19. Review published in *Mercure de France*, in *Comprehensive Edition*, reel 3, frame 0348; review published in *Goettingische Anzeigen* in *Comprehensive Edition*, reel 3, frame 0417.

20. Margherita Marchione, "Philip Mazzei and the Last King of Poland," *Italian Americana*, 4 (1978):185–99.

21. Marchione, *Philip Mazzei: World Citizen*, 82.

22. *Selected Writings*, 1:583.

23. Howard R. Marraro, trans., *Memoirs of the Life and Peregrinations of the Florentine Philip Mazzei, 1730–1816* (New York, 1942), xii. For a careful presentation of the complex financial dealings of Jefferson and Mazzei, see Dumas Malone, *The Sage of Monticello*, vol. 6 of *Jefferson and His Time* (Boston, 1981), 509–10.

24. The "Mazzei Letter" appears in its entirety in *Selected Writings*, 3:180–82.

2

"Moral Suasion Has Had Its Day": From Temperance to Prohibition in Antebellum Kentucky

Thomas H. Appleton, Jr.

Intoxicating liquors entered Kentucky with the earliest frontiersmen and soon became an imperative of pioneer life. From the older settlements of the Atlantic seaboard the early pioneers brought to the wilderness the custom of drinking ardent spirits as beverages. Because money was often scarce and difficult to obtain, liquor served not only as a drink but also as a medium of exchange with the Indians. Pioneer families relied on alcoholic liquors as medicine and used them as preventives and remedies. In the view of one historian, "the jug of 'bitters' was deemed as essential in the family as bread and meat, and far more so than coffee and milk."[1] In the pioneer household the distillation of liquor or brandy and the brewing of beer were chores as routine as making soap. By the time it entered the Union in 1792, Kentucky was the home of some five hundred stills. During the same decade at least one commercial brewery operated in the state.[2]

Most frontiersmen did not object to the drinking of spirits when done in moderation. In fact, the consumption of liquors was commonplace in pioneer life. The eminent religious historian William Warren Sweet believed that "practically everyone on the frontier drank liquor." "Everyone on the frontier seems to have indulged, including women and children," he concluded, "and until as late as the eighteen twenties, it was a rare thing to find a teetotaler even among the preachers."[3]

Indeed, some clergymen themselves were involved directly in the liquor traffic. The Reverend Elijah Craig is credited with having made bourbon whiskey in Georgetown, Kentucky, in 1789, while another Baptist minister, the Reverend James Garrard, had been indicted two years earlier by the

Bourbon County grand jury for retailing whiskey without a license. Among the gifts that the Reverend John Schackelford received in 1798 for preaching were thirty-six gallons of whiskey.[4] At least one church gave the traffic in liquors its tacit blessing. When questioned specifically in 1796 whether a congregation could refuse to accept into fellowship a member of a sister church solely on the grounds that he sold intoxicants, the Elkhorn Baptist Association ruled that such a denial of membership would not be justifiable.[5]

In early Kentucky churches, moral standards were often strikingly inconsistent. Though dancing was sometimes regarded as a sin for which one should be expelled from church membership, drinking in moderation or engaging in the whiskey business proved no barrier to full fellowship in the church. The clerk's book of the Bryan Station Baptist Church in the Lexington area states that in May 1795 an inquiry was made as to whether it was "consistent with true religion and the gospel of Christ" for a church member to be involved in the distillation of spirits. After much discussion the church ruled that distilling *was* consistent with Christian principles. As a result, two church members were appointed to invite one Elizabeth Smith to appear before the next congregational meeting to answer complaints that she had spoken disrespectfully of the distilling business. Three months later, this same woman was excluded from the church because she had permitted dancing in her home.[6]

Although they posed no objection to the moderate use of spirits, the early churches in Kentucky did frown on the excessive use of intoxicants. When he brought his family to settle in Kentucky in October 1783, David Rice, the so-called Father of Presbyterianism in Kentucky, was shocked to find so many Kentuckians in what he considered a quarrelsome and intemperate condition.[7] Early church records contain numerous references to offenses variously listed as "drinking to excess," "intoxication," "drunkenness," and "Drinking too much Spiritual liquor."[8] Baptist documents reveal that in frontier Kentucky "cases of discipline for drunkenness or 'drinking too much' were frequent."[9] One student of the early Baptist church in the state declared flatly that "the most frequent single cause for breach of fellowship involving disciplinary action appears to have been the uncontrolled use of alcoholic liquors."[10]

Independent congregations evaluated each allegation of drunkenness on its own merit. Sometimes the judgment rendered was harsh. In April 1801, for example, the Boone's Creek Baptist Church agreed to suspend Brother Leonard Bradley and withhold from him the privileges of the church "for drinking to excess." The Forks of Elkhorn Baptist Church reached a like verdict in 1807 when it excluded Jack, "the property of Sister Samuel," for gambling and drunkenness. Yet, at other times, a congregation dealt leniently with offenders, especially if the accused appeared contrite. In July 1803 the Mount Tabor Baptist Church heard a charge of "drinking too much" leveled against one Sister Arnett. The congregation delegated three ladies of the church to meet with the accused and bring her to the next meeting. At the August assembly the committee reported that Sister Arnett seemed to be "humble" and "very sorry for what she had done." She was then restored to full fellowship. Similarly, at a meeting of the Forks of Elkhorn Baptist Church in October 1801, a Brother Clift came forward and confessed his drunkenness, and the congregation agreed "to bear with him."[11]

The excessive use of intoxicants remained a problem throughout the antebellum period in both town and country. As early as the War of 1812, Louisville had gained a reputation among some English visitors as the home of "hard-drinking, hard-gambling rivermen."[12] Drunkenness was particularly evident in river towns, with their unique mixture of laborers, immigrants, boatmen, and prostitutes. Historian F. Garvin Davenport has observed that "it was a common occurrence for screams, curses, and the sound of breaking glass to interrupt the peaceful slumber of law abiding citizens." Holidays were especially boisterous. Townspeople of every class consumed such large amounts of liquor that the police were often hard-pressed to maintain "a semblance of peace and tranquility."[13] The early court records of Ohio County demonstrate that, although there were few criminal prosecutions, charges of drunkenness were "very numerous."[14]

The imbibing of alcoholic spirits in liberal quantities by no means was restricted to the larger cities that bordered the Kentucky and Ohio rivers. In Kentucky towns of every size, taverns and tippling houses served as centers of recreation and gossip, scenes of political rallies, and sites of lectures and exhibits. Taverns located in the various county seats were also welcome oases for the many hundreds who poured in each month on Court Day to register deeds, have petitions heard, or conduct various other types of legal business.[15]

For many, though, the serious "business" of Court Day began only after the legal transactions had been concluded. On one Court Day in Casey County, for example, after hearing the verdict rendered in a case, the men poured out of the courthouse and headed for the nearby tavern to treat and be treated.[16] In certain areas of the state, Court Day meant the setting up of tables on the sidewalk outside the village tavern, where men could play poker, sip juleps, or "take short, potent draughts from a bottle that was passed and repassed with solemn regularity."[17] One historian has written that "in some places the intake of alcoholic beverages took on many of the characteristics of an athletic competition."[18] Brawling often resulted.

These highly visible excesses called into question the doctrine of moderation. By the late 1820s many Kentuckians had lost faith in the efficacy of individual self-control and had embraced the philosophy of total abstinence. Numerous "temperance societies" sprang up across the state. Some of these groups, such as the Woodford Church Temperance Society, were established as auxiliaries of church congregations. Many were small, nonaffiliated, and autonomous. Still others were allied with the American Society for the Promotion of Temperance (or American Temperance Society), which had been founded in 1826 in Boston, Massachusetts.[19] By 1828 only one society in Kentucky had affiliated with the national organization. Within three years, however, there were at least twenty-three such societies, with approximately sixteen hundred members.[20]

The Franklin Temperance Society in Franklin County was one of the most influential of the local societies. Founded on July 4, 1829, as an auxiliary of the American Temperance Society, the organization elected Benjamin Mills its first president. In its constitution the group pronounced the use of intoxicating liquors "hurtful" and "unnecessary." Members pledged themselves not to traffic in spirits and to abstain from the use of distilled liquors, including "foreign wines," except in cases of "bodily infirmity" or religious sacrament. Further, the seventy-three signatories agreed to refrain from serving alcoholic beverages to family members or employees and to "discountenance" their use in the community.[21]

Unlike many other fledgling temperance groups, the Franklin County society survived and prospered. During its first year the organization enrolled some 290 members.[22] On July 4, 1830, delegates from four other temperance societies in Henry, Owen, and Woodford counties appeared at the first anniversary meeting of the group to urge that the Franklin Temperance Society become a state organization. After adopting a new constitution the following day, the Franklin Temperance Society assumed the title the Kentucky Temperance Society.[23]

The four other societies joined immediately as auxiliaries. By July 1831 there were at least eighteen auxiliary chapters scattered throughout the state, including those in Bourbon, Edmonson, Garrard, Logan, Mercer, Pendleton, Robertson, and Warren counties. The largest auxiliary, and indeed the largest temperance group in Kentucky, appears to have been the Fayette County Temperance Society, which boasted some 530 members.[24] A separate organization in Frankfort for free blacks "and other persons of color" contained 94 members. By April 1832 Frankfort was also the home of a Juvenile Temperance Society that had enrolled 88 children.[25]

The record book of the Columbia Temperance Society in Adair County documents both the rationale and the history of one such temperance group. Between March 15, 1837, and February 25, 1840, a total of 139 persons took the total abstinence pledge and became members of the Columbia Society. Fifty-four of the enrolled members were women; at least one was a slave. Members promised to abstain from the drinking, buying, or selling of spirituous or intoxicating liquors, "except as a medicine or Sacramentally." Any person who accepted the constitution of the group and took the pledge, it was stated, was making a public declaration of his promise to abstain totally from drinking, "upon pain of not being considered as entitled to the confidence of any person whatever." Each member had the "especial duty" to report any violations of the pledge that he might discover. The society would then either expel the offending member or determine to give him a second chance.[26]

From time to time the society was indeed called upon to consider allegations of misconduct. At a meeting of the Columbia Temperance Society in August 1837, an acknowledgment by John Richards that he had drunk ardent spirits led to his expulsion. When offered a chance to retake the pledge, Richards refused. On another occasion the following year, one member pointed an accusing finger at two fellow members. One of the men admitted he had sold intoxicants and was subsequently expelled "for Sufficient reasons." The second accused man stated he had drunk liquor "as a medicine." After the society voted to release him from the charge, he requested permission to resign. In all, some ten persons—all males—were excluded from the official rolls of the society between 1837 and 1840.[27]

Newspapers devoted to the temperance cause greatly assisted these societies in spreading the total abstinence message. Particularly influential were the *Temperance Herald of the Mississippi Valley* and the *Harbinger of the Mississippi Valley*, published at Lexington and Frankfort, respectively.[28] The two publications frequently carried editorials or other items that the societies had prepared. For example, the *Temperance Herald* in 1832 published the results of an inquiry undertaken by the Louisville Temperance Society to determine the proportion of crime and disease that could be traced to intemperance. In late 1832 the society had posed the question to a number of judges and physicians throughout Kentucky. Their published responses seemed to enhance the credibility of the dry argument. One jurist in Hopkinsville estimated that ninety-nine out of every one hundred cases of assault and battery, and perhaps as many as one-half of all slander cases, could be blamed on intemperance. A Greenville judge attributed three-fourths of assault and battery actions there to overindulgence.[29]

The mounting temperance crusade extended to the halls of the Kentucky legislature. In 1832 a nationwide campaign began to establish temperance societies in the U.S. Congress and the various state houses. Lawmakers were to be assembled not for the purpose of enacting additional legislation to restrict the liquor traffic but rather to serve as examples for their constituents.[30] At the state house in Frankfort on January 13, 1834, the Kentucky Legislative Temperance Society was born. The constitution of the group denounced the use of ardent spirits as "not only unnecessary" but "injurious" and asserted that it led to "pauperism, crime, and wretchedness." One of the best means to counter the liquor traffic, it stated, was by example. Therefore, the object of the society would be "by example and by kind moral influence, to discountenance the use of ardent spirit and wines, and the traffic in them, throughout the community." Any present or former legislator or official of the state government could become a member. The incumbent governor, John Breathitt, was selected president;

Lieutenant Governor James T. Morehead was chosen as one of the five vice-presidents.[31]

Such temperance leaders and their societies encountered fierce opposition from some quarters. The distilling industry obviously was no friend of an abstinence movement. Interestingly, church members at times also objected to temperance societies on the grounds that the signing of pledges was improper.[32] In 1839 Robert Wilkins Lucas of Bowling Green noted in his journal that he had discovered only recently there were some "who would contend that it was unchristianlike and derogatory to the christian character to become members of a temperance society." Some of his fellow Baptists, he wrote, believed they would be "lowering their moral dignity" if they united with a society that contained nonchurchmembers. Rejecting any notion that the church should "withdraw entirely from the world," Lucas exclaimed: "I doubt not that had these sticklers for Christian dignity lived in Christs [sic] day but they would have joined with the Scribes and Pharisees in condemning Him for eating with publicans and sinners." The resident of Warren County concluded that Christ had come into the world to save sinners, not the righteous.[33]

An early advocate of the temperance cause in Kentucky was the Reverend Robert J. Breckinridge. Although he was then residing in Baltimore, Breckinridge maintained close ties with his native state. The Presbyterian minister urged fellow Christians to join a temperance society. Believing it was "incompatible with Christian duty" to manufacture, sell, or use intoxicating liquors, Breckinridge declared that one of the greatest obstacles to the destruction of the liquor traffic was the support it received from "persons of respectability in society." People who professed to be Christians yet expressed hostility toward temperance groups, he said, formed "an effective stumbling-block in the way of weak Christians." Breckinridge encouraged Christians to join a temperance society at once. Christians who failed to heed the call, the minister warned, would have "just grounds to fear that they are greatly declined from the life of God in their souls." Such Christians might at the last be denied by Jesus because of their transgressions. Those who obeyed the spirit of His Son, however, would receive "the approving smile of God."[34]

The vast majority of the temperance societies founded in the late 1820s and 1830s were short-lived. Few survived the decade of the thirties. In interpreting the significance of these early temperance societies in Kentucky, one scholar has observed:

Most of them were ephemeral, and multitudes of them organized and dissolved, in a single decade. Yet they subserved important ends. Many drunkards were temporarily, and a few permanently, reformed; and the rising generation was educated to see and abhor the evils of drunkenness.[35]

Thus, despite the brevity of their existence, these temperance groups contributed greatly to the growing public awareness of the excesses of intemperance. By October 1839, for example, the General Association of Baptists in Kentucky adopted a resolution petitioning the legislature either to repeal "all laws authorizing the sale of intoxicating drinks" or to fashion other measures "best calculated to put a stop to the *crime* of intemperance."[36]

Early in the next decade the colorful Washingtonian crusade reached the commonwealth. The original Washingtonians had been unlikely allies of the temperance cause. In 1840 six friends who met frequently at Chase's Tavern in Baltimore, Maryland, to drink and gamble were converted dramatically to teetotalism. Regretting their past excesses, the men formed the Washington Temperance Society, named in honor of the nation's first president. These men pledged themselves to total abstinence from all intoxicants. Further, they proclaimed their intention of drawing fellow tipplers to the dry banner.[37]

Kentucky was among the states selected for proselytizing. In early December 1841, two reformed drunkards entered the commonwealth at Maysville to begin a statewide tour to relate the tale of their personal salvation from the clutches of John Barleycorn.[38] The revival-like emotionalism of the testimony persuaded many Kentuckians of all ages and professions to enlist in the dry army.[39] Entire communities apparently signed the pledge; even some saloonkeepers "were converted and closed their shops."[40] Washington Societies flourished for a time in Louisville and Lexington, as well as in smaller communities such as Athens in Fayette County.[41] By April 1842 an estimated thirty thousand Kentuckians had signed the total abstinence pledge.[42]

The methods and philosophy of the Washingtonian movement troubled some Kentuckians, particularly the Reverend Dr. William Louis Breckinridge, perhaps the most eloquent critic of the societies. Unlike his brother Robert, Dr. Breckinridge believed the universal moral obligation of total abstinence was "radical" and derived no countenance from the word of God. The Saviour, he asserted, had neither practiced nor preached total abstinence. After all, had He not made wine at Cana and then left each one there free to partake or not as he saw fit? Breckinridge disputed the contention of some, including his brother, that one must join a temperance society. In his view, God had created but one society on earth—the Church. "I humbly conceive," he said, "that this is the only society on earth, which it is the absolute Christian duty of all to join."[43]

William Louis Breckinridge adhered to the Biblical promise of "an immediate and thorough reform, as the only true personal reformation." When one was truly reformed, he abandoned all of his vices at once. The Washingtonians, Breckinridge alleged, stood on a "radically different" principle: they sought to correct merely one vice at a time. Washingtonians would free a man of his drink habit and only then combat his lying, cheating, and the like. Breckinridge declared: "God says, a personal reformation reaches all sins at once—and he is not reformed, who, though he drinks no more, indulges other vices." The Presbyterian clergyman also made the acute observation:

The influence of these societies sets a sort of bounty upon past intemperance. There is no one in so high repute among them as a reformed drunkard. And he no sooner takes the pledge, than he becomes a public lecturer, a teacher and enforcer of the true principles of sobriety and decency.[44]

Like most of the temperance societies of the 1820s and 1830s, the Washingtonian movement did not survive long as a distinct phase of the temperance crusade. It appears to have peaked in Kentucky in 1842 and thereafter declined. Its influence, however, was profound. Prior to the Washingtonian crusade, temperance arguments had been reasoned, factual, and based on moral and religious conviction. The zealous Washingtonians injected drama and emotionalism. As one student of the national antebellum temperance movement noted, "The most distinctive contribution of the Washingtonian movement to American temperance was the experience meeting."[45] Whereas the earlier temperance groups often had been composed of the virtuous and chaste attempting to prevent future transgressions, the Washingtonians were the recently converted endeavoring to reclaim the inebriate from a drunkard's grave.[46]

The medical profession in Kentucky also sought to eliminate the dire effects of habitual drunkenness. In December 1841 the eminent physician Dr. Daniel Drake organized the Physiological Temperance Society of the Medical Institute of Louisville (later the University of Louisville).[47] The charter asserted that the purpose of the group was to study and make known the causes and consequences of the excessive use of intoxicating drinks "and other narcotic stimulants." Members agreed to abstain from all such drinks for a period of five years.[48] Anyone violating his oath would be "obnoxious to expulsion." Within a short time some 137 students, "six more than half the class," had taken the oath. By early 1847 some 610 students and 7 officers of the institute had joined.[49]

The society investigated the widely held notion that alcoholic spirits served as preventives in warding off disease. Many Kentuckians had traditionally endowed liquors with medicinal properties. In 1819 Dr. Henry McMurtrie of Louisville, for example, advised newcomers to the city that to avoid bilious fevers they should follow a careful diet, wear flannel next to the skin, avoid early-morning air and evening dew, and imbibe moderate amounts of "sound wines" and "good malt liquor."[50]

In 1842 a committee of the Physiological Temperance Society reported, however, there was no discernible evidence that the habitual use of alcohol would fend off diseases. The group would not declare categorically there was no epidemic whatsoever in which alcoholic spirits might not act as a preventive, but it did affirm "fearlessly" that in any such epidemic the individual who had been "rigidly abstinent" to that time would be better able than a drinker to meet the crisis. The society contended that intemperance multiplied disease and shortened human life. Dr. Drake warned that intemperance "destroyed" females "more certainly and in a shorter time than males."[51]

Still another organization, the Sons of Temperance, represented a significant departure from earlier temperance groups. An offshoot of the Washingtonians, the Order of the Sons of Temperance began in September 1842 in New York City. Its sixteen founders, each of whom had been a Washingtonian, proposed three objects for themselves and the new society: "To shield us from the evils of intemperance; afford mutual assistance in the case of sickness; and elevate our characters as men."[52]

A "closed" total abstinence society, the Sons initiated new members in secret, wore regalia, issued passwords, and posted sentinels to bar intruders from meetings. The names of officers, however, were made public. The secrecy of the organization provoked residual anti-Masonic sentiment and criticism, which the Sons countered by declaring they were not so much a secret society as a society with a secret. Adhering to a rigid hierarchical organization, the National Division of the Sons of Temperance permitted "grand" and "subordinate" divisions of the order to be established on both the state and local levels.[53]

On January 21, 1846, Governor William Owsley approved and signed an act of the legislature incorporating a subordinate division of the Sons of Temperance under the title Covington Division No. 1 Sons of Temperance of the State of Ky.[54] At a meeting in Louisville on August 1 of that year, the Grand Division of the State of Kentucky was born.[55] Additional subordinate divisions quickly proliferated throughout the commonwealth.

The constitution of the group at Sharpsburg in Bath County is typical of the rules and procedures of these subordinate divisions in Kentucky. On May 12, 1847, James B. Redd, Grand Worthy Patriarch of the Grand Division of Kentucky, granted formal dispensation to Dr. Henry Ellis Guerrant and others to organize a division of the Sons at Sharpsburg.[56] Their constitution included the following injunction: "No brother shall make, buy, sell or use as a beverage, any Spirituous or Malt Liquors, Wine or Cider." Any male eighteen years of age or older possessing good moral character and not "incapacitated from earning a livelihood" was eligible to take the pledge and become a member. If a brother violated his total abstinence oath, he could be fined, reprimanded, suspended, or expelled as two-thirds of the membership determined. Should a member learn of another's transgression and fail to prefer charges within three weeks, he would be fined one dollar.[57]

While devoted chiefly to the cause of temperance, the subordinate divisions of the Sons of Temperance throughout the nation served as beneficent societies as well. The Sharpsburg group was no exception. Its constitution contained prudential features designed to protect the membership from the hardships associated with death, sickness, and unemployment. A sick or disabled brother was entitled to receive from the treasury not less than three dollars per week, provided he had not feigned illness or caused his own disability. Any member who lost his wife would be given a funeral benefit of fifteen dollars. A like amount would be presented to the family of a deceased brother.[58]

The Sons of Temperance was the largest temperance organization in antebellum Kentucky. By mid-1853 it claimed at least 146 functioning societies in the commonwealth.[59] The Sons, however, was not the only such order that prospered in the state at this time. In 1846 the Templars of Honor and Temperance established its first Kentucky temple at Louisville. The Temple of Honor there adopted rules strikingly similar to those of the various subordinate divisions of the Sons. For example, only white males eighteen years of age and older could take the membership pledge of lifelong commitment to total abstinence. Also, various benefits were accorded sick and disabled brothers. The constitution of the Louisville Temple of Honor, though, contained an additional prudential feature. If a brother found himself unemployed, he was encouraged to notify the officers of the society and specify to them the type of work he was seeking. The leadership in turn would announce the fact "in open Temple." All brothers were then enjoined to aid the unemployed Templar in his search.[60]

By the early 1850s many temperance advocates in Kentucky had begun to despair of their ultimate success. Despite a quarter-century of vigorous agitation, the specter of intemperance still haunted the commonwealth. Churches continued to be plagued by drunkenness. In 1850 four Baptist churches in northeastern Kentucky, for example, withdrew from the Greenup Association because of that body's alleged failure to expel drunkards from fellowship. The moderator of the association himself, it was charged, had often "taken too much of that bowl."[61]

In the last antebellum decade, many Kentuckians concluded that moral suasion alone could not solve the enormous problems associated with intemperance. The aid of government must be sought, not simply to regulate the liquor traffic but also to prohibit it. The manner of the temperance movement in Kentucky thus would no longer be persuasive; it would be coercive. Indeed, "temperance" would now be defined as "prohibition."

As early as 1851 Kentucky's temperance leadership began advocating statewide prohibition. The recent success of Neal Dow in securing prohibition for Maine greatly inspired Kentucky drys.[62] At its annual session in Louisville in October 1851, the Grand Division of the Sons of Temperance agreed to petition the legislature to authorize a statewide referendum on the proposed suppression of the liquor traffic.[63] This effort to secure a direct vote of the people proved to be unsuccessful. Nonetheless, Kentucky drys remained steadfast. One national official of the Sons reported in 1852 that Kentucky was among the states "buckling on their armor for the contest."[64]

Temperance reformers continued to rally and exhort. A multitude of temperance meetings took place throughout the state. On April 15, 1853, for example, a large and enthusiastic throng of Scott Countians assembled at Georgetown to endorse a statewide prohibitory law. In describing the scene for the official state temperance organ, the *Kentucky New Era*, one correspondent characterized the region as "ripe for action on the subject of Temperance" and exclaimed: "The Lord is on our side—the preachers are for us—the ladies are with us—who can resist."[65]

On April 22, 1853, the friends of temperance gathered in mass meeting at Springfield in Washington County. In his address to the group, the Reverend Dr. Robert J. Breckinridge urged the legislature to prepare and submit to the voters a proposed law that would prohibit the manufacture and sale of all intoxicating liquors, except for medical, mechanical, or sacramental purposes. If it received popular approval, the bill should become law. Though he was willing for legislators to work out the particulars, Breckinridge declared that the bill should end the retail traffic and public tippling. The measure must also "prohibit minors and slaves from all dealing in said liquors under any circumstances whatever."

Reminding his audience that elections for the state legislature would be held in August, Breckinridge encouraged each friend of temperance to make as a condition of his vote that every candidate pledge to assist in drafting and passing such a bill. If they were unable to secure this commitment from any aspirant in a district, temperance folk should advance their own candidate for the legislature. In this case, Breckinridge advised, they should nominate someone who belonged to the dominant party in the district, whether Whig or Democrat. The meeting adopted his plan of action "with loud acclaim."[66]

The *Kentucky New Era* gave ringing editorial endorsement to the so-called Springfield Platform. Editor Charles Eginton wrote that the watchword of the day must be *organize*. Each county had to be made ready for the coming battle. Even without the franchise, he stressed, Kentucky women could render great assistance to the cause by speaking eloquently of the foul injustices that drink had perpetrated on their families. The editor cautioned temperance men, however, not to be deterred by those who might protest that the temperance issue should remain out of politics. Anyone who made such a complaint, he admonished, in truth opposed the spread of temperance and was "no friend of sobriety." Eginton proclaimed: "*Now* is the time—*now* is the hour."[67]

The *Frankfort Commonwealth*, which had not heretofore been allied with the dry forces, reprinted the Springfield Platform and expressed pleasure that the "more moderate" wing of the temperance movement had taken charge. The idea of nominating distinct temperance candidates, it said, would be "suicidal." The paper suggested having each candidate for the legislature agree simply to obey the will of his constituents in voting for or against submission of a prohibitory law. County courts could then order a separate poll to be taken on the day of the August election. If a county court refused to authorize such a referendum, temperance men could question the voters outside of, but not at, the polls. The *Commonwealth* reasoned that "this course would enable every man to vote his sentiments on the question, without the least interference with his political or personal preferences among candidates." The *Kentucky New Era* promptly rejected this proposal, however, and encouraged temperance advocates not to be "seduced" by "*faint-hearted* or false friends."[68]

The two major parties viewed with alarm the entrance of the temperance forces into politics. Whig and Democratic leaders alike were suspicious of the drys' motives and feared that a separate temperance ticket on the August ballot would spell doom for their respective parties. One Democratic editor pronounced the prohibition issue a "Whig trick" to rule or ruin. He named the dry leaders, whom he said were all Whigs. At the same time, the foremost Whig editor in Kentucky, George D. Prentice of the *Louisville Journal*, regarded prohibition as a Democratic ploy. On May 3 he wrote:

> The attempt to bring the Maine Liquor Law into the politics of Kentucky is all a Locofoco device. It is a party stratagem cunningly planned and perfectly understood by the Democratic leaders. They may have a few coadjutors or tools calling themselves Whigs or neutrals, but the stratagem is of Locofoco origin, and is intended to subserve Locofoco purposes.

He declared further that temperance leaders desired "to have an espionage over the parlor, cupboard, and sideboard of private individuals."[69]

In his *Kentucky New Era* Eginton responded to the criticisms leveled by Whig and Democratic leaders. He emphasized that the temperance movement in Kentucky was bipartisan and not designed to injure either party. The editor noted that he himself had long been associated with the Whig Party and indeed had served twice as a delegate to its national convention. Despite the vehement opposition of Prentice, at least six Whig editors had come out "unflinchingly supporting" the submission of a prohibitory law. Moreover, "nearly all" of the Democratic press was willing to hold a popular vote. The agitation, he acknowledged, *was* "democratic" in that it sought to destroy the "privileged class" of whiskey sellers. Eginton concluded: "In this sense it is a Democratic movement, but in no wise is it true that the Democratic party either originated or are now carrying on this movement."[70]

Kentucky Whigs were especially concerned about the possible political consequences of the prohibition effort. Still smarting from their loss of the governorship two years earlier, some Whigs in 1853 worried that their long domination of Kentucky politics might be irreparably destroyed.[71] The Reverend Dr. Robert J. Breckinridge attempted to allay the suspicions of his fellow Whigs, many of whom had entreated him to cease the drive for prohibition. He assured them that the movement was "deep and fervent" and desired no quarrel with either party. Nevertheless, Whigs had "no alternative" but to accept the Springfield Platform. If it failed to do so, the party would "break itself to pieces." Breckinridge also maintained that it was not "casual events" that destroyed political parties, but the "incompetency" of party leadership.[72]

Temperance men throughout the commonwealth began the process of examining candidates for the state legislature. At a rally in Cadiz, residents of Trigg County learned that an announced candidate for the General Assembly in that district had denounced publicly "anything like a prohibitory law." The convention then resolved "to use all honorable means" to elect Major Matthew Mayes, a temperance advocate, instead.[73] Similarly, prohibitionists in Woodford County, who had grown tired of "the shuffling, hide-and-go-seek game pursued towards them," named Squire James Carter of Mortonsville for the legislature.[74] Whenever possible, however, drys endorsed the nominee of a major party. In Mercer County, for example, friends of temperance backed Dr. W. G. Armstrong, a Democrat, in his race against the Whig, Elijah Gabbert. In Boyle County, the temperance candidate withdrew once the Whig nominee agreed to vote for submission.[75]

The most colorful contest took shape in Harrison County. There temperance advocates persuaded Joseph M. Hawkins to announce his candidacy on a platform that endorsed submission. Almost immediately, J. T. Rickerson declared his intention to run for the legislature as an antiprohibitionist. Strongly opposed to a "Maine Law" for Kentucky, Rickerson charged that a prohibitory law would be the same "as telling a man what church he should belong to, or how often he should kiss his wife." As the dispenser of J. T. Rickerson's Hoarhound and Sarsaparilla, "a general invigorator of the human system," the Harrison Countian then trumpeted: "I flatter myself that I have contributed to the health and comfort of my fellow-citizens; and if you elect me, I will endeavor also to invigorate your political system."[76]

Prohibitionists expressed particular satisfaction with political developments in Fayette County. At its convention in Lexington on May 28, the Whig Party tapped Major M. C. Johnson and F. K. Hunt as its standard-bearers. Although they had hoped to avoid making public assurances on any matter, the two lawyers felt compelled several days later to issue a joint statement on temperance. Believing that the will of the people must rule, they agreed to work for submission in the General Assembly. Nonetheless, the pair announced forthrightly that they would most likely vote against a prohibitory measure once a popular vote was held. The temperance organ of Kentucky praised the two for having spoken "like honest men" and for allowing drys "an open field and a fair fight." Eginton declared: "The example set by Messrs. Johnson and Hunt is worthy of the consideration of the political parties in this State; and if said parties will follow it, will save much anxiety and trouble."[77]

Temperance leaders often reminded their followers that the most they should expect from a candidate for the General Assembly was his simple pledge of support for the submission effort. He was not required to subscribe to the "propriety" of a prohibitory law itself. The *Kentucky New Era* opined: "We should be proud of a candidate who grants to us our request, and at the same time in honesty and good faith, tells us he believes our proposed law will not meet our expectations."[78]

Throughout the 1853 campaign the *Louisville Journal* was the nemesis of the prohibition forces. Insisting he personally would be "perfectly willing" to see the liquor traffic halted in Kentucky, editor Prentice maintained that drys had not given adequate thought to how a prohibitory law would be executed. "If the present law is not enforced," he asked, "what reason is there to suppose that a far severer law would be enforced?" A more prudent course would be to seek more rigid enforcement of existing statutes. Prentice also warned Kentucky drys that they risked injuring their cause by thrusting it into politics as the abolitionists had done.[79]

One of the most influential journalists in Kentucky history, Prentice eloquently upheld the Whig cause in state politics.[80] As the election neared, he cautioned fellow Whigs that they might lose the legislature, not from lack of zeal or numbers but because of "divisions and dissensions upon the subject of the liquor law." He reminded his partisans that the legislators to be elected in August would choose a U.S. senator, reapportion the state into congressional districts, and, for the first time, serve for a two-year term. Prentice urged Whigs not to allow prohibition to obscure the paramount issue: whether Whiggism or Democratic "Locofocoism" would reign in the commonwealth. All eyes would be on the Kentucky contest, he explained, as the first state verdict on the acts of the national Democratic administration of President Franklin Pierce. The editor declared:

> We earnestly trust that the Whigs of Kentucky will save their State. It is enough for us to be tyrannized over and proscribed by a Locofoco Government at Washington, without being also tyrannized over and proscribed by a Locofoco Government at Frankfort.[81]

On August 1, Kentuckians went to the polls and returned a Whig majority to both houses of the General Assembly. In the Senate, Whigs would enjoy a 22-to-16 edge over the Democrats; in the House the advantage stood at 55 to 45.[82] At the same time, constituents in at least two counties had the opportunity to register their sentiment on the question of submission by means of a separate straw poll. In both counties the drys triumphed. Residents of Boyle County voted 424 in favor of submission, with 262 opposed; in Garrard County the ballot was 529 to 430.[83]

The eventual fate of prohibition in the General Assembly was not certain. Each side advanced its own interpretation of the election results. For their part, temperance forces expressed pleasure at the outcome. They pointed with particular pride to their success in Muhlenberg County, where they claimed to have elected temperance Whigs as state representative, presiding judge of the county court, and county attorney. The *Kentucky New Era* proclaimed confidently that a majority of the new legislature was committed to submission of a prohibitory law. Eginton bitterly assailed the *Louisville Journal* for having raised the specter of a Whig Party ripped asunder by the temperance issue. The editor asserted that Whigs would surely have constituted a minority of the incoming House had it not been for the Whigs who were elected from normally Democratic counties as a result of temperance agitation.[84]

Opponents of submission, on the other hand, announced that "unconditional temperance" candidates had been almost universally defeated.[85] Boasting that prohibitionists had met "with a signal rebuke," Prentice rejoiced: "We believe that but one Maine liquor law or temperance candidate is elected to the Legislature from the whole State. How he managed to get elected we don't know, but we presume that he will not give much trouble in the Legislature." Nonetheless, he warned that drys might attempt to inject the liquor issue into future contests.[86]

Subsequent events revealed Prentice to be a better prognosticator than Eginton. The General Assembly that convened in December 1853 never submitted a prohibitory law to the voters. The session concentrated on the election of a U.S. senator and the reapportionment of congressional districts.[87] Indeed, legislators gave scant consideration to prohibition. On January 26, 1854, drys presented to the General Assembly a memorial requesting a prohibitory law. The Senate received the petition and referred it to a select committee. The House, however, refused to accept the memorial, voting 45 to 42 to lay the document on the table.[88]

By October 1854 the Sons of Temperance was leading the drive to organize temperance forces into a distinct political party.[89] In issuing its call for friends to meet in convention in Louisville on December 13, the Sons proposed to debate the wisdom of nominating candidates to run in the statewide races the following year.[90] Although amicable, the delegates were deeply divided on the question. Edgar Needham of Louisville and George Robertson of Fayette County were among those who opposed naming a slate of temperance candidates. Needham preferred for drys to withhold nominations until the Whig and Democratic parties had revealed their tickets. Robertson, the president of the convention, encouraged the delegates to endorse the American, or Know-Nothing, Party.[91]

On December 14, the convention ended its spirited debate. By a vote of 31 to 18, the delegates agreed to field a temperance ticket in 1855.[92] The convention selected George W. Williams of Bourbon County, a Whig, for governor and James G. Hardy of Glasgow, a Democrat, for lieutenant governor. However, Williams, an attorney and prominent member of the Sons of Temperance, requested additional time to consider his position and whether he could accept the nomination.[93]

Before adjourning, the State Temperance Convention adopted a declaration of principles. Insisting it was "neither right nor politic" for the state to afford legal sanction and protection to a system that increased crime and debauched citizens, the delegates repeated their demand for statewide prohibition. Liquor regulation, they maintained, had proved impossible, because the liquor traffic itself was "mischievous in its tendencies." They asserted that legislative prohibition would be entirely compatible with considerations of liberty, justice, and commerce. Appreciative of trends outside the commonwealth as well, the drys further resolved: "That in support and furtherance of their views and aims we insist on the widest extension of popular education, the most vigilant guarding of the purity of the elective franchise, and the perpetuation of the union of these States."[94]

After a short period of deliberation, Williams informed temperance leaders he felt compelled to decline the gubernatorial nomination. He believed that an aroused public sentiment would soon allow drys to accomplish their goals without the formation of a new political party. In April 1855 a subsequent temperance convention at Lexington once again endorsed Hardy for lieutenant governor. The assembly declared, however, that it would be "inexpedient" to make a further nomination for governor and urged instead that temperance friends select from the available candidates the one who seemed most favorable to the dry cause.[95]

Several noted temperance leaders, including Hardy and Dr. Robert J. Breckinridge, embraced the Know-Nothing Party. Indeed, the Know-Nothings bestowed on Hardy their nomination for lieutenant governor as well. By election day in August the temperance party had become associated with the Know-Nothings. Perhaps its identification with temperance provided the Know-Nothing Party in 1855 with its narrow margin of victory. The Know-Nothing candidate for governor, Charles Slaughter Morehead, emerged with a majority of 4,403 votes over his Democratic opponent, Beverly L. Clarke. In the race for lieutenant governor, Hardy received 68,104 votes, while his Democratic challenger, Beriah Magoffin, polled 64,430.[96]

As the decade of the 1850s neared an end, Kentucky prohibitionists remained convinced of the rightness of their cause and confident of ultimate victory. In several sermons at the Chestnut Street Presbyterian Church in Louisville in 1855, the Reverend Dr. Leroy Jones Halsey portrayed the failures of the license system. Despite the Herculean efforts of noble temperance men to arrest the spread of debauchery, he said, there were then at least a half-million "confirmed drunkards" in the United States. Exclaiming that "moral suasion has had its day," Halsey advanced legal prohibition as "the only certain and effective safeguard against drunkenness." The minister asserted: "The quackery and nostrums of the license system have been tried long enough; and all other remedies are but child's play in the path of this destroyer." Halsey said that under prohibition there would still be drunkards, just as there were murderers and counterfeiters contrary to the law. He foresaw, however, that a prohibitory law would drive drunkards "from the ranks of respectability and decency."[97]

The Sons of Temperance in Kentucky also predicted that the objective of constitutional prohibition would soon be achieved. In July 1856, the Reverend A. C. Dickerson, the Grand Worthy Patriarch of the Grand Division of the South of Kentucky, reported to the annual session at Hartford that temperance sentiment in the commonwealth was "widening and deepening every day" and was more advanced "than ever before." The Sons adhered to the conviction that "none but the strong arm of the law" could eradicate permanently the liquor curse.[98]

In his discussion of the national temperance movement prior to the Civil War, Russel Blaine Nye declares that prohibition "was never an issue in the South." Ian Tyrrell also minimizes the importance of temperance agitation in that region. He states that his research has concentrated on the Northeast rather than on the South, "where temperance was weakest, and where prohibition was virtually non-existent."[99] Clearly, the Kentucky experience belies this conclusion. By the early 1850s prohibition had become a major political issue in the commonwealth. In the legislative contests of 1853 and again in the gubernatorial election of 1855, temperance advocates sought to achieve politically the submission of a prohibitory law to the voters. Although their encouraging predictions of a dry Kentucky were not realized during the antebellum years, temperance reformers never abandoned their faith that the evils they perceived could be eradicated. The crusade for a society freed from intemperance would continue.

NOTES

1. Henry G. Crowgey, *Kentucky Bourbon: The Early Years of Whiskeymaking* (Lexington, KY, 1971), xiv, xv, 25, 62, 74; Willard Rouse Jillson, *Early Kentucky Distillers, 1783–1800* (Louisville, 1940) xi; Robert Peter, *History of Fayette County, Kentucky*, William Henry Perrin, ed. (Chicago, 1882), 205 (quotation).

2. Stanley W. Baron, *Brewed in America: A History of Beer and Ale in the United States* (Boston, 1962), x, 130; Crowgey, *Kentucky Bourbon*, 25; Thomas D. Clark, *Kentucky: Land of Contrast* (New York, 1968), 185.

3. William Warren Sweet, *Religion in the Development of American Culture, 1765–1840* (New York, 1952), 138, as cited in James Edward Humphrey, "Baptist Discipline in Kentucky, 1781–1860" (Th.D. diss., Southern Baptist Theological Seminary, 1959), 149. J. H. Spencer agrees that "the most pious christian [*sic*] had no hesitancy about the propriety of drinking in moderation." See his *History of Kentucky Baptists, From 1769 to 1885*, 2 vols. (Cincinnati, 1886), 1:706.

4. Paul C. Conley and Andrew A. Sorensen, *The Staggering Steeple: The Story of Alcoholism and the Churches* (Philadelphia, 1971), 26; Alonzo Willard Fortune, *The Disciples in Kentucky* (Lexington, KY, 1932), 28; also cited in Humphrey, "Baptist Discipline in Kentucky," 151.

5. Humphrey, "Baptist Discipline in Kentucky," 151. Spencer apparently errs in setting the date at 1797. See Spencer, *History of Kentucky Baptists*, 2:15.

6. Fortune, *The Disciples in Kentucky*, 28; also cited in Humphrey, "Baptist Discipline in Kentucky," 150–51n.

7. William E. Arnold, *A History of Methodism in Kentucky*, 2 vols. (Louisville, 1935), 1:13–14.

8. Humphrey, "Baptist Discipline in Kentucky," 152. See also George F. Doyle, transcriber, *A Transcript of the First Record Book of Goshen Baptist Church, Clark County, Kentucky* . . . (n.p., 1927), 19, and William Warren Sweet, *Religion on the American Frontier: The Baptists, 1783–1830* (New York, 1931), 257, 285, 287.

9. Sweet, *Religion on the American Frontier*, 51.

10. Humphrey, "Baptist Discipline in Kentucky," 151–52. See also John B. Boles, *Religion in Antebellum Kentucky* (Lexington, KY, 1976), 132.

11. Sweet, *Religion on the American Frontier*, 257, 260–61, 285, 337. The confidence of the congregation was often misplaced. Frequently the same parishioners were charged with further acts of drunkenness. For example, see the 1801 cases of Brother Steven Deavenport of Clark County, in Doyle, *A Transcript of the First Record Book of Goshen Baptist Church*, 19–21.

12. Carl E. Kramer, "Images of a Developing City: Louisville, 1800–1830," *Filson Club History Quarterly*, 52 (1978):186–87.

13. F. Garvin Davenport, *Ante-Bellum Kentucky: A Social History, 1800–1860* (Oxford, OH, 1943), 22.

14. Harrison D. Taylor, *Ohio County, Kentucky, in the Olden Days* (Louisville, 1926), 24.

15. Davenport, *Ante-Bellum Kentucky*, 29–30; Robert M. Ireland, *The County Courts in Antebellum Kentucky* (Lexington, KY, 1972), 4.

16. Willie Moss Watkins, *The Men, Women, Events, Institutions & Lore of Casey County, Kentucky* (Louisville, 1939), 105. Watkins does not give a precise date for this anecdote. Internal evidence indicates that the period under discussion is roughly 1825 to 1835.

17. Davenport, *Ante-Bellum Kentucky*, 29.

18. Robert M. Ireland, *The County in Kentucky History* (Lexington, KY, 1976), 22.

19. John Allen Krout, *The Origins of Prohibition* (New York, 1967; orig. pub. 1925), 108.

20. *Permanent Temperance Documents of the American Temperance Society* (Boston, 1835), 1:23, 38. Apparently, no other volumes in the series were published. In his report to the national society, one Kentucky correspondent claimed that many of the auxiliaries of the state had failed to submit reports. He estimated there were perhaps one hundred societies in Kentucky, with some fifteen thousand members. Ibid., 39.

21. *Frankfort Commentator*, July 14, 1829; *Harbinger of the Mississippi Valley*, 1 (March 1832): 6. The University of Kentucky Library owns several rare issues of the *Harbinger*, a serial devoted to the temperance issue.

22. *Harbinger of the Mississippi Valley*, 1 (March 1832): 7. Not all of the 290 remained in the society. Some seven or eight withdrew, claiming that their busi-

ness required dealing in ardent spirits. Another three were expelled for "repeated" violations of the pledge. Thus, by July 4, 1830, the official membership in good standing stood at 279.

23. Ibid. The reorganized society again selected Mills as its president. Upon his death in December 1831, he was succeeded by Colonel James Davidson. Ibid., 5.

24. Ibid., 7, 8. The large Louisville Temperance Society, which had approximately 280 members, may not have been affiliated with the Kentucky Temperance Society. See *Temperance Herald of the Mississippi Valley*, 1 (April 2, 1832): 1, in folder titled "Temperance," General File, Library, Kentucky Historical Society, Frankfort. In *The Origins of Prohibition*, Krout notes vaguely (p. 144) that the Kentucky Temperance Society at one point had some ninety auxiliaries, which claimed to have closed forty-six distilleries in the commonwealth.

25. *Harbinger of the Mississippi Valley*, 1 (March 1832): 11; ibid. (April 1832): 18.

26. Record Book of the Columbia (Kentucky) Temperance Society, March 15, 1837-March 6, 1843 (microfilm), Special Collections, Margaret I. King Library, University of Kentucky. The regulations of these societies were remarkably similar. See also the Minute Book of the Newtown (Kentucky) Temperance Society, November 26, 1831-November 10, 1832, Special Collections, Margaret I. King Library, University of Kentucky.

27. Record Book of the Columbia (Kentucky) Temperance Society, August 31, 1837, September 1, 13, 20, 1838.

28. According to editor Thomas T. Skillman, the bimonthly *Temperance Herald* was the only periodical published west of the Allegheny Mountains that was devoted solely to the cause of temperance. See *Temperance Herald*, 1 (April 2, 1832): 1. The *Harbinger*, edited by Dr. Luke Munsell, upheld the causes of temperance, black colonization, and Sunday schools. A noted Kentucky mapmaker, Munsell served simultaneously as secretary of the Kentucky Temperance Society and as corresponding secretary of the Kentucky Colonization Society. See *Harbinger*, 1 (March 1832): 12. At a meeting of the Presbytery of West-Lexington the delegates resolved to recommend "earnestly" the two publications to the churches in their jurisdiction. Ibid. (April 1832):2.

29. *Temperance Herald of the Mississippi Valley*, 1 (April 2, 1832): 1–2.

30. Krout, *The Origins of Prohibition*, 136–37. The American Congressional Temperance Society was formed on February 26, 1833.

31. *Frankfort Commonwealth*, January 21, 1834; *Harbinger of the Mississippi Valley*, 1 (March 1832): 9. When asked to sign the constitution, one legislator observed that in his district there was an active temperance society composed of men from every political party. The group agreed that they would not vote for any candidate who directly or indirectly furnished ardent spirits. During the last election, he said, none was furnished. The legislator then commented wistfully: "Had that course been adopted five years ago, it would have saved me a thousand dollars." See *Permanent Temperance Documents*, 1:348.

32. Some Protestant churches in Kentucky took the extraordinary step of expelling from their congregations members who joined temperance societies. In particular, the "antimissionary" faction of the Baptist church strongly opposed the signing of pledges. One such Baptist church in Barren County is especially interesting. The congregation excluded Brother James Gillock for intoxication and his son, R.R.H. Gillock, for joining a total abstinence society! One wag claimed to have had

this conversation with a member of the Barren County church: "I have been thinking of joining your church, and if I do so, I desire to be a faithful member. I learn that you have excluded a father for drinking too much, and his son for drinking too little. I wish to know just how much whisky a man must drink in order to be an acceptable member of your church." These antimissionary Baptists were frequently dubbed "Whiskey Baptists." As late as 1854 a church of that denomination in Franklin County expelled several members who had joined a temperance society. Spencer, *History of Kentucky Baptists*, 1:709; 2:295; Frank Mariro Masters, *A History of Baptists in Kentucky* (Louisville, 1953), 232.

33. Entry titled "Bro Buck" in Journal of Robert Wilkins Lucas of Bowling Green, Lucas Collection, Manuscript Division, Kentucky Library, Western Kentucky University.

34. Robert J. Breckinridge, *The Immorality of the Traffic, Manufacture, and Use, of Ardent Spirits As A Drink* . . . (Baltimore, 1834), 3, 10–11, 22, 23.

35. Spencer, *History of Kentucky Baptists*, 1:708.

36. Masters, *A History of Baptists in Kentucky*, 273. Italics added.

37. Alice Felt Tyler, *Freedom's Ferment: Phases of American Social History from the Colonial Period to the Outbreak of the Civil War* (New York, 1962), 339; Ian Robert Tyrrell, "Drink and the Process of Social Reform: From Temperance to Prohibition in Ante-Bellum America, 1813–1860" (Ph.D. diss., Duke University, 1974), 132–74, passim; Ronald G. Walters, *American Reformers, 1815–1860* (New York, 1978), 130. A less "whimsical" account of the origins of the Washingtonians appears in Jack S. Blocker, Jr., *American Temperance Movements: Cycles of Reform* (Boston, 1989), 40–41.

38. Krout, *The Origins of Prohibition*, 190; Spencer, *History of Kentucky Baptists*, 1:708. Some confusion exists about the dates of this tour. Thomas D. Clark, *A History of Kentucky*, rev. ed. (Lexington, KY, 1960), 397, places the two Washingtonians in the state as early as 1840. The year 1842 is cited by William Elsey Connelley and E. Merton Coulter, *History of Kentucky*, ed. by Charles Kerr, 5 vols. (Chicago, 1922), 2:795.

39. The personnel of the Washingtonian movement in Kentucky never has been investigated. In February 1842 a newspaper account reported that a large temperance parade conducted by the Louisville society had embraced individuals "of all ages and professions" (*Louisville Daily Journal*, February 23, 1842). Youngsters often took the pledge. For example, an elderly Fayette County resident recalled in 1913 that he had embraced lifelong teetotalism at Athens, Kentucky, in 1842, when as a ten-year-old he signed the total abstinence pledge. See *Lexington Leader*, January 27, 1913. Further study is needed to determine whether Kentucky fits the national pattern as outlined (p. 137) by Tyrrell, who believes that Washingtonians appealed especially to the artisan groups, and by Barbara Leslie Epstein, who concludes that the Washington Societies "marked a further popularization of temperance and eventually led to the greater inclusion of women in the movement." See Epstein, *The Politics of Domesticity: Women, Evangelism, and Temperance in Nineteenth-Century America* (Middletown, CT, 1981), 42, 93 (quotation).

40. Connelley and Coulter, *History of Kentucky*, 2:795.

41. *Louisville Daily Journal*, February 22, 23, 1842; Women's Temperance Society of Lexington, "Programme of the Temperance Procession In Celebration of the

Fourth of July, 1842," Special Collections, Margaret I. King Library, University of Kentucky; *Lexington Leader*, January 27, 1913.

42. Lewis and Richard Collins, *History of Kentucky*, 2 vols. (Louisville, 1924; orig. pub. 1874), 2:47. Tyler and Krout caution that such figures should be used carefully since few societies left permanent records. As Tyler observes (p. 341) in *Freedom's Ferment:* "No one could know how many pledge-signers returned to their cups when the excitement was over."

43. William Louis Breckinridge, *The New Test of Christian Character Tested, Or, The Bible Doctrine of Temperance* (Frankfort, KY, 1842), 7, 3, 11, 21–22.

44. Ibid., 35–37, 39.

45. Tyrrell, "Drink and the Process of Social Reform," 135 (quotation); Walters, *American Reformers*, 131–33.

46. Daniel Dorchester, *The Liquor Problem in All Ages* (New York, 1884), 271; August F. Fehlandt, *A Century of Drink Reform in the United States* (Cincinnati, 1904), 88; Joseph R. Gusfield, *Symbolic Crusade: Status Politics and the American Temperance Movement* (Urbana, IL, 1972), 48–49; Tyler, *Freedom's Ferment*, 338–39.

47. Daniel Drake, *Pioneer Life in Kentucky, 1785–1880*, ed. by Emmet Field Horine (New York, 1948), 42n. In January 1848 Drake wrote two letters to his family in which he mentioned that he had been in his boyhood "a dealer in whiskey." He declared to his daughter: "It is curious and lamentable to observe how much of our time in later life is necessarily devoted, or ought to be, to the correction of the effects of the mistakes and errors of youth." Ibid., 85, 177.

48. Reuben Anderson, *The Annual Oration of the Physiological Temperance Society of the University of Louisville, Delivered by Appointment February 6th, 1847* (Louisville, 1847), 3.

49. *Proceedings of the Physiological Temperance Society of the Medical Institute of Louisville, 1842* (Louisville, 1842), 4, 3 (quotations); Anderson, *Annual Oration of the Physiological Temperance Society*, 3.

50. Kramer, "Images of a Developing City," 184.

51. *Proceedings of the Physiological Temperance Society*, 9–11, 7.

52. Donald Weldon Beattie, "Sons of Temperance: Pioneers in Total Abstinence and 'Constitutional' Prohibition" (Ph.D. diss., Boston University, 1966), viii; Krout, *The Origins of Prohibition*, 209.

53. Beattie, "Sons of Temperance," xi, 137–38, 149, ix; Krout, *The Origins of Prohibition*, 209, 211–12.

54. Kentucky *Acts* (1845), 77–78.

55. Beattie, "Sons of Temperance," 410.

56. Dispensation from James B. Redd, Grand Worthy Patriarch of the Grand Division of Kentucky, Sons of Temperance, to H. E. Guerrant and others to organize a division of the Sons of Temperance at Sharpsburg, Signed May 12, 1847, in Henry Ellis Guerrant Papers, The Filson Club, Louisville.

57. *Constitution, By-Laws, and Rules of Order, of Sharpsburg Div., No. 71, Sons of Temperance, Revised by Natl. Div. June 1847*, 1, 3, 5, 6 (hereafter cited as *Sharpsburg Constitution*). A copy is contained in Box 2 of the Guerrant Papers. This constitution made no reference to race as a criterion for joining the society. In 1850, however, the National Division ruled that the admission of blacks into subordinate or grand divisions was "improper and illegal." This stand later received the commendation of the Grand Division of Kentucky. Beattie, "Sons of Temperance,"

174–75. Although the National Division never introduced a "tobacco pledge" into the order for adults, Hancock Division, No. 12, of Kentucky, required its members to swear against use of tobacco in the division room. Those who would not sign the pledge were assessed five cents per month. Any brother who partook of tobacco during a division meeting was subject to a fine of one dollar per offense. Both the Grand Division of Kentucky and the National Division deemed the actions of the Hancock Division to be illegal. Ibid., 62.

58. *Sharpsburg Constitution*, 4. The founders of the Sons of Temperance considered the benefit program "as second only in importance to the pledge." In many areas, however, the scheme proved unworkable; the expenses of the program exceeded cash on hand. As early as June 1854, the National Division ruled that subordinate divisions could suspend payments if necessary. See Beattie, "Sons of Temperance," 77–81; quote on 80–81.

59. [Lexington] *Kentucky New Era*, May 27, 1853. On June 7, 1855, the Grand Division of Kentucky was divided into two jurisdictions. The new division received the designation: "The Grand Division of the South of Kentucky." Beattie, "Sons of Temperance," 411.

60. *Constitution, By-Laws, and Rules of Order, of Kentucky Temple of Honor, No. 1, Of the State of Kentucky; Instituted in the City of Louisville, August 31, 1846* (Louisville, 1850), 5, 14, 16. A microfilm copy of the constitution appears on reel 2, Burrell H. Thurman Papers, Special Collections, Margaret I. King Library, University of Kentucky.

61. Masters, *A History of Baptists in Kentucky*, 314.

62. Jack S. Blocker provides the most succinct appraisal of the Maine Law and its impact on temperance during the fifties. See *American Temperance Movements*, esp. 55–60.

63. [Lexington] *Kentucky New Era*, May 6, 13, 1853.

64. Beattie, "Sons of Temperance," 205–6.

65. [Lexington] *Kentucky New Era*, April 29, 1853. In its third year of publication the paper was printing over four thousand copies per week.

66. Ibid.

67. Ibid., May 6, 1853. For an additional discussion of how women could further the cause, see Eginton's editorial on July 15, 1853.

68. Ibid., May 6, 1853.

69. *Louisville Daily Journal*, May 3, 1853; [Lexington] *Kentucky New Era*, May 13, 1853.

70. [Lexington] *Kentucky New Era*, May 13, 1853.

71. Wallace B. Turner, "Kentucky State Politics in the Early 1850's," *Register of the Kentucky Historical Society*, 56 (1958): 129, 132.

72. [Lexington] *Kentucky New Era*, May 13, 1853.

73. Ibid., May 27, 1853.

74. Ibid., July 8, 1853.

75. Ibid., June 24, 1853.

76. *Cynthiana News*, as cited in [Lexington] *Kentucky New Era*, June 10, 1853.

77. [Lexington] *Kentucky New Era*, June 3, 10, 1853.

78. Ibid., June 17, 1853.

79. *Louisville Daily Journal*, July 19, 22 (quotation), 1853.

80. Connelley and Coulter, *History of Kentucky*, 2:774. Editor Henry Watterson of the *Louisville Courier-Journal* later said of Prentice: "From 1830 to 1861 the influence of Prentice was perhaps greater than the influence of any political writer who ever lived; it was an influence directly positive and personal." Ibid.

81. *Louisville Daily Journal*, July 19, 26, 1853.

82. Frederick A. Wallis and Hambleton Tapp, eds., *A Sesquicentennial History of Kentucky*, 4 vols. (Hopkinsville, KY, 1945), 1:397. In fact, the Whig majority in the Senate increased from two to eight seats. See Turner, "Kentucky State Politics in the Early 1850s," 138.

83. [Lexington] *Kentucky New Era*, July 22, August 5, 1853.

84. Ibid., August 12, 19, 26, 1853.

85. For example, *Covington Journal*, August 6, 1853.

86. *Louisville Daily Journal*, August 11, 1853.

87. Turner, "Kentucky State Politics in the Early 1850s," 138–39.

88. Wallace B. Turner, "Kentucky In A Decade Of Change, 1850–1860" (Ph.D. diss., University of Kentucky, 1954), 274–75; Kentucky *Senate Journal* (1853–54), 155–56; Kentucky *House Journal* (1853–54), 164–66.

89. Connelley and Coulter, *History of Kentucky*, 2:847.

90. Turner, "Kentucky In A Decade Of Change," 275.

91. *Louisville Daily Journal*, December 14, 15, 1854; *Covington Journal*, December 16, 1854; Connelley and Coulter, *History of Kentucky*, 2:847.

92. *Louisville Daily Journal*, December 15, 1854. Kentucky was not the only southern state where prohibitionists formed a separate political party to seek the governorship in 1855. For an account of the famous Overby campaign in Georgia, see Henry A. Scomp, *King Alcohol in the Realm of King Cotton* (Chicago, 1888), 495–516.

93. *Covington Journal*, December 16, 1854; *Louisville Daily Journal*, December 15, 1854; [Lexington] *Kentucky New Era*, May 13, 1853; *Biographical Encyclopaedia of Kentucky Of The Dead and Living Men of the Nineteenth Century*, 2 vols. (Cincinnati, 1878), 1:98.

94. *Louisville Daily Journal*, December 15, 1854.

95. Turner, "Kentucky In A Decade Of Change," 275–76: *Biographical Encyclopaedia*, 1:98; *Paris True Kentuckian*, February 2, 1870.

96. Wallis and Tapp, *A Sesquicentennial History of Kentucky*, 1:398; Connelley and Coulter, *History of Kentucky*, 2:847; Sister Agnes Geraldine McGann, *Nativism in Kentucky in 1860* (Washington, DC, 1944), 47. The latter study is disappointing. Although she devotes an entire chapter to the 1855 election, Sister Agnes treats the temperance party in a single sentence (p. 47).

97. Leroy Jones Halsey, *Legal Prohibition: The Only Remedy For Drunkenness; Being the Substance of Two Discourses, Delivered In The Chestnut Street Church, Louisville, On the First Sabbaths of April and July, 1855* (Louisville, 1855), 11, 12, 18, 19.

98. Sons of Temperance of North America, Grand Division of the South of Kentucky, *Journal of the Proceedings of the Grand Division of the South of Kentucky of the Sons of Temperance, At Its Third Quarterly Session, On the 23rd July, 1856* (Russellville, KY, 1856), 4, 9.

99. Russel Blaine Nye, *Society and Culture in America, 1830–1860* (New York, 1974), 50; Tyrrell, "Drink and the Process of Social Reform," 8. Two scholars who do acknowledge the extent of the movement in the South are Clifford S. Griffin,

who observes, "Southern support for the Maine Law grew steadily." *The Ferment of Reform, 1830–1860* (Arlington Heights, IL, 1967), 74; and Ronald Walters, who pronounces temperance "among the least sectional of the antebellum crusades." *American Reformers*, 138.

3

Medical Education in the South: The Case of Louisville, 1837–1910

Dwayne Cox

In 1910 Abraham Flexner wrote that in years past "crude boys thronged from the plantations" to attend medical school in Louisville. This began in 1837 with the opening of the Louisville Medical Institute, which later became the Medical Department of the University of Louisville. Subsequently, a host of rivals appeared, including the Kentucky School of Medicine, the Louisville Medical College, and the Hospital College of Medicine. Any white man who paid his fees could gain admission to these institutions, which competed for the corporate income generated by large enrollments. Furthermore, instruction consisted of lectures uninformed by the germ theory of disease and unsupported by clinical and laboratory requirements. Traditionally, historians have considered the Flexner report a turning point for reform in medical education.[1]

This stereotype rests upon an invidious comparison of nineteenth-century medical schools with their twentieth-century counterparts. Actually, the proliferation of medical schools during this period paralleled the geographic expansion of the United States. Furthermore, competition among schools reflected the nation's unregulated business climate. Louisville's first medical school possessed considerable academic merit, but was compromised by factors largely beyond the faculty's control. These included urban rivalry, party politics, and sectional animosity, in addition to competition among rival physicians and schools. Well before publication of the Flexner report, local medical educators recognized the need for a more orderly environment and moved to create it. The case of Louisville demonstrates that the Progressive interpretation of nineteenth-century medical education was overly harsh. Flexner leveled his most severe criticism at the South, including his native Kentucky.[2]

The Louisville Medical Institute assembled an enviable faculty. By the early 1840s, this group included several individuals of regional and even national prominence. Collectively, their careers exemplified passage of the gentleman naturalist, emergence of scientific specialization, conflict and change within the medical community, and the role of medical schools in scientific education. Several of the professors received their training at the University of Pennsylvania, the best American medical school of the day. Some of them made significant contributions to science and medicine. Others were forced into retirement because of their failure to keep pace with change.[3]

Charles Wilkins Short received his M.D. degree in 1815 from the University of Pennsylvania. Working there with Benjamin Smith Barton, he developed a lifelong interest in the identification and classification of medicinal and other plants. For almost a decade, Short practiced medicine in frontier Kentucky, but devoted his leisure to botany. In 1825 he was called to the Medical Department of Transylvania University in Lexington, Kentucky, where he began his career as a teacher of materia medica. Short continued his botanical studies, collecting and classifying native plants, carrying on extensive correspondence with other botanists, and financing botanical expeditions. In 1838 he joined the faculty of the Louisville Medical Institute, where he remained for more than a decade. The foremost American botanist of the day, Asa Gray, named the North Carolina wildflower *Shortia galacifolia* in his honor. Josiah Gregg, one of Dr. Short's students, also achieved distinction as a botanist.[4]

Like Short, Daniel Drake studied at the University of Pennsylvania (M.D., 1816), where he learned the importance of accurate observation and recording of data. In 1838, when he joined the Louisville Medical Institute faculty, Drake possessed an excellent reputation as a teacher, researcher, and civic-minded physician. In Louisville, he completed much of the research and writing for his two-volume study of climate, geography, disease, and social conditions in the Mississippi Valley. Reviewers hailed the work as a scientific treatise, as well as a handbook for practicing physicians. Drake also edited the *Western Journal of Medicine and Surgery*, which he brought with him to the Louisville Medical Institute. Few, if any, physicians were better known than he in the trans-Appalachian West.[5]

In 1840 Samuel David Gross came to the Louisville Medical Institute as professor of surgery, a position he held for all but one of the next sixteen years. Gross had studied at the Jefferson Medical College in Philadelphia (M.D., 1828). Shortly before accepting the appointment in Louisville, he had published *Elements of Pathological Anatomy*, which established his reputation as an authority on this topic. While in Louisville, Gross enjoyed regional acclaim for his skills in surgery. He also refined techniques for resection and suturing of the intestines, using dogs as his subjects. In 1859 Gross published *A System of Surgery*, which became a standard treatment of the subject. In his *Autobiography*, Gross recalled the years in Louisville as some of the more productive of his career.[6]

John Esten Cooke (M.D., University of Pennsylvania, 1805) served on the original Louisville Medical Institute faculty, but eventually stepped down in the face of professional criticism. Dr. Cooke believed that all disease arose from an imbalance of the body's four humors: blood, phlegm, yellow bile, and black bile. Based on this assumption, he considered bleeding and purging sovereign remedies because these procedures balanced the humors. This had been the accepted wisdom at one time, but was coming under increasing attack. Eventually, Cooke became known as "the high priest of calomel," a mercury-based purgative. In 1838 Henry Miller, a faculty colleague, published a scathing attack upon Cooke's theories of the origin and treatment of disease. Criticism continued, and in 1844 he retired.[7]

Some considered Charles Caldwell the founder of the Louisville Medical Institute. A graduate of the University of Pennsylvania (M.D., 1796), Caldwell possessed a commanding personality and a firm belief in his own rectitude. At sixty-five, he was the oldest member of the original faculty. Consequently, Caldwell sympathized with the textbook medicine and deductive reasoning of the eighteenth century. He believed in phrenology, the study of the skull's shape as a predictor of personality; he advocated polygenesis, the separate creation of the races; and he defended the traditional notion that a mysterious, vital principle regulated body chemistry. Caldwell's defense of vitalism put him at odds with Lunsford P. Yandell, who taught chemistry at the Medical Institute. In 1849 Caldwell retired involuntarily, in part because of his outmoded doctrines.[8]

Daniel Drake's *Western Journal of Medicine and Surgery* was a credit to the editor, its contributors, and the sponsoring institution. It contained many fine articles by Medical Institute faculty: Short on Kentucky flora, Gross on surgical methods, and Drake on health and the environment. It also carried Professor Yandell's hard-hitting review of Caldwell's *Physiology Vindicated*, a defense of vitalism. Perhaps the most significant studies that appeared in the *Western Journal* came from Edward Jarvis, a local physician not wholly friendly toward the Louisville Medical Institute, who contributed pioneering pieces on medical statistics and the humane treatment of the mentally ill.[9]

If bricks and mortar provided an indication, the Louisville Medical Institute was confident, successful, and respectable. The Louisville city council erected and furnished the school building at the cost of approximately $50,000. The three-story, Greek Revival structure offered ample classroom, office, and laboratory space. Professor Short boasted that it equaled or surpassed any other medical school facility in the nation; Yandell wrote that the structure's inspired design cured the blues; and civic leaders

considered the new building physical evidence that in Louisville intellectual pursuits had eclipsed the rougher passions of the frontier.[10]

The faculty's reputation, the school's facilities, and the city's strategic
location at the falls of the Ohio River attracted large enrollments. Most
students came from Kentucky, but significant numbers hailed from Alabama, Mississippi, Tennessee, and other states linked to Louisville by river.
The first class consisted of twenty-four graduates, a number that rose
steadily until it peaked at 113 in 1850. Between 1837 and 1860, the school
produced nearly 1,500 graduates. This was only a fraction of those who
enrolled but never took a degree.[11]

Classes began in the fall and ran for approximately five months. Degree
candidates attended two terms, the second of which repeated the first. This
was the standard degree requirement in American medical schools of the
day, but at least some educators recognized shortcomings in the curriculum.
Daniel Drake, for example, described the need for a three-term program of
progressive difficulty. In the absence of such a requirement, he urged
students to take three terms anyway; concentrate on the basic sciences
during the first; and continue their medical studies abroad. Professor Short
advised students to develop a study routine and the discipline to follow it.
The school published the advice of both professors, each of whom provided
excellent professional role models.[12]

Both faculty and students at the Louisville Medical Institute devoted
considerable attention to the study of human anatomy. In fact, the availabil-
ity of anatomical material provided one justification for establishing a
medical school in the city. Louisville had a large river transient population,
as well as slaves and free blacks. These three groups undoubtedly provided
a disproportionate number of cadavers. At least some of the school's
anatomical specimens had been stolen, which indicates the importance
attached to laboratory work. The director of the laboratory acquired cadavers, collected fees, oversaw dissection, and had the title Demonstrator of
Anatomy. Occupants of the position included Tobias G. Richardson, a
graduate of the Louisville Medical Institute who later taught at Tulane
University and published a standard textbook on human anatomy. The
anatomy laboratory consisted of several adjoining rooms designed specifically for this purpose. Generally, the dissecting course was not mandatory
at American medical schools, including the Louisville Medical Institute, but
by their words and deeds the faculty stressed its importance.[13]

The existence of the Louisville Marine Hospital provided another argument for establishing a medical school in the city. The facility consisted of
three stories, a center edifice and two wings; received an annual budget of
$3,500; and employed several attending physicians and one resident.
Drake's *Western Journal* carried reports of student activity in the hospital;
Henry Clay Lewis described his work there in anecdotes about student life;
and the faculty enjoyed free access to the facility for teaching purposes.

They even added a 400-seat clinical amphitheater at their own expense. Clinical experience at the Louisville Marine Hospital was not a graduation requirement, but many students clearly availed themselves of the opportunity. The faculty's financial investment in the hospital provided the strongest possible evidence of the importance they attached to it.[14]

Nineteenth-century medical students have been depicted as social and academic misfits. Considerable anecdotal evidence supports the conclusion that some were. In Louisville, students robbed graves, drank whiskey, and chased women, but this was not necessarily the behavioral norm. In fact, reports of indiscretions undoubtedly received an unrepresentative share of contemporary attention and probably were embellished in retrospect. Furthermore, many students entered school at a relatively late age. Daniel Drake reported that some were as old as the professors. Often, they worked as apprentice physicians and enjoyed a degree of financial independence. Not surprisingly, some medical students had adult vices and were unintimidated by faculty authority.[15]

Candidates for the M.D. degree were required to submit a thesis. Professor Drake, at least, took the requirement seriously. He advised students to prepare their essays between sessions, when they had more time for research, reflection, and revision. He even suggested possible topics: the impact of chemistry upon medicine, native medicinal plants, and endemic diseases of the United States. Drake concluded that the thesis should be "a positive contribution to science." The faculty published some theses, including Joseph W. Brooks's essay on creosote, in which he discussed the history of the substance, reviewed the current literature, and described its use as an antiseptic. Charles Wilkins Short complained that some students knew "little or nothing" about their topics, but like Drake he had a rigorous vision of what a thesis should be.[16]

Degree candidates stood for final oral examinations, which were not a formality. Although he made light of the process, Henry Clay Lewis worried about the upcoming ordeal. The examination consisted of a fifteen-minute private session with each of seven professors, a total of almost two hours. Lewis was tested on the pros and cons of vitalism and the types and amounts of drugs to administer in specific situations. Dr. Gross considered the candidate talented but overconfident, and administered a dose of humility to him. Most of those who took the examination probably passed, but many who enrolled never reached that point. Even David W. Yandell, the son of Lunsford P. Yandell, almost failed to graduate.[17]

Faculty members were aware of shortcomings in the medical profession and urged students to avoid them. In 1844, for example, Daniel Drake described the typical western physician as ignorant, greedy, and disorderly. To combat these problems, he urged Louisville Medical Institute graduates to stay abreast of professional developments and devote their full attention to medical practice. Furthermore, he advised them to maintain thorough records of their scientific observations and to publish significant findings. Their lifetime goal should be to hand down the profession "enlarged, purified, and embellished." Drake gave this advice in an introductory lecture that was open to all matriculates.[18]

The Louisville Medical Institute grew out of a rivalry between Louisville and Lexington. Prior to the War of 1812, Lexington had been the economic and cultural capital of Kentucky. Its leadership in the latter category rested in large part on the reputation of Transylvania University and its Medical Department. Lexington never recovered from the Panic of 1819, but Louisville prospered with its growing river trade. When Transylvania came under political and religious attack, Louisvillians took the opportunity to strike Lexington at a vulnerable point. They were aided by some members of the Transylvania medical faculty, who saw a more prosperous future in Louisville. Charles Caldwell, John Esten Cooke, Lunsford P. Yandell, and Charles Wilkins Short all came to Louisville directly from Transylvania. James Guthrie, head of the Louisville city council and later president of the Louisville and Nashville Railroad, led the drive to bring a medical school to the city.[19]

Some considered the Louisville Medical Institute a component of what would be a larger institution of higher learning. Charles Caldwell, for example, proposed that it constitute one of several "grand departments." Shortly after the medical school opened, the city council created the Louisville Collegiate Institute, which attracted few students and struggled to survive. Over the next several years, proponents of the Collegiate Institute advocated a combination with the medical school. They intended to divert a portion of the latter's fee revenue to a common account. Initially, the medical professors did not oppose an administrative combination, but they resisted the invasion of their treasury. This dispute was carried on in the political rhetoric of the day. The Louisville Medical Institute represented selfish economic interests that thwarted the people's desire for a comprehensive university.[20]

The debate involved fratricidal warfare as well as egalitarian politics. Some local physicians resented the Louisville Medical Institute faculty, which Edward Jarvis described as "conceited, supercilious, and overbearing." Dr. William A. McDowell led the attack, which was joined by Drs. Henry M. Bullitt and Joshua Barker Flint, the latter of whom had been dismissed from the Louisville Medical Institute faculty because of his poor lecture performance. The dispute became especially bitter between McDowell and Professor Yandell. At one point, Yandell wrote of McDowell's work on tuberculosis that the latter could no more cure the disease than he could "make a pig's stump tail grow out again." In 1842 McDowell and others distributed a tract that accused the Louisville Medical Institute faculty of selfishness, mismanagement, and incompetence.[21]

These ill feelings propelled a series of events that sapped the time, energy, and morale of the faculty. In 1846 the state legislature chartered the University of Louisville, which combined the Medical Institute and the Collegiate Institute under a single board, but kept each unit financially independent. Afterwards, the city tried but failed to revive the Collegiate Institute as the Academic Department of the University of Louisville. Meanwhile, in 1849 Short and Drake retired. Their decisions may have been influenced in part by attacks upon the school, but their departure undoubtedly left a void difficult to fill. In 1850 the Kentucky School of Medicine opened its doors, with a faculty that included Henry M. Bullitt and Joshua Barker Flint. The Kentucky School and Transylvania University established a joint degree program under which students could take back-to-back terms in the fall and spring and thus complete the required course in half the usual time. Yandell predicted that "Flint and his new corps will not cause much alarm," although by this time they already had done so.[22]

Efforts continued to place the medical school under public control and divert a portion of its revenue to a common account. John Hopkins Harney, editor of the *Louisville Democrat*, led the campaign. In 1851 the Kentucky state legislature approved a new charter for the city of Louisville, which called for the financial integration of all departments of the University of Louisville and the direct election of trustees. The medical faculty took legal action against these changes in the 1846 charter. As the case worked its way through the courts, Professor Yandell published a history of the medical school in which he complained bitterly of selfish, unprovoked attacks upon the institution. In 1854 the state's highest court ruled in favor of the medical faculty, citing the 1819 decision in the Dartmouth College case, which had held that the college charter was a private contract protected against legislative action. The professors won their case but lost the momentum of the school's initial success. In 1856 Dr. Gross resigned, citing the faculty's decline as the primary reason for his decision. Later that year, a fire swept through the original Medical Institute building and destroyed another link with the heady days of the early 1840s. An 1860 act of the state legislature cut off the possibility of municipal support for the University of Louisville.[23]

The Civil War and readjustment fueled an already tense situation within the local medical community. Owing to low enrollments, the University of Louisville offered no classes during the 1862–63 term. In 1863 Joseph W. Benson, the medical school dean, was convicted by court-martial for failure to honor a government contract for horse feed. During 1866 and 1867 the University of Louisville and the Kentucky School of Medicine merged, but professional and sectional animosities ended the venture after one term. Around the same time, Dr. Benson and other southern sympathizers were accused of abusing privileges at the Freedmen's Bureau Hospital. According to some witnesses, Benson performed needless surgery on U.S. soldiers, stole government whiskey, and sold dead babies to medical schools.[24]

In 1868 Henry M. Bullitt organized a third medical school in the city— the Louisville Medical College. The University of Louisville faculty claimed that the name of the new school was designed to confuse prospective students with that of their own, which was undoubtedly true. The Medical College faculty included Edward S. Gaillard, who edited the *Richmond and Louisville Medical Review*. In the late 1860s and early 1870s, Gaillard published a series of mean-spirited attacks upon the Medical Department of the University of Louisville in general and Professor David W. Yandell in particular. Yandell responded in a more moderate tone, but the dispute continued to escalate.[25]

Competition peaked during the 1870s. In 1873, when the Hospital College of Medicine opened, the University of Louisville attempted to form an alliance with the new school. Under the terms of the proposal, the Hospital College would have rented the University of Louisville building and hired the faculty to offer spring lectures. In effect, this would have allowed students to complete their course requirements in half the usual time. The offer was rejected. Two years later, however, the Kentucky School of Medicine and the Louisville Medical College entered a similar agreement. The two schools maintained separate legal identities but shared faculty and offered back-to-back fall and spring sessions. In addition, they cut fees through the guise of tuition scholarships.[26]

The Medical Department of the University of Louisville responded by establishing the *Louisville Medical News*. As the title indicated, this was less a scientific journal than a medical newspaper. It covered a variety of topics, but specialized in bashing the Kentucky School of Medicine and the Louisville Medical College. At the same time, L. R. Sale sued the Louisville Medical College, charging that the school solicited students under false pretenses. The *Medical News* covered the case with perverse delight. In 1877 the Louisville Medical College agreed to reduce the number of tuition scholarships offered. Competition continued but began to subside.[27]

The movement away from competition had begun as early as 1866, when the University of Louisville's medical faculty showed an interest in cooperative efforts to standardize fees and raise academic requirements. During the next three years, several initiatives were discussed but not implemented. In 1874 the medical faculty called for regional negotiations regarding fees and academic standards, yet cautioned that unilateral changes were unrealistic. Two years later, Dean James M. Bodine of the University of Louisville attended the organizational meeting of the American Medical College Association (AMCA). The university endorsed the association's call for a three-year course, but the AMCA failed to gain a wide following among the nation's medical schools. In 1884 Bodine reported to the faculty that the organization was "virtually nonexistent." He was instructed to resign the University of Louisville's membership.[28]

During this period, David W. Yandell provided strong individual leadership for higher standards in medical education, particularly in clinical facilities and instruction. Following his graduation from the Louisville Medical Institute, Yandell had continued his medical studies in Europe. During the Civil War, he served the Confederacy as a military physician and medical administrator. Following the war, Yandell returned to the University of Louisville, where beginning in the mid-1860s he carried on a dispute with other faculty members regarding the quality of the school's dispensary. Yandell sometimes became impatient and overwrought with his colleagues' inaction, but he persistently advocated improved clinical facilities and instruction. Early in the 1870s, he worked with the Sisters of Charity to erect a teaching hospital. By this time, the University of Louisville required clinical instruction, which earlier had been optional. Finally, in 1888, the University of Louisville opened a dispensary that at least approximated Yandell's specifications. Dr. Yandell also served as president of the American Medical Association and edited the *American Practitioner*, a journal which generally avoided the morass of medical politics.[29]

In 1890 the founding of the Association of American Medical Colleges (AAMC) brought permanent changes in academic requirements. Initially, the University of Louisville did not apply for membership, but pledged to lobby other southern schools for cooperation with the association. In 1891 the faculty urged the dean to attend the organization's meeting "at whatever sacrifice," but instructed him to move no faster than other southern schools on the three-year requirement. In 1892 representatives of eleven southern schools convened in Louisville and agreed upon a three-year course. Three years later, the University of Louisville raised its entrance requirements in conformity with AAMC standards. In 1899 the four-year course became a requirement. Despite these changes, in 1906 the Council on Medical Education of the American Medical Association deemed Louisville one of "five especially rotten spots" in American medical education.[30]

By this time, combining resources offered the best hope of survival. In 1907 the Louisville Medical College and the Hospital College of Medicine came together as the Louisville and Hospital College of Medicine. Meanwhile, the state legislature gave the University of Kentucky legal authority to open a medical school in Lexington. The Kentucky School of Medicine and the Louisville and Hospital College of Medicine made a joint proposal for affiliation with the University of Kentucky, provided the medical school remain in Louisville. The University of Louisville made the same offer, but both were declined. In July 1908 the University of Louisville absorbed the Kentucky School of Medicine and the Louisville and Hospital College of Medicine.[31]

The next year, Abraham Flexner visited Louisville in preparing his report on medical education for the Carnegie Foundation. By that time, the local

situation had undergone substantial change. Flexner noted the recent mergers but saw little hope for the financial resources needed by the Medical
Department of the University of Louisville. In 1910 the publication of his
harsh assessment inspired some municipal support for the university, but
it did not result in decisive action. The ten years prior to the report brought
changes at least as significant as the decade following its publication.[32]

The Flexner report was, among other things, a well-publicized, Progressive interpretation of nineteenth-century medical education. Others followed and likewise influenced subsequent views of the topic. In the case of
Louisville, the recollections of John Allen Wyeth, Louis Frank, and Simon
Flexner did so. The medical careers of all three spanned the period before
and after the bacteriological revolution. Understandably, these and other
observers judged earlier conditions by later standards. Generally, they
viewed medical education as a story of progress. In their view, the nineteenth century represented a retarded phase in medical education.[33]

Actually, nineteenth-century medical knowledge compared favorably
with other fields. The eighteenth-century rule of *caveat emptor* dominated
tort law well into the twentieth century, long after the Industrial Revolution
had compromised its original utility. During much of the nineteenth century, many American theologians rejected textual criticism of the Penta-
teuch, which eventually undermined the traditional concept of scriptural
inerrancy. As an intellectual achievement, the germ theory of disease at least
equaled comparable developments in theology and law. Furthermore, it
probably achieved a greater degree of popular acceptance.[34]

The Louisville Medical Institute exemplified how medical schools
sprang up in response to demographic changes. This and other schools that
appeared along the nation's urban frontier filled a demand for physicians.
Medical leaders such as Daniel Drake recognized their deficiencies and
recommended corrections. In doing so, they demonstrated an acute awareness of their profession's low status in the trans-Appalachian West and the
Old South. In this sense, they exhibited a variety of sectionalism that was
professional rather than political.[35]

The middle of the nineteenth century was a period of unregulated
capitalism in U.S. history. This spirit prevailed in medical education as well
as the business community. The move toward consolidation reflected the
medical profession's growing realization that uncoordinated expansion
had become counterproductive. Business and government engaged in a
comparable "search for order." In the case of Louisville, the medical school
mergers of 1907 and 1908 exerted more of an immediate, measurable impact
than the 1910 Flexner report.[36]

The consolidation and cooperation that Flexner foresaw throughout the
nation he found "especially urgent" in the South. He recommended closing
all but six four-year medical schools in the region, whereas Ohio alone
would retain half that number. The six southern schools he envisioned

would be located in Virginia, Tennessee, Georgia, Alabama, Louisiana, and Texas. Nevertheless, the Medical Department of the University of Louisville, successor to the Louisville Medical Institute, survived his recommendation. It remained the only medical school in the state until the University of Kentucky established a second in Lexington following World War II.[37]

The new order of regulation and consolidation created its own set of problems. For example, it brought standards that eliminated Flexner's "crude boys" from medical school but failed to provide an adequate supply of physicians to rural and depressed areas. This problem persisted in Kentucky as in other southern states. Flexner reported the existence of a small black medical school in Louisville, which closed within a few years because it lacked the financial resources demanded by Progressive reformers. As medicine became more sophisticated, it also became more expensive and exclusive.[38]

Nineteenth-century Louisville was a regional center for medical education. Several distinguished medical educators taught in the city. Their students filled a demand fueled by geographic expansion and an unregulated economic climate. From the beginning, local medical educators acknowledged their shortcomings. Gradually, they reached enough of a consensus to turn away from competition and move toward consolidation. Rather than being a retarded phase in the history of medical education, the nineteenth century was an important stage in the evolution of the profession. This was no less true in the South than in the rest of the United States.

NOTES

1. Abraham Flexner, *Report on Medical Education in the United States and Canada* (New York, 1910), 230; John H. Ellis, *Medicine in Kentucky* (Lexington, 1977), 8–22; Martin Kaufman, *American Medical Education: The Formative Years, 1765–1910* (Westport, 1976), 36–56, 164–82.

2. James H. Cassedy, *Medicine and American Growth, 1800–1860* (Madison, 1986), 67–72; Flexner, *Report on Medical Education*, 148.

3. George Daniels, "The Process of Professionalization in American Science: The Emergent Period, 1820–1860," *Isis*, 58 (1967): 151–66; George Daniels, *American Science in the Age of Jackson* (New York, 1968), 1–5.

4. Percy Albert Davis, "Charles Wilkins Short, 1794–1863: Kentucky Botanist and Physician," *Filson Club History Quarterly*, 19 (1945):131–55, 208–49; Deborah Skaggs, "Charles Wilkins Short: Kentucky Botanist and Physician, 1794–1863" (Master's thesis, University of Louisville, 1982), iii.

5. Emmett F. Horine, *Daniel Drake, 1785–1852: Pioneer Physician of the Mid-West* (Philadelphia, 1961), 324–67; Henry D. Shapiro, "Daniel Drake: The Scientist as Citizen," in *Physician to the West: Selected Writings of Daniel Drake on Science and Society*, Henry D. Shapiro and Zane L. Miller, eds. (Lexington, 1970), xi–xxii.

6. J. Chalmers DaCosta, "Samuel David Gross," *Dictionary of American Biography* (New York, 1926–), 8: 18–20; Samuel David Gross, *Autobiography*, 2 vols. (Philadelphia, 1887), 1:96–99.

7. Frederick Eberson, "A Great Purging—Cholera or Calomel?" *Filson Club History Quarterly*, 50 (1976):28–35; Henry Miller, "Vulgar Errors in Medicine," *Louisville Journal of Medicine and Surgery*, 1 (1838):268–75.

8. Emmett F. Horine, *Biographical Sketch and Guide to the Writings of Charles Caldwell* (Brooks, KY, 1960), 1–17; Nellie H. Carstens, "Charles Caldwell, M.D.: A Biographical Sketch" (Master's thesis, University of Louisville, 1979), iii.

9. Samuel D. Gross, "A Case of Axillary Aneurism," *Western Journal of Medicine and Surgery*, 3 (1841):401–42; Daniel Drake, "The Northern Lakes: A Summer Resort for Invalids of the South," *Western Journal of Medicine and Surgery*, 6 (1842):401–26; Charles Wilkins Short, "A Fourth Supplementary Catalogue of the Plants of Kentucky," *Western Journal of Medicine and Surgery*, 8 (1843):430–61; Gerald N. Grob, *Edward Jarvis and the Medical World of Nineteenth-Century America* (Knoxville, 1978), 43–56; James H. Cassedy, *American Medicine and Statistical Thinking, 1800–1860* (Cambridge, 1984), 172–77.

10. Joan Titley, "The Library of the Louisville Medical Institute, 1837–46," *Bulletin of the Medical Library Association*, 52 (1964):343–69; Lunsford P. Yandell to Charles Wilkins Short, June 3, 1838, Charles Wilkins Short to William Short, July 29, 1838, Short Papers, The Filson Club, Louisville; Louisville Medical Institute, *Catalogue* (Louisville, 1838), 6; W. N. Haldeman, *Picture of Louisville and Business Advertiser* (Louisville, 1844), 66; George M. Bibb, "Laying the Cornerstone of the College Edifice," *Louisville Journal of Medicine and Surgery*, 1 (1838): appendix.

11. These statistics were compiled from lists of graduates that appeared in the school's annual catalog.

12. William G. Rothstein, *American Physicians in the Nineteenth Century: From Sects to Science* (Baltimore, 1972), 85–100; Louisville Medical Institute, *Catalogue* (Louisville, 1837), 3–8; Daniel Drake, "The Means of Promoting Moral and Intellectual Improvements of Students and Physicians of the Mississippi Valley," in Miller and Shapiro, *Physician to the West*, 295–314; Charles Wilkins Short, *Duties of Medical Students during Attendance of Lectures* (Louisville, 1845), 11–23.

13. Ellis, *Medicine in Kentucky*, 13; Todd L. Savitt, "The Use of Blacks for Medical Experimentation and Demonstration in the Old South," *Journal of Southern History*, 48 (1982):331–48; Charles A. Hentz, "Autobiography," n.d., 64, 74–75, Southern Historical Collection, University of North Carolina, Chapel Hill; Henry Clay Lewis, "Stealing a Baby," in *Louisiana Swamp Doctor: The Life of Henry Clay Lewis*, John Q. Anderson, ed. (Baton Rouge, 1972), 151–58; Kentucky Writer's Project, *A Centennial History of the University of Louisville* (Louisville, 1939), 42; Rudolph Matas and Virginia Gray, "Tobias Richardson," *Dictionary of American Biography*, 8: 575–76.

14. W. H. Donne, "Wound of the Antrum Highmore," *Western Journal of Medicine and Surgery*, 6 (1842):186–89; Henry Clay Lewis, "Cupping an Irishman," in Anderson, ed., *Louisiana Swamp Doctor*, 158–64; Ellis, *Medicine in Kentucky*, 13; Richard W. Otis, ed., *The Louisville Directory* (Louisville, 1832), 143–44; "Louisville Marine Hospital," *Western Journal of Medicine and Surgery*, 2 (1840):319–20; "Clinical Medicine in Louisville," *Western Journal of Medicine and Surgery*, 3, 3rd series (1849): 453; Joan Titley, "Edward Jarvis, M.D.: A New England Physician's Activities in Louisville, 1837–42," *Tractions*, 3 (1967–68):20–23.

15. Kaufman, *American Medical Education*, 46–47; *Louisville Cardinal*, April 16, 23, 1936; John Q. Anderson, "Henry Clay Lewis: Louisville Medical Institute Student, 1844–1846," *Filson Club History Quarterly*, 32 (1959):30–37; Drake, "Promoting

Moral and Intellectual Improvement," 295–314; David F. Allmendinger, *Paupers and Scholars: The Transformation of Student Life in Nineteenth-Century New England* (New York, 1975), 1–5.

16. Drake, "Promoting Moral and Intellectual Improvement," 295–314; Joseph W. Brooks, "On Creosote: A Thesis Submitted to the Managers and Faculty of the Louisville Medical Institute," *Louisville Journal of Medicine and Surgery*, 1 (1838):275–94; Charles Wilkins Short to John Cleves Short, February 16, 1848, Symmes, Short, and Harrison Papers, Library of Congress.

17. Lewis, "Being Examined for My Degree," 164–74; Nancy D. Baird, *David Wendel Yandell: Physician of Old Louisville* (Lexington, 1978), 14–15.

18. Drake, "Promoting Moral and Intellectual Improvement," 295–314.

19. Richard C. Wade, *The Urban Frontier: The Rise of the Western Cities, 1780–1830* (Cambridge, 1959), 197–200; John D. Wright, *Transylvania: Tutor to the West* (Lexington, 1980), 145–57; Ellis, *Medicine in Kentucky*, 8–22.

20. Charles Caldwell, "A Succinct View of the Influence of Mental Cultivation on the Destinies of Louisville," *Louisville Journal of Medicine and Surgery*, 1 (1838):1–34; Louisville, Legislative Records, November 27, 1837, 370–71, Louisville City Archives; Jefferson County, Deed Books, November 21, 1837, 19:385–86, Jefferson County Archives, Louisville; Lunsford P. Yandell, *History of the University of Louisville* (Louisville, 1852), 19–22.

21. Rothstein, *American Physicians in the Nineteenth Century*, 85–100; Joseph F. Kett, *The Formation of the American Medical Profession: The Role of Institutions, 1780–1860* (New Haven, 1968), 32–96; Edward Jarvis, "Autobiography," n.d., 92, Harvard University Archives, Cambridge; Horine, *Daniel Drake*, 336–40; Edgar Erskine Hume, "Henry Massie Bullitt," *Dictionary of American Biography*, 3:256–57; Lunsford P. Yandell, "Dr. McDowell and His Pretensions, *Western Journal of Medicine and Surgery*, 7, 2d series (1844):242–47; [William A. McDowell], *Some Account of the Faculty of the Louisville Medical Institute* (Louisville, 1842), 3–5; Louisville Medical Institute, *Some Account of the Origin and Present Condition of the Louisville Medical Institute* (Louisville, 1842), 3 ff.

22. *A Collection of the State and Municipal Laws . . .* Applicable to the City of Louisville, Oliver H. Stratton and John M. Vaughn, eds. (Louisville, 1857), 363–67; Board of Trustees, Minutes, August 3, 1846, 216, November 23, 1846, 284–85, University Archives, University of Louisville; Skaggs, "Charles Wilkins Short," 133–35; Horine, *Daniel Drake*, 324–67; "A New Medical School," *Western Journal of Medicine and Surgery*, 6, 3d series (1850):80–92; Lunsford P. Yandell to Susan Yandell, May 5, 1850, Yandell Papers, Filson Club.

23. *Louisville Democrat*, March 7, 1851; Kentucky *Acts* (1851):231–36; Lunsford P. Yandell, *History of the University of Louisville*, 19–22; City of Louisville v. University of Louisville (1854), 15 Monroe 642; Gross, *Autobiography*, 1:103; "Destruction of the University of Louisville," *North American Medico-Chirurgical Review*, 1 (1857):306–8; Kentucky *Acts* (1860): 432.

24. Ellis, *Medicine in Kentucky*, 17; *Centennial History*, 65, 76–77; Medical Faculty Minutes, November 28, 1863, 65, Health Sciences Library, University of Louisville; Case of Joseph W. Benson, January 7, 1865, Records of the Judge Advocate General, National Archives; Medical Department, *Record of the Facts in Relation to the Dismissal of the Faculty* (Louisville, 1869), passim; *Louisville Journal*, May 17, June 22,

1866; B.R.S. Beomand, Testimony, July 29, 1867, Gustave Meiser, Testimony, August 18, 1867, Freedmen's Bureau Records, National Archives.

25. Ellis, *Medicine in Kentucky*, 18–29; Baird, *Yandell*, 93–94; Emmett F. Horine, "A Forgotten Medical Editor: Edwin Samuel Gaillard (1827–1885)," *Annals of Medical History*, 2, 3d Series (1940):375–82; David W. Yandell, "Supplement," *American Practitioner*, 29 (1884):4.

26. Ellis, *Medicine in Kentucky*, 19–20; Medical Faculty Minutes, June 2, 1873, 263.

27. Ellis, *Medicine in Kentucky*, 18–20; *Louisville Medical News*, January 1, February 19, 1876; Kaufman, *American Medical Education*, 143; Yandell, "Supplement," 1–14; Kentucky School of Medicine, *Response to Charge and Specification Preferred before the American Medical College Association* (Louisville, 1879), 13.

28. Medical Faculty Minutes, March 29, 1866, 930, February 20, 1867, 135–36; May 15, 1869, 209–10; May 14, 1874, 280; June 9, 1877, 305–6; June 27, 1879, 327; May 8, 1884, 359; University of Louisville, *Annual Announcement* (Louisville, 1878), 5, 12–13; Kaufman, *Medical Education*, 133–40.

29. Baird, *Yandell*, 59–84.

30. Kaufman, *Medical Education*, 154–61; *Centennial History*, 79–80; Ellis, *Medicine in Kentucky*, 20–21; University of Louisville, *Annual Announcement* (Louisville, 1891), 5–6; *Annual Announcement* (Louisville, 1893), 9–10; *Annual Announcement* (Louisville, 1896), 11–12; Arthur Dean Bevan, "Cooperation in Medical Education and Medical Service," *Journal of the American Medical Association*, 90 (1928): 1173–81.

31. *Centennial History*, 81–86; James F. Hopkins, *The University of Kentucky: Origins and Early Years* (Lexington, 1951), 258–59; *Louisville Courier-Journal*, June 20, 1907, June 10, July 19, 29, 1908; *Louisville Herald*, June 20, 1908.

32. Flexner, *Medical Education*, 229–31; *Louisville Times*, June 7, 1910; Louisville Board of Trade, Resolution, February 23, 1910, Legislative Records of the City of Louisville, Supplementary Series; *Centennial History*, 128.

33. *Louisville Cardinal*, April 16, 23, 1936; John Allan Wyeth, *With Sabre and Scalpel: The Autobiography of a Soldier and Surgeon* (New York, 1914), 327; Simon Flexner, "A Half Century of American Medicine," in *A Century of Municipal Higher Education* (Chicago, 1937), 29–56.

34. G. Edward White, *Tort Law in America: An Intellectual History* (New York, 1980), 125–27; Ernest R. Sandeen, *The Roots of Fundamentalism: British and American Millenarianism, 1800–1930* (Chicago, 1970), 121; Robert H. Wiebe, *The Search for Order, 1877–1920* (New York, 1967), 113–16.

35. Cassedy, *Medicine and American Growth*, 67–72, 103–4; Drake, "Promoting Moral and Intellectual Improvement," 295–314; John Harley Warner, "A Southern Medical Reform: The Meaning of the Antebellum Argument for Southern Medical Education," in Ronald L. Numbers and Todd L. Savitt, eds., *Science and Medicine in the Old South* (Baton Rouge, 1989), 206–25.

36. Richard Hofstadter, *The American Political Tradition and the Men Who Made It* (New York, 1948), 44–66; Wiebe, *The Search for Order*, 111–63; James G. Burrow, *Organized Medicine in the Progressive Era: The Move Toward Monopoly* (Baltimore, 1977), 14–28.

37. Flexner, *Medical Education*, 148, 153.

38. Ibid., 230; Paul Starr, *The Social Transformation of American Medicine* (New York, 1982), 70–144; Ellis, *Medicine in Kentucky*, 77.

4

Compromiser or Conspirator? Henry Clay and the Graves-Cilley Duel

Melba Porter Hay

Few rituals have captured the imagination of Americans as much as the code duello. At once fascinating and romantic, repulsive and malevolent, the practice experienced its heyday in the famous duels of the nineteenth century—Alexander Hamilton and Aaron Burr, Stephen Decatur and James Barron, Henry Clay and John Randolph, to name a few. As the century progressed, it became more and more a practice relegated to the Deep South, where concepts of honor were frequently defended by the sword or the pistol. But rarely did the practice extend to two sitting members of Congress, as it did in the duel between William J. Graves of Kentucky and Jonathan Cilley of Maine, held on February 24, 1838.

The Graves-Cilley encounter had many peculiarities. Graves, the challenger, represented a border state where the practice was tolerated, if not applauded, by public opinion, but it was almost universally condemned in Cilley's native state. Because the meeting resulted from words spoken by Cilley in debate in the House of Representatives, he could have honorably declined the challenge for that reason, yet he refused to do so. Both men professed to have no personal animosity toward the other, yet the action continued to the third firing, when Cilley lay dead. It produced a huge public outcry, as well as a congressional investigation and threats of expulsion or censure for the surviving principal and the seconds. Moreover, many errors and unconfirmed assertions abound in both contemporary and historical accounts of the duel. But perhaps the strangest factor of all was that it became a prominent issue used against Henry Clay in the 1844 presidential campaign, when he was accused of having fomented a conspiracy against Cilley that resulted in a virtual assassination—and this in spite of the fact that Clay had not been mentioned in the report issued as a result of the House investigation or in the extensive journalistic coverage the duel received in 1838.

What, then, were the facts surrounding the encounter? Did the fight follow the proper ritual of the code duello? Why was it fought? Why was it pushed to the death? And why did the incident become an issue in the presidential campaign of 1844? What had been Clay's role? Was he a conspirator, as his opponents in 1844 charged, or was he a compromiser, as he himself claimed? The answers to these questions reveal much about the highly partisan, uncivil, acrimonious, even violent state of politics during the second-party system. To understand Clay's involvement and determine how the duel became an issue in the 1844 presidential election, it is necessary to examine the events leading to the confrontation, the conduct of the parties on the field, and the role of political rivalries both at the time of the encounter and later.

The events leading to the duel were set in motion on February 7, 1838, with publication of a column in the *New York Courier and Enquirer*, written by "The Spy in Washington," which charged that a member of Congress had sold his influence to an executive department of government. The article claimed that the member had explained to an applicant for a contract: " 'Merit! . . . *why things do not go here by merit, but by pulling the right strings. Make it my interest and I will pull the strings for you.'* " Two days later, an editorial written by the *Courier and Enquirer*'s volatile editor, James Watson Webb, called upon Congress to investigate the "Spy's" charge.[1]

On February 12, Congressman Henry A. Wise of Virginia, at that time a Whig known for his hot-headedness, referred to Webb's editorial and moved that the House investigate the charge. His motion was opposed by Cilley, a Democrat whose baiting of Whigs in debate had aroused the admiration of southern Democrats.[2] Cilley, like many members of his party, believed Webb had changed his affiliation from Democrat to Whig after receiving a loan from the Whigs' ally, the Second Bank of the United States. Replying to Wise's demand for an investigation, Cilley said he "knew nothing of this editor; but if it was the same editor who had once made grave charges against an institution of this country, and afterwards was said to have received facilities to the amount of some $52,000 from the same institution, and gave it his hearty support, he did not think that his charges were entitled to much credit in an American Congress."[3]

Wise snarled back: "Who is it that has influence to sell? It is those who belong to that party with which the gentleman from Maine acts." This heated exchange, which Wise later described as "a slight misunderstanding," was only one of several clashes between the two congressmen. A few days earlier Cilley had ridiculed Wise's effort to reduce the appropriation for conducting the Seminole War by comparing his "sympathy for the dark red man which seemed to be akin to that expressed in some quarters for the man of yet darker hue." It is doubtful that the Virginian would overlook this attack. Both men, proud and ambitious, exhibited the extreme partisan spirit then prevalent in the U.S. Congress.[4]

Whig Congressman John Quincy Adams characterized the charge made by "The Spy in Washington" as "a design, stimulated by party tactics, to blow up some individual member of the Administration party, and thereby to cast obloquy upon the whole party." This had caused a number of Democrats to vent "their unutterable indignation upon Matthew L. Davis," Adams charged, referring to the journalist widely reputed to be the "Spy."[5]

Wise's House resolution to investigate the "Spy's" charge passed on February 13 by a vote of 140 to 46, and Speaker of the House James K. Polk issued a subpoena directing the sergeant-at-arms to summon Matthew L. Davis to appear. While testifying, Davis refused to state whether he was, in fact, the "Spy," but admitted knowing the author of the charge and said the person accused of influence peddling was not then a member of the House. Earlier that same day Wise had noted a report in the *Newark Daily Advocate* stating that the person so charged was actually a U.S. senator. The object of the accusation was John Ruggles of Maine, who soon called upon Senator Daniel Webster to ask for a Senate investigation. Webster reluctantly did so, and a special committee subsequently found no evidence to support the charge.[6]

Events moved swiftly after Cilley's speech as Webb hurried to Washington intent on challenging Cilley to a duel if he refused to apologize. Webb persuaded Congressman William J. Graves of Kentucky to bear his note to the Maine congressman, inquiring "whether I am the editor to whom you alluded, and, if so, to ask the explanation which the character of your remarks renders necessary." According to the rules of the code duello, the Kentuckian, by accepting the responsibility of delivering the note, in effect assumed the role of second to Webb if a duel resulted. Since he and Webb were not close friends, why he agreed to do this remains a mystery.

When Graves attempted to present the note on February 21, the Maine congressman refused to accept it on the grounds, as the Kentuckian understood it, that he would not "be drawn into personal difficulties with the conductors of public journals for what he might . . . say in debate . . . [but] that he said nothing against Col. Webb as a gentleman." Graves urged Cilley "to receive the note and to adopt such ulterior course . . . by which I would be relieved from a most unpleasant situation, of the responsibilities of which, from my inexperience in the rules that regulate such matters, I should have to deliberate." When Cilley again refused the note, Graves stated that he "regretted it extremely; that I feared, unless he would reconsider, and change his determination, that I could not avoid a responsibility which I would very much regret."[7]

In such instances contemporaries consulted the standard rule book for the practice of dueling: John Lyde Wilson's booklet, *The Code of Honor or, Rules for the Government of Principals and Seconds in Dueling* (1838). According to Wilson:

If the party called on refuses to receive the note you bear, you are entitled to demand a reason for such refusal.—If he refuses to give you any reasons, and persists in such refusal, he treats, not only your friend, but yourself with indignity, and you must then make yourself the actor, by sending a respectful note, requiring a proper explanation of the course he has pursued towards you and your friend; and if he still adheres to his determination, you are to challenge or post him.

Wilson also explained that if the person to whom a second delivers a note refuses to accept it on grounds of inequality—that is, that the writer of the note is not a "gentleman"—the second is bound to tender himself instead. In such cases the substitute's second should interpose and adjust the matter if at all possible, because "the true reason of substitution, is the supposed insult of imputing the like inequality which is charged upon your friend, and when the contrary is declared, there should be no fight."[8]

When Graves consulted his friends and repeated what he thought the Maine congressman had said, they told him there was no reason for him to be offended by Cilley's refusal, because it had not been made upon objection to Webb as a gentleman. After reflection, Graves decided to ask Cilley to put his reasons in writing, but Cilley suggested instead that Graves address a note to him to which he would then reply.[9]

Graves delivered his first note to Cilley in the House of Representatives on February 21:

you will please say whether you did not remark, in substance, that in declining to receive the note, you hoped I would not consider it in any respect disrespectful to me, and that the ground on which you rested your declining to receive the note was distinctly this: that you could not consent to get yourself into personal difficulties with conductors of public journals, for what you might think proper to say in debate upon this floor in discharge of your duties as a representative of the people; and that you did not rest your objection in our interview, upon any personal objections to Colonel Webb as a gentleman.[10]

Late that evening, Graves received Cilley's reply, stating:

I declined to receive it, because I chose to be drawn into no controversy with him [Webb]. I neither affirmed nor denied any thing in regard to his character; but when you remarked that this course on my part might place you in an unpleasant situation, I stated to you, and now repeat, that I intended by the refusal no disrespect to you.[11]

The following day, Graves wrote his second note to Cilley, which was delivered by Kentucky Congressman Richard H. Menefee. It called Cilley's reply "inexplicit, unsatisfactory, and insufficient," in part because "in your declining to receive Colonel Webb's communication, it does not *disclaim* any exception to him personally as a gentleman." He concluded: "I have, therefore, to inquire *whether you declined to receive his communication on the ground of any personal exception to him as a gentleman or man of honor?* A categorical answer is expected."[12]

Cilley's second note was terse: "Your note of this date has just been placed in my hands. I regret that mine of yesterday was not satisfactory to you, but I cannot admit the right on your part to propound the question to which you ask a categorical answer, and therefore decline any further response to it."[13]

Graves later recalled: "On perusing this note, I perceived Mr. Cilley had determined not to state in writing what he had said in my personal interviews with him. I therefore felt there was no other alternative left me but to make the call contained in my third note." He said he then drafted the third note, his formal challenge, without asking anyone's opinion about the course he should pursue. He asked Representative Wise to deliver the challenge. Wise agreed but suggested they wait until the next day. According to Graves, the following day he changed "the date and some of the phraseology," and Wise delivered it to Cilley. The challenge stated:

As you have declined accepting a communication which I bore to you from Colonel Webb, and as by your note of yesterday you have refused to decline on grounds which would exonerate me from all responsibility growing out of the affair, I am left no other alternative but to ask that satisfaction which is recognised among gentlemen. My friend, Hon. Henry A. Wise, is authorized by me to make arrangements suitable to the occasion.[14]

Following protocol, Cilley chose General George Wallace Jones of Wisconsin as his second on the advice of a close friend and adviser, Senator Franklin Pierce of New Hampshire. Soon after refusing to accept Webb's note from Graves on February 21, Cilley had consulted Pierce. After receiving Graves's note, Cilley reportedly told Pierce and Dr. Alexander Duncan, congressman from Ohio, that he, Cilley, would "not be forced to place his [own] refusal to accept, either on the grounds of privilege, or that James W. Webb was or was not a gentleman, though a battery of artillery were arrayed before him." Pierce replied: "That could not be expected, but you should make your reply acceptable to Mr. Graves, if possible." Duncan interjected that Cilley ought to say that he "could not accept a communication from James W. Webb at the hand of any man," because Webb is "an unprincipled scoundrel, a degraded coward, and a bought-up vassal." Pierce cautioned that a southwestern man might be able to use such language, but a northern man must couch his answer so that if Cilley had to put his life in jeopardy "it must clearly appear that he is forced to do so in defence [*sic*] of his honor and of his rights."[15]

On February 22, Cilley, Duncan, Pierce, and Congressman Jesse A. Bynum of North Carolina met to discuss Graves's second note. Cilley complained that the note was not respectful and said that Graves "was put up to this . . . but if *they* thought to break him down by frightening him, they were mistaken." The following day Pierce asked General Jones to be Cilley's second. He at first refused on the grounds that his acquaintance with Cilley was "too limited . . . to accept so *important, responsible,* and *delicate a position,*" but finally, at Cilley's personal request, he agreed.[16]

Because the rules of the code duello provided that the person challenged set the conditions, Jones presented Wise with Cilley's terms—rifles at eighty yards. Each principal could have on the field his second, two friends, and a surgeon. Graves chose Congressman Menefee and Senator John J. Crittenden, both of Kentucky, as his friends and Dr. J. M. Foltz of the U.S. Navy as his surgeon, while Cilley chose Bynum and Colonel James W. Schaumburg of Louisiana as his friends and Dr. Duncan as his surgeon. Although he considered the terms "unusual and objectionable," Wise nonetheless accepted. The encounter was to take place at noon on February 24, provided Graves could procure a rifle by that time.[17]

Cilley was reputed to be an expert with that type of weapon, so apparently that was his reason for making such an unusual choice. Despite the fact that his friends later claimed otherwise, contemporary accounts indicate that he was a crack rifleman, while Graves decidedly was not. Writing to his wife on February 23, Congressman John Fairfield of Maine predicted that the duel would be fought "not with pistols, but with rifles, as the person challenged has a right to select his weapon." During the subsequent congressional investigation Bynum testified that Cilley had called himself "a tolerable fair shot," while Jones swore that Cilley had told him he chose rifles because he thought Graves was "adept in the use of" pistols. After the duel Philip Hone of New York received a letter from fellow New Yorker Charles King informing him of Cilley's death and saying that friends of the deceased had been confident Graves would be the one killed. King further stated that the day before the duel, Cilley had shot eleven balls in succession into a space not bigger than a man's hand.[18]

Virtually no one disputed Graves's lack of experience with the rifle. Wise testified that Graves had told him he was not practiced in the use of any weapon. The Virginian and Graves's other friends who accompanied him to the dueling field thought Cilley's terms were "barbarous, and such as might properly be declined"; but "that they were intended to intimidate; that the distance was so great as, in some measure, to mitigate the severity of the weapon, and, therefore, I was advised that they should be accepted." In fact, Graves's advisers thought that acceptance might actually avoid the duel altogether, "inasmuch as the plain object of such a proposition was either to *make the duel fatal*, or to *deter Mr. Graves from accepting them*; and, if the latter was the object, the party proposing was most likely to fly from the terms himself."[19]

On February 23, after accepting the terms, Wise embarked on a search for a rifle. Jones and Wise would later dispute whether or not the Virginian had asked for Jones's help in that endeavor. At 10:00 A.M. on February 24, Wise left a note for Jones saying that Graves had been unable to find a weapon and put it in order in time to meet at noon, but that he still wanted to have the meeting that day. A half-hour later Jones left a note saying that he had a rifle "in good order which is at the service of Mr. Graves." Meanwhile, a rifle procured by Richard Menefee at two o'clock that morning was being cleaned and Graves had begun to practice. Wise observed that Graves handled the weapon very awkwardly and shot badly. When Wise returned to his room, he found Jones had left a rifle and concluded that the encounter could be postponed no longer without an imputation of cowardice. The Virginian decided that Graves should not use the rifle Jones had offered, because "though 'an excellent rifle, in good order,' *Mr. Cilley had, of course preferred another to it*; and if Mr. Graves had missed with it, and been killed, I would have been justly chargeable with his death." Thus, the two seconds set the meeting for 3:00 P.M. that same day, February 24, on the road to Marlborough, Maryland, near the Anacostia Bridge.[20]

Confusion reigned about where the parties were meeting, and even some modern secondary accounts have subsequently erred in placing it on the road to Bladensburg, Maryland, the most common dueling site. Early on the morning of February 24, James Watson Webb went with two friends to Cilley's boardinghouse with the determination to force the congressman to fight with pistols on the spot or to promise that he would fight Webb before Graves. It was the editor's intention to disable Cilley by shooting him in the right arm if he refused both propositions. Not finding Cilley, Webb and his friends departed for Bladensburg, where they thought the duel would take place. One of the men accompanying Webb later said that he understood the site of the duel had been changed "to avoid interruption by Colonel Webb."[21]

When they arrived at the dueling field, Graves remarked to Dr. Foltz, his surgeon, that "he had not fired a rifle for two years, until that morning . . . and that in shooting off-hand, at eighty yards, he thought he would shoot very badly . . . and he supposed he was the worst shot, with a rifle, in his [congressional] delegation." He added that he knew little of Cilley and "had no personal ill feelings toward him."[22]

When stepping off the eighty yards, the seconds were generous in their measurements because, according to later testimony, they hoped the extra distance would help prevent a deadly hit. Wise later estimated that it was nearer a hundred yards, while another testified he had measured the ground afterwards, and it was ninety-two yards. Several conditions worked against Cilley, despite his better marksmanship. It was alleged that his nearsightedness made it virtually impossible for him to shoot accurately at the distance measured. Further, his rifle was one-half the caliber of his opponent's. Moreover, he was shooting against the wind as he stood on rising ground in open light, while Graves was shaded by a woodland.[23]

On the first exchange, Cilley's gun misfired and Graves missed. On the second exchange, the reverse occurred, though it initially appeared that Graves had been hit. Graves said at once that he must have another shot. After both firings, the seconds and friends parleyed in an attempt to resolve the conflict, but no agreement was reached. On the third exchange, Cilley fell dead, probably from a severed aorta.[24]

On February 28, 1838, four days after the duel, with public feeling running high, Maine Congressman John Fairfield moved that the House of Representatives investigate the cause of Cilley's death. The ostensible duty of the investigative committee was to see whether the encounter involved a breach of the privileges of the House. Appointed to the committee were Isaac Toucey of Connecticut (Democrat), chairman; William W. Potter of Pennsylvania (Democrat); Franklin H. Elmore of South Carolina (Democrat); Andrew D. W. Bruyn of New York (Democrat); James Rariden of Indiana (Whig); George Grennell, Jr., of Massachusetts (Whig); and Seaton Grantland of Georgia (Whig).[25]

Controversies quickly erupted during the investigation. Part of the disagreement centered on what actually happened on the dueling field, especially during the parleys between firings: Did the seconds make a sincere attempt to settle the dispute before it became deadly? Did Wise insist that Cilley avow that James Watson Webb was a "gentleman" before the proceeding could end? Did Crittenden insist that the confrontation end after the second firing? Also, debate arose among the participants over the true cause of the duel: Had Cilley impugned Graves's honor as a "gentleman" by refusing to accept Webb's note, thus forcing Graves to substitute himself? Or was the real cause the fact that by refusing to put in writing what Graves had told his friends Cilley had said, the Maine congressman had impugned the Kentuckian's veracity? Was there a partisan conspiracy to force a duel between the two congressmen, as some on both sides implied?

Both seconds declared that the proceedings had been conducted according to the code of honor. Defending his own responsibility to see that the encounter was fair to Cilley, George Jones maintained that because of the wind and the way the sun fell, Cilley had the best position on the field. Jones further testified that Cilley had said that "Mr. Graves and his party meant either to make him [Cilley] recognise Mr. Webb as a gentleman, shield himself behind his privilege as a member of the House of Representatives, or disgrace himself and his family." Jones added that "Mr. Wise frequently said to me, he 'hoped the difficulty would end,' and appeared to me to desire it, but [he] continued to require from Mr. Cilley concessions" in regard to his reasons for refusing to accept Webb's note. Jones also said that no one ever indicated to him that a question of veracity existed between Graves and Cilley.[26]

Wise, who already was receiving the lion's share of the blame for the deadly result of the duel, not only stoutly defended himself to the investigating committee and on the floor of the House but also wrote a letter to his constituents explaining his role in the affair. The Virginian swore he had received no prior knowledge that Graves was bearing Webb's note to Cilley. Indeed, when informed by Graves of that fact on February 21, Wise "rebuked him for having done so, upon the ground that his own previous relations with Colonel Webb did not justify the latter in imposing upon him such an office and its responsibilities." When Graves revealed what Cilley had verbally stated about his reasons for refusing the note, Wise had told him the reasons were satisfactory, and Graves left saying he would get the statement in writing. The Kentuckian had then returned "highly incensed" after receiving the first note from Cilley. Wise added that Graves regarded the note:

First: *As denying what he had alleged to his friends Mr. Cilley had said to him in conversation.*

Second: *As contemptuous and insulting to Colonel Webb, whose note he had borne.*

Third: *As placing Mr. Graves himself in the humiliating attitude of supplication to him (Mr. Cilley) to relieve him (Mr. Graves) from "an unpleasant situation."*

Fourth: *As saying, in effect, "I do not recognise COLONEL WEBB to be a gentleman, sir, but I respect YOU as one," thereby inviting Mr. Graves to substitute himself for Colonel Webb.*[27]

Since Wise had agreed with Graves's interpretation of the situation, he accepted the role of second. He denied having any personal enmity toward Cilley that would have precluded his serving as the Kentuckian's second.[28]

Wise repeatedly asserted that the basis of the dispute was Cilley's attack on Graves's veracity, though Jones and Cilley's friends denied that truthfulness had ever been stated as an issue. Wise "understood positively from Mr. Graves, that he would not be satisfied with any admission short of what Mr. Cilley had made to him, verbally, in their interviews. Our object, then, was to adopt or suggest some form of explanation or admission, which would be as easy as possible for Mr. Cilley to make, and which should satisfy Mr. Graves." They attempted and failed after both the first and the second firing to find a compromise. Further, the *"reason why* Mr. Graves insisted upon such admissions . . . was, because he confidently alleged Mr. Cilley had made them to him in conversation." Wise swore that every decision made on the dueling ground was done in consultation with Crittenden and Menefee. Further, he asserted that at any time in the proceedings Graves would have been satisfied if Cilley had made the plea that he could not be held accountable for words spoken in debate. The Virginian also admitted proposing that if no one was hit on the third firing, the distance should be shortened.[29]

James Watson Webb agreed with Wise's assertion that the true cause of the duel was Cilley's impugning Graves's truthfulness. He charged that Cilley had been willing to put into writing what he had said to Graves until he was influenced by Missouri Senator Thomas Hart Benton and Dr. Alexander Duncan. Webb referred to these men as *"ruffians"* who believed that "the life of Mr. Graves was at stake, in consequence of Mr. Cilley's wonderful accuracy in rifle shooting." Indeed, they had persuaded Cilley "to withhold his assent to what Mr. Graves had already reduced to writing, and thereby indirectly implicated his veracity."[30]

Graves had chosen Crittenden to serve as one of his friends on the field because, "in Kentucky and wherever else he was well known, no man was more distinguished for his mildness and humility." Graves believed Crittenden's presence would be "the best evidence I could offer at home that I did not intend to act rashly or go beyond the requirements of those laws under which I went to the field." Crittenden reluctantly agreed to serve, although he knew little about dueling procedures and opposed the practice in principle. Therefore, his actions on the field became a subject of some dispute during the investigation. Bynum, Duncan, and Foltz all understood him to say that honor had been satisfied after the first firing and the duel should be terminated. After the second firing, several understood Crittenden to say it should stop and that if the third attempt was unsuccessful, he would take a firm stand to that effect. Apparently in an effort to shield his friends from criticism and to accept his own share of the blame, Crittenden denied in testimony to the investigating committee that he had disagreed in any way with Wise and Menefee and said others must have been misled by his attempt to perform "a sort of mediation." He admitted, however, saying between the second and third firings that both men had shown their courage.[31]

If Crittenden rejected the role of peacemaker, Cilley's friend Congressman Jesse A. Bynum gladly accepted it. Bynum said that he believed honor had been satisfied on the first firing and had wanted to call it off, but found his own friends disagreed. He concluded that Wise and Menefee "manifested every disposition, and did persevere in its prosecution, to the death of one of the parties," while Crittenden manifested "every intention and disposition to arrest the fight."[32]

Menefee maintained that Cilley's friends believed the proceedings were intended *"to extort from Mr. Cilley an admission that Colonel Webb was a gentleman."* He thought that notion was erroneous and had directed his efforts to suppressing it. Although Cilley's friends could not recall these statements, Menefee testified that he had repeated over and over that "all Mr. Graves insisted on, connected with Colonel Webb, was *that when Mr.*

Cilley refused the note, he placed his refusal on other grounds than of exception to character." Menefee also stated that he and his friends had perceived Cilley's intent to be deadly because of the "extraordinary and ferocious nature of the weapons selected by Mr. Cilley," the precipitation of the time of the duel by providing a weapon, and the report they heard "of the excellence of Mr. Cilley's marksmanship with the rifle."[33]

On the other hand, Cilley's friend James Schaumburg testified that Cilley had said Graves's demand was for Cilley to say that Webb was a man of honor, but he could not do so. Furthermore, Schaumburg reported that Cilley had referred to Wise as his "enemy." When Schaumburg asked Cilley why he had not objected to Wise as Graves's second, the congressman replied that he regretted not doing so, but it was too late. Schaumburg also protested to Wise during the parleys between firings that it was unusual and absurd for the challenger to demand an explanation from the party challenged after the demand for satisfaction had been granted.[34]

It is not surprising that after this often contradictory testimony, given in the aftermath of the duel, the investigating committee divided primarily along party lines. A majority report, signed by Democrats Toucey, Potter, and Bruyn, and by Whig Grantland, concluded that the words spoken by Cilley in debate and his refusal to explain those words except that he chose not to be drawn into debate on the subject were the causes that led to his death. The majority also concluded that there had indeed been a breach of the privileges of the House and recommended that the House expel Graves and censure Wise and Jones. They made no recommendation regarding other friends on the field.[35]

Democrat Franklin Elmore, in a separate report, concluded that Graves was "as much a victim as the member who fell by his hand." While Elmore agreed with the majority that demanding an explanation for words spoken in debate was a breach of the privileges of the House, as was issuing or bearing a challenge, or acting as a second, he also contended that *accepting* a challenge was equally a breach of those privileges. He favored "mildness in the present proceeding" and greater severity in the future through passage of a new law against dueling and amendments to House rules.[36]

Whigs George Grennell and James Rariden issued a minority report saying that they concurred with the majority that a breach of House privileges had taken place. However, they argued that the greater purpose of the investigating committee had been to determine the facts surrounding Cilley's death and to arouse sentiment against dueling. Moreover, they disagreed "with the manner in which the majority have selected and arranged portions of the testimony, with a view to conclusions." They contended that instead of proposing punishment, the committee should devise a "just, well-conceived, and efficient law of Congress against duel-ling" and a standing House rule providing for the expulsion of any member who participated in a duel.[37]

When the whole report was laid on the table, no action was taken toward either the censure or the expulsion of any of the participants. Congressman John Quincy Adams summed up the result best:

Laying the whole [report] on the table is, in fact, smothering the report; but it leaves the resolutions of expulsion and of censure suspended over the heads of the members implicated. And perhaps this is the most equitable result of the whole affair that could occur. It is a strong though indirect censure of the House upon the principals and seconds to the duel, and upon the practice itself; and it is a censure alike indirect, not less strong, and as just, upon the report of the committee laid upon the table, outrageous as it is upon every sense of impartial justice. All the parties to the duel are severely censurable; none more so than the man who fell. The majority of the committee who presented this report are still more censurable; for, instead of holding an impartial balance between the parties, they have turned the whole subject into an electioneering engine of party.[38]

To be sure, the Democrats sought to gain politically from the proceedings. For example, Congressman John Fairfield, Cilley's colleague from Maine, wrote his wife on two occasions about the approbation he received for his resolution demanding an investigation. In one instance Fairfield remarked that he was "reaping a harvest of glory for my course upon this subject."[39]

Another example of the Democrats' use of the incident was an article in the *United States Magazine & Democratic Review*, titled "The Martyrdom of Cilley." The writer blamed the Whigs for the congressman's death and singled out Wise for special criticism. The article charged that a "bitter and ferocious spirit of party" had made its way into politics and "no person has done more to create and foster this, than the wretched individual who has enacted the principal part in this drama of death—we refer . . . not to the weak-minded and unhappy man who drew the fatal trigger, but to the hand which held and directed that *comparatively* innocent and passive will." The writer defended Cilley's acceptance of the challenge by saying that "He believed it to be a conspiracy to browbeat him into insignificance before the House and the country." While Graves was described as "a criminal of an inferior order of intellect and malignity" who was "bad and weak, though not . . . demonic," Wise was called a "deliberate assassin" who would cause the flesh to "creep with disgust and the blood" to "curdle with horror."[40]

Crittenden, though one of Graves's friends on the field, managed to escape most of the opprobrium for the affair. He noted, however, that the duel was being used by "all the *little politicians*," with the vilest abuse being poured out by the administration presses on Graves and "on *Wise* particularly." Crittenden continued to maintain that Graves acted from a sense of honor, even "if he went a step too far."[41]

And so the matter stood until 1842. Henry Clay's name had not been mentioned during the House investigation or in any press report or commentary related to the duel. Graves, who maintained he had never dreamed of the consequences that would result from delivering Webb's note, was reelected to another term in the House and then returned to the state legislature.[42]

Though public commotion about the duel died down, party rivalries only intensified in the 1840s. Wise was allied with Henry Clay, the Whig Party's leader, until fellow Virginian John Tyler succeeded to the presidency in 1841 after the death of William Henry Harrison. Tyler, who had never really accepted the nationalistic program of the majority of the Whig Party, soon began vetoing legislation sponsored by Clay and eventually broke with the party completely. When that occurred, Wise, who had become one of Tyler's closest advisers, deserted the Whig Party and its leader.[43]

Slavery also contributed to the escalating party and sectional tensions and helped bring the Graves-Cilley duel back to the forefront of debate in 1842. In the House of Representatives John Quincy Adams led the opposition to the so-called gag rule by which antislavery petitions were tabled without debate. Adams supported diplomatic recognition of the black republic of Haiti. In January 1842 he presented a petition from the citizens of Haverhill, Massachusetts, calling for a dissolution of the Union because of the continued practice of slavery in the southern states. Wise, who opposed recognition of Haiti, demanded that Adams be censured for presenting this petition, and the two engaged in venomous debate for several days, with Wise implying at one point that Adams was an English agent working for dissolution of the Union. Adams defended himself on January 26, referring to his adversary's role in the Graves-Cilley duel. He reminded his colleagues that four or five years earlier "there came to this house . . . a man with his hands and face dripping with the blood of murder," who was more guilty than the man who "happened to draw the trigger."[44]

Two days later Wise replied, declaring that he would vindicate himself from the charge of instigating and advising in the Graves-Cilley duel. Without calling names, he appealed to Clay and Crittenden, who were spectators in the House, to witness that "his was not the advice relied upon or followed in the preliminaries of that duel—it was the advice of another, higher, better, and more distinguished man which was relied on."[45]

By this time the Democratic press had begun to insinuate that Clay, who was expected to be the Whig presidential candidate in 1844, had been the main force behind the duel. An article in the *Boston Morning Post* of February 4, 1842, reported that a congressman declared he had proof not only that Clay dictated the challenge "but for the officiousness and rancor he displayed on the occasion, the duel never would have been had. . . . Mr. Cilley was a victim to the rapacity of Mr. Clay, rather than a victim to the rifle of his antagonist." The writer further asserted that the Whig leader had *"compelled"* Graves to assume Webb's cause in order to get the *New York Courier and Enquirer* to abandon its support of Daniel Webster for president and endorse the Kentuckian instead. While admitting that the *Courier and*

Enquirer "was from the year 1832 very favorably inclined to Mr. Clay," the writer noted that it had become "a thoroughgoing Clay paper" immediately after the duel. Moreover, the writer claimed to have observed "in the manner and expression of Mr. Clay's countenance . . . the smile of exultation that lighted [his face] . . . when he was informed that *'the Yankee had fallen'* and *'the chivalric Graves, the noble Kentuckian'* had escaped unharmed!" The writer said he voiced these sentiments at the time and was denounced as a liar and a scoundrel; he was now glad that Wise had stepped forward to prove "that Jonathan Cilley was murdered to propitiate the fortunes and ambition of Henry Clay."

On February 12 the *Courier and Enquirer* countered that if Wise and his associates had not deceived Clay about the time and place of the duel, civil authorities at Clay's instigation would have interfered and prevented the meeting. A denial appeared four days later in *The Madisonian*, the Tyler administration paper, in an article widely believed to have been written by Wise himself. *The Madisonian* asserted that all who were concerned in the duel had known from the beginning that Graves had relied upon Clay's advice. "We mean not to say, but to repel the idea that he [Clay] *instigated* that duel; far from it. . . . [But] we deny that Mr. Wise ever deceived Mr. Clay as to the *day*. . . . And we affirm, equally positive, that the *place* of meeting was *not* changed, by Mr. Wise."

Clay's friends soon came to his defense. On February 25, the *Daily National Intelligencer* in Washington published a letter from Graves to Clay, as well as statements written by Charles King, editor of the *New York American*, and Reverdy Johnson of Maryland, explaining Clay's role in the affair. Graves stated that he did not remember mentioning to Clay his problem with Cilley until the morning before the duel. He recalled that Clay "suggested to me some modification in the praseology [*sic*] of the challenge, which I had written but had not sent by which milder language was empolyed [*sic*] & the door was not so completely closed against adjustment." Graves then adopted Clay's draft. He also wrote Clay that it was "utterly untrue that you ever exhibited to me any wish that the meeting should take place. I believe I had no fr[i]end in Washington who more regreted [*sic*] it.[46]

In their statements Johnson and King insisted that they had been urged by James Watson Webb to seek out Clay and ask his assistance in preventing the encounter. Clay had told them he ought not to have been consulted by Graves, but because Graves had sought him out, he could not take any action to stop the meeting without compromising his friend's honor. When Johnson and King learned the following morning that the parties had gone out, they again went to Clay, who, though sick in bed, advised them to seek the aid of Virginia Congressman Charles Fenton Mercer and U.S. District Attorney Francis Scott Key on how to stop the duel. The civil authorities were called out, but thinking the meeting would take place at Bladensburg, the usual dueling site, they failed to locate the parties.[47]

On February 25, the day Graves's letter and Johnson and King's statements appeared in the *Intelligencer*, Wise wrote Clay demanding to know whether, by his publication of these statements and by the February 12 editorial in the *Courier and Enquirer*, Clay meant "to give countenance to the imputation . . . that *I ever deceived you, either as to the time or place of meeting.*" He also commanded Clay to state whether or not he had drawn the form of the challenge and whether or not it was his advice that had been followed in the affair.[48]

Three days later Clay replied, denying he had ever said or thought that Wise had deceived him as to the time and place of the meeting. Rather, having no previous knowledge of either, Clay simply thought the duel could not occur on February 24 because Graves did not have a rifle. Clay further stated that he had known nothing of the affair until Graves informed him of Cilley's verbal explanation for refusing the note. At that time he advised Graves to get Cilley's explanation in writing. Clay said he never saw the rest of the correspondence until Graves showed him the challenge, which appeared to close the door to all accommodation. For that reason Clay sketched a draft in his own hand that he hoped would admit of an amicable adjustment. The Kentuckian added that a few weeks earlier, "prior to any allusion to the unfortunate duel made in the H. of Representatives by Mr. Adams and yourself . . . a letter . . . appeared in the *N. York Herald*, charging me with having instigated and caused the duel and with having prepared the challenge." In this way, "the naked fact of my having prepared the challenge, suppressing the attending circumstances, and especially the motive of an amicable adjustment . . . was thus brought before the public." He added: "Now, you [Wise] Mr. Graves and I were only present when I proposed that modification. Not for a moment could I believe that He [Graves] furnished the fact of the challenge to the writer of the letter to the *N. York Herald*, I did not; and my conclusion was not unreasonable that you did."[49]

Wise maintained that Clay's friends in 1838 had sought to keep his name out of the duel. He claimed Clay had said to him: "Sir, it is a nine days' bubble! If they want to know what I did in the matter, tell them to call me before them, and I will tell them!" The Virginian said this excited his admiration "and was effectual to prevent me from unnecessarily bringing his name before the committee."[50]

While it is doubtful that these revelations in 1842 had much of an impact on public opinion toward Wise, they subsequently provided the Democrats with considerable ammunition against Clay. In the campaign of 1844, all of the correspondence and charges from 1842 were brought forward and repeated again and again. In fact, the same statements were quoted by Democrats to prove that Clay instigated the duel and by Whigs to prove that he had not done so. On July 2, 1844, one of the most virulent anti-Clay newspapers, the *Delaware Gazette*, called on its readers to picture Mrs. Cilley as she shrieked at the news of her husband's death. "And then let them contemplate Mr. Clay the *cause* of her miseries, the author of her calamities. Let them see him rejoicing . . . over the death of her husband and exclaiming . . . that 'it was only a nine-day bubble.' " Later, the *Gazette* charged that Clay had "assisted in planning the murder of Jonathan Cilley, of Maine. He counseled with Graves, urged on the duel, and actually penned the challenge with his own hand." The article erroneously concluded that "it is said" that Cilley's "young wife died in a mad house and his two children are left destitute." (Actually, Mrs. Cilley did not die until October 1844.) On July 23, in an article titled "Henry Clay, The Duellist, Who Pronounced The Murder of An Innocent Man 'A Nine Days Bubble,' " the *Gazette* proclaimed Clay to be *"so excessively bad"* that it was difficult to get the public to understand how *"corrupt, vicious, and dangerous"* he was.[51]

The *Washington Globe*, another Democratic paper, charged that the "blood of the murdered Cilley rests upon [Clay's] soul; its crimson is upon his head." According to the *Globe*, Clay's motive for promoting the duel was to protect James Watson Webb, the "chattel" of the Bank of the United States, from risk. Clay did not want the bank to lose its valuable "property" in the form of Webb. The *Globe* graphically summed up its points by presenting Clay's alleged involvement in dueling in a story shaped like a body. Over this was a coat of arms—supposedly Clay's—consisting of a brandy bottle, a pack of cards, a dueling pistol, and the words "Shoot lower!!"[52]

Amos Kendall, former tutor to Clay's sons but in 1844 the anti-Clay editor of *Kendall's Expositor*, wrote numerous articles and tracts accusing Clay of every moral defect imaginable. In one publication, Kendall gave eight reasons why Clay should not be elected president, including the charge that it would encourage dueling, gambling, and cursing. On another occasion the editor proclaimed in bold capitals: "MR. CLAY WAS THE CAUSE OF CILLEY'S MURDER."[53]

On the other hand, a pro-Clay paper, the *Kennebec* (Maine) *Journal*, called Kendall a notorious "ingrate" and reported that his slanderous pamphlet, *Clay's Duels*, had been franked by members of Congress, including John Fairfield of Maine, and had been sent throughout Maine and Connecticut. The paper called on the Democratic Party to repudiate such tactics from which "every honest man must turn with loathing and disgust . . . lest the pestilence which flows from his dirty soul should, like the effluvia of a polecat, infect everyone who might come in contact with it." The true culprits, the paper charged, were certain northern Democrats who had groomed Cilley for the encounter and, "confident that Graves and not Cilley would be slain," had prevented Cilley from making the proper explanation to Graves. These men also advised the use of rifles because Cilley was the best shot in Washington. Taking the offensive, the *Journal* noted that Democrats, having by accident nominated one who had never fought a duel, had suddenly much to say on the subject, whereas, when Andrew Jackson had been their candidate, they had been completely silent on the issue.[54]

Charles King and William J. Graves traveled around Kentucky and Tennessee during the 1844 campaign, defending Clay's actions in the affair. King recalled that when he and Johnson had informed Clay that the parties had gone out, "the surprise and grief evinced by Mr. Clay . . . his solicitude that no time should be lost by us . . . and the steps he immediately took to aid us in discovering the route of the combatants—all bespoke the most anxious desire on his part to prevent the fatal meeting." He concluded that "Partisan malignity has never been exhibited in a fouler and falser way than in the attempt to make Mr. Clay responsible for the blood of Cilley."[55]

The Whig press accused the Democrats of concentrating on personal attacks rather than national issues. "Tell them that the Whig tariff has been beneficial in its operations, and ought not to be repealed, and they reply by asserting that Mr. Clay planned the murder of Cilley," one paper decried. A Baltimore paper lamented that of the many calumnies used to vilify Clay "there is scarcely any that is more frequently resorted to than the slander of the Cilley duel." The *Washington Daily National Intelligencer* claimed that the issue of the Graves-Cilley duel had "risen to the dignity of a formidable lie; formidable . . . for its magnitude and its power of mischief." Rather, the *Intelligencer* argued, no man had accommodated or prevented more duels than Clay, and it was in this same pacific spirit that he attempted to settle the affair between Graves and Cilley.[56]

During the 1844 campaign Clay defended himself against charges concerning his role in the duel in at least two letters. Citing the correspondence between himself, Graves, and Wise in 1842, he noted: First, that the evidence established that "the draft which I suggested of the challenge was made expressly with the view of leading to an adjustment of the dispute . . . and not, as alleged . . . to close the door." Second, "that I never believed the controversy would occasion a hostile meeting, but continually thought that it ought to be, and would be, amicably settled." Third, "that I was ignorant that the parties were to meet in combat, and at what hour they were to meet." Fourth, "that when I accidentally heard that they had gone out to fight . . . I advised the police to be called out; but they missed the parties, in consequence of their having taken an unexpected route."[57]

After losing the 1844 presidential election to James K. Polk by a mere 38,000 popular votes, Clay noted that he had been accused of "a thousand and one calumnies." Of those, exactly what influence the Graves-Cilley duel had in the outcome of an election that was also influenced by the momentous issue of Texas annexation, the rise of the Liberty Party, charges of nativism against the Whigs, and a variety of other issues is impossible to say. Certainly, it would be a mistake to place too much emphasis on the duel in a campaign notable for its use of myriad falsehoods and dirty tricks.[58]

Yet, taken together, the testimony at the 1838 congressional investigation, the revelations of 1842, the subsequent campaign charges in 1844, and secondary references to the duel confuse as much as they clarify. In considering whether the rules of the code duello were followed, it is clear that Wise should never have acted as Graves's second. Craig M. Simpson, one of Wise's biographers, has accurately noted that the Virginian understated his differences with Cilley. The Maine congressman was his enemy as a result of the personal attacks they had made against each other in House debate. Since it was the duty of the second to attempt to effect a reconciliation that would avert combat and, failing that, to decide after an exchange of fire whether or not honor had been satisfied, the second should have been someone who was calm and cool and had no personal animosity toward the other party.

Wise's behavior as second, however, was anything but conciliatory. For example, Wise could have rejected the use of rifles as being unusually severe, but he claimed that Clay advised acceptance of the terms by saying that Graves was "a Kentuckian and can never back from a rifle." This statement remained uncorroborated. Wise also could have stopped the fight after the first fire by declaring that honor had been satisfied. Instead, he seems to have been unsure of what exactly Cilley was required to say in apology before the firing ceased. And since on the dueling field Cilley obviously was not going to say what he had already refused to state about his reasons for rejecting Webb's note, it seems strange that Wise added that condition as the only means of halting the duel other than the wounding of one of the parties. Wise had said that the reason the duel went to three firings was because Cilley misfired on the first round, Graves on the second, and the third was the only true exchange. Yet he had suggested that if no one was hit on the third fire, the distance should be shortened. This could only be interpreted as a deadly intent. Thus, Wise deserved at least part of the condemnation he encountered.[59]

What of Cilley's responsibility for the affair? Clearly, he could simply have deflected the problem by saying he was not accountable for words spoken in debate, but on several occasions, including on the dueling field itself, he refused to do so. Although he couched his participation in terms of upholding the honor of his family and New England, the majority of both would undoubtedly have supported him if he had declined the challenge, because the practice was generally condemned in the North. His close friend Nathaniel Hawthorne lamented that Cilley threw his life away "in so miserable a cause" and asked: "Why, as he was true to the Northern character in all things else, did he swerve from his Northern principles in this final scene?" Yet sectional differences can be exaggerated. As Bertram Wyatt-Brown has pointed out in *Southern Honor: Ethics & Behavior in the Old South* (1982), the degree of difference between northerners and southerners in notions of honor was often slight, and Cilley seems to have subscribed to a concept of chivalry and honor akin to that of the most fire-eating southerner. One must also take into account the repeated testimony that Cilley was an expert rifleman and that his friends, as well as Graves's, apparently expected him to emerge the winner. Moreover, from their own testimony, he was clearly encouraged to proceed by friends such as Alexander Duncan. Ultimately, it must be concluded that he was as culpable as the victor.[60]

Then there is the question: What was the real cause of the duel? Was it that Graves was substituting himself for Webb as the code demanded, or was it that Cilley denied saying to Graves what the Kentuckian had reported to his friends Cilley had said, thereby impugning Graves's veracity? This is a key question that remained unresolved in the 1838 investigation. If the former caused the duel, then the affair was over a mere point of honor and would customarily have been settled with one firing. If the latter, it meant that deadly issues existed between the two men, issues that involved much more than a mere point of honor. Truthfulness was an extremely serious matter. Nothing was more insulting than calling a man a liar.

The 1842 revelations favor the issue of veracity as the cause of the duel. Certainly, that was what Wise maintained all along, and Graves's statements support this argument. As two of the parties most intimately involved, surely they knew what the fight was about. Yet confusion has resulted because veracity was not mentioned in the challenge, and at least some of the parties on the field did not recognize it to be an issue. Those who have written about the duel have subsequently also misinterpreted the cause.

Steven M. Stowe, for example, in *Intimacy and Power in the Old South: Ritual in the Lives of the Planters* (1987) has depicted the Graves-Cilley duel as a classic example of how the "ritual power of the affair of honor was fully displayed" because the episode stemmed from a point of honor rather than from personal animosity. He concludes that Graves's self-esteem was threatened because, in refusing to accept Webb's note, Cilley was implying not only that Webb was less than an equal but that the bearer was not his equal as well. This echoes an 1855 account that concluded the duel was "upon a mere point of honor." In fact, although the two men had apparently borne no personal animosity toward each other previously, the very fact of Cilley's implying that Graves had lied in reporting the reasons Cilley had given for refusing the note created personal animosity of the most dangerous sort on Graves's part, while Cilley apparently viewed the other congressman's bearing of the note as part of a conspiracy to threaten his honor, thus causing him to have personal animosity toward Graves. Indeed, a public meeting in Maine in March 1838 adopted a resolution charging Cilley's death to "a foul conspiracy, concerted and approved among a few political leaders to take advantage of Mr. Cilley . . . in order . . . to gratify personal feelings of private malice and revenge."[61]

In light of these considerations, Clay's role in drafting a new challenge becomes clearer. Although the wording of the original challenge was never made public, it appears that it based Cilley's insult on his impugning Graves's veracity. Clay, thus, changed it to a mere point of honor, with Graves substituting himself for Webb. The only logical reason for doing this was to attempt to couch the dispute in terms more easily reconcilable than impugning a man's truthfulness. The action backfired, however, in the sense that Clay eventually bore the opprobrium of being the author of the challenge. And it also made Wise look worse for pursuing the match until the third firing, because most people were unaware that the dispute involved such a serious issue. Clay admitted in 1842 that he had advised Graves to get Cilley's reason for refusing the note in writing, but it seems unlikely he could have foretold that Cilley would deny the words he had spoken to Graves.[62] While evidence suggests that Clay was not a conspirator promoting the duel—he in fact feared for his friend Graves's life in facing a marksman like Cilley—he certainly might have played a more assertive role as a compromiser in mediating the dispute. Merely changing the wording of the challenge and subsequently advising that the police be called to stop the duel were apparently his only contributions.

In the end, there appears to have been no concerted conspiracy on the part of any party in the famous Graves-Cilley duel. The underlying culprit in the entire episode, and one that would increase in the next two decades until it finally resulted in civil war, was the increasing stridency in political debate, the loss of civility in speech and conduct, and the making of every political difference into a cause for personal animosity. The episode was a warning against the dangers of excess, but it was one that went unheeded. This spirit of extremism was evidenced to an even greater degree in the campaign of 1844. Although at that time it was couched in terms of party and personality, it was soon to be phrased in terms of sectionalism, division, and civil war.

NOTES

1. *New York Courier and Enquirer*, February 7, 9, 1838. The "Spy in Washington" was widely known to be Matthew L. Davis. A number of newspapers and other published sources cited used italics for emphasis; this has been reproduced as published in all direct quotations.

2. Roy F. Nichols, *Franklin Pierce, Young Hickory of the Granite Hills* (Philadelphia, 1931), 103; Craig M. Simpson, *A Good Southerner: The Life of Henry A. Wise of Virginia* (Chapel Hill, 1985), 38–39.

3. *Congressional Globe*, 25 Cong., 2d sess., 173–76. For a discussion of whether or not Webb was actually bribed by the Second Bank of the United States, see *U.S. House Report No. 460*, 22 Cong., 1st sess. (which concludes that he was bribed); Thomas P. Govan, *Nicholas Biddle, Nationalist and Public Banker, 1786–1844* (Chicago, 1959), 193–204 (which concludes that Biddle intended to bribe Webb); and James L. Crouthamel, "Did the Second Bank of the United States Bribe the Press?" *Journalism Quarterly*, 36 (Winter 1959):35–44 (which proves fairly conclusively that

although Biddle probably intended for the loan to influence Webb, it did not, because Webb did not realize at the time he changed his editorial stance that the loan had come from the B.U.S.). Crouthamel makes the same point, more briefly, in *James Watson Webb, A Biography* (Middletown, CT, 1969), 36–45.

4. *Congressional Globe*, 25 Cong., 2d sess., 173–76; Simpson, *A Good Southerner*, 38–39.

5. Charles Francis Adams, ed., *Memoirs of John Quincy Adams, Comprising Portions of the Diary From 1795 to 1848*, 12 vols. (Philadelphia, 1876), 9:493.

6. *Congressional Globe*, 25 Cong., 2d sess., 178–79, 186, 194–95, 302–3; *New York Courier and Enquirer*, February 19, 1838.

7. Bayard Tuckerman, ed., *The Diary of Philip Hone, 1828–1851*, 2 vols. (New York, 1889), 1:292–93; *House Report No. 825*, 25 Cong., 2d sess., 3, 127–28.

8. John Lyde Wilson, *The Code of Honor or, Rules for the Government of Principals and Seconds in Dueling* (Charleston, SC, 1838), reprinted in Jack K. Williams, *Dueling in the Old South: Vignettes of Social History* (College Station, TX, 1980), 40, 91. Wilson's was the standard text on the rules of dueling and was consulted throughout the South.

9. *U.S. House Report No. 825*, 128.

10. Ibid., 41.

11. Ibid., 41–42.

12. Ibid., 42.

13. Ibid., 5.

14. Ibid., 42, 128–29.

15. Ibid., 102–3, 120–22. A number of published sources have erroneously identified Cilley's second as George Jones of Tennessee, who did not go to Congress until 1843. See, for example, William O. Stevens, *Pistols at Ten Paces, The Story of the Code of Honor in America* (Boston, 1940), 223.

16. *U.S. House Report No. 825*, 48, 103.

17. Ibid., 5–6.

18. Arthur G. Staples, ed., *The Letters of John Fairfield* (Lewiston, ME, 1922), 202–3; *U.S. House Report No. 825*, 73, 48; Tuckerman, *Diary of Philip Hone*, 1:295.

19. *U.S. House Report No. 825*, 57; *Niles' Register*, 54 (March 24, 1838):54.

20. *U.S. House Report No. 825*, 6–7, 57–58.

21. Albert D. Kirwan, *John J. Crittenden, the Struggle for the Union* (Lexington, KY, 1962), 119, incorrectly places the duel on the Bladensburg Road. See David Morrell's statement, *U.S. House Report No. 825*, 11, 139–40, also published in *New York Courier and Enquirer*, March 3, 1838.

22. *U.S. House Report No. 825*, 116.

23. Ibid., 138; Horatio King, "History of the Duel Between Jonathan Cilley and William J. Graves," *Collections and Proceedings of the Maine Historical Society*, 2d Series, 3 (Portland, ME, 1889), 396.

24. *U.S. House Report No. 825*, 8–9, 107.

25. Staples, *Letters of John Fairfield*, 204–5.

26. *U.S. House Report No. 825*, 49, 52–53.

27. Ibid., 55–56. For Wise's account of the duel many years later, see John A. Wise, "Henry A. Wise's Account of the Duel," *Saturday Evening Post*, June 2, 1906, and Barton H. Wise, *The Life of Henry A. Wise of Virginia, 1806–1876* (New York, 1899), 81–83.

28. *U.S. House Report No. 825*, 56–61; *Niles' Register*, 54 (March 24, 1838):54.

29. *U.S. House Report No. 825*, 59–60, 63; *Niles' Register*, 54 (March 24, 1838):54. Kirwan, *Life of Crittenden*, 119–20, erroneously says the distance was shortened on each firing.

30. *New York Courier and Enquirer*, March 2, 1838.

31. Kirwan, *Life of Crittenden*, 119–20; *U.S. House Report No. 825*, 9–10, 69, 92–101, 106, 108, 118.

32. *U.S. House Report No. 825*, 68–76.

33. Ibid., 80–81.

34. Ibid., 85–89.

35. Ibid., 15–17.

36. Ibid., 29–34.

37. Ibid., 19–25.

38. Adams, *Memoirs of John Quincy Adams*, 9:527.

39. Staples, *Letters of John Fairfield*, 210–12.

40. "The Martyrdom of Cilley," *U.S. Magazine and Democratic Review*, 1 (March 1838): 493–504.

41. John J. Crittenden to Leslie Combs, March 20, 1838, printed in *The Life of John J. Crittenden, with Selections From His Correspondence and Speeches*, Mrs. Chapman Coleman, ed., 2 vols. (Philadelphia, 1871), 1:107–8.

42. Graves was reelected to the U.S. House in 1838 and to the Kentucky House of Representatives in 1843. He served as a Whig elector in 1844 and died in Louisville in 1848. *Biographical Directory of the American Congress* (Washington, DC, 1928). An example of one of the many errors written about the duel is in Hamilton Cochran, *Noted American Duels and Hostile Encounters* (Philadelphia and New York, 1963), 141, which says that Graves was not reelected "for it was a tradition in Kentucky that no man who killed another in a duel would ever be elected again to public office."

43. President Tyler broke with the Whig Party when he vetoed bills passed by Congress creating a new national bank. His entire cabinet, with the exception of Daniel Webster, resigned, and he eventually tried unsuccessfully to create a political party of his own. See James F. Hopkins et al., *The Papers of Henry Clay*, 11 vols. (Lexington, KY, 1959–1992), 9:524–29, 538, 548–50, 602, 614–18, 827.

44. *Congressional Globe*, 27 Cong., 2d sess., 158–62, 168, 170–94.

45. Ibid., 194.

46. Graves to Clay, February 16, 1842, printed in Hopkins et al., *Papers of Henry Clay*, 9:656–58.

47. King and Johnson's statements are summarized in ibid., 9:644. They are printed in *Kendall's Expositor*, 4:72–73.

48. Wise to Clay, February 25, 1842, in Hopkins et al., *Papers of Henry Clay*, 9:661.

49. Clay to Wise, February 28, 1842, in ibid., 9:662–65.

50. Wise, *Life of Henry A. Wise*, 86.

51. *Wilmington Delaware Gazette*, July 2, 19, 1844; King, "History of the Duel," 407, 409.

52. *Washington Globe*, June 7, July 23, 31, 1844.

53. *Kendall's Expositor*, 4:71–77, 176, 244–48, 443–47, 450–53.

54. *Kennebec* (ME) *Journal*, April 5, July 7, 19, September 20, 1844.

55. *Lexington Observer and Reporter*, September 4, 1844.

56. Ibid., August 22, 28, September 4, 21, October 2, 1844; *Washington Daily National Intelligencer*, August 10, 22, 1844; *Baltimore American and Commercial Daily Advertiser*, July 20, 1844.

57. Clay to Dr. J. G. Noble, August 16, 1844, in "Mr. Clay and the Cilley Duel," *The Campaign of 1844* (Frankfort, KY, 1844), 198; Clay to Alexander Plumer et al., August 1, 1844, in *Kendall's Expositor*, 4:333.

58. Hopkins et al., *Papers of Henry Clay*, 10:75, 121–22, 125–26, 141–44, 152–53, 162–63, 177, 245–47; Wise, *Life of Henry A. Wise*, 86. For the Senate's investigation of fraud during the 1844 election, see *Senate Documents*, 28 Cong., 2d sess., No. 173, 1–197. See also John Bach McMaster, *History of the United States, From the Revolution to the Civil War*, 8 vols. (New York, 1883–1913), 7:386–87.

59. Stevens, *Pistols at Ten Paces*, 132–33; Simpson, *A Good Southerner*, 40–41; Wise, *Life of Henry A. Wise*, 82; Williams, *Dueling in the Old South*, 90–92; J. Winston Coleman, Jr., *Famous Kentucky Duels* (Lexington, KY, 1969), 170, 173; Steven M. Stowe, *Intimacy and Power in the Old South: Ritual in the Lives of the Planters* (Baltimore, 1987), 44.

60. Simpson, *A Good Southerner*, 40–41; Bertram Wyatt-Brown, *Southern Honor: Ethics and Behavior in the Old South* (New York, 1982), 559n; Nathaniel Hawthorne, *Miscellanies, Biographical and Other Sketches and Letters* (Boston and New York, 1900), 74.

61. *U.S. House Report No. 825*, 56, 128; Stowe, *Intimacy and Power*, 39; King, "History of the Duel," 397, 400; Lorenzo Sabine, *Notes of Duels and Duelling* (Boston, 1855), 89–90.

62. Hopkins et al., *Papers of Henry Clay*, 9:662–65.

5

The Slave Insurrection Panic of 1860 and Southern Secession

Donald E. Reynolds

Although full-fledged slave insurrections were rare in the antebellum South, slave insurrection *panics* were not.[1] Indeed, periodic scares over possible uprisings were about as common to most whites of the Old South as grits and red-eye gravy. In part, the easy susceptibility to rumors of slave conspiracies may have resulted from the southerners' uneasiness with the obvious contradictions between their high ideals and the gross inequities of their peculiar institution; in part, it may have stemmed from deep psycho-sexual fears that ensured that the hobgoblins of imagined horrors were never far beneath the level of individual and community consciousness. Whatever the underlying causes, such panics occurred periodically through the slaveholding states, usually during times of great stress. Bertram Wyatt-Brown has said that punishment of those blacks or alleged white abolitionists who were pinpointed as culprits served as a kind of catharsis that reaffirmed community values and class relationships, thus restoring equilibrium and normality to the community.[2]

Whether or not the slave panic typically served to reaffirm southern values and reassure white citizens, as Wyatt-Brown suggests, potentially it was an ideal vehicle for those southern radicals who desired a separate southern nation. No other sectional issue carried with it the emotional impact of threatened race war. Politicians could rage about northern economic exploitation of the South, about limitations on slavery's extension to the West, about "bleeding Kansas," and about states' rights, but none of these divisive questions came as close to hearth and home for all white southerners as the specter of blacks rising up to wreak vengeance on their oppressors. The ghosts of Toussaint L'Ouverture and Nat Turner constantly reminded white southerners of what could happen if their vigilance were to flag.[3] The great slave panic of 1860, following as it did hard on the heels of John Brown's raid, was seized upon by William Lowndes Yancey, Edmund Ruffin, Robert Barnwell Rhett, and other secessionists as "proof" that the Republican Party and John Brown's supporters were co-conspirators in a plot to destroy the South's peculiar institution and instigate race war among the southern people.

The panic began in the aftermath of damaging fires that struck the little north Texas towns of Dallas, Denton, and Pilot Point on the afternoon of July 8, 1860. The conflagration in Dallas was the most damaging of the three, destroying nearly all of the business houses in the town and causing an estimated $400,000 damage. A lengthy drought had made wooden structures tinder-dry and high winds spread the fires so quickly that efforts to extinguish the flames were largely ineffective. The first reaction of the press was to attribute the fires to a combination of the exceedingly hot temperature—in Dallas the mercury on the day of the fires rose to 108 degrees—and the recent introduction into stores of "prairie matches," phosphorous-tipped sticks that were known to be unstable when subjected to excessive heat.[4]

Nevertheless, Dallas and the neighboring communities were ripe for a slave insurrection panic. Not only had the unusually hot, dry weather strained nerves to the breaking point, but for the past year or so the citizens had been especially concerned about the activities of Northern Methodists, who had apparently staked out northern Texas as a mission field and whom the Texans regarded as abolitionists. In March 1859, indignant citizens of the nearby town of McKinney had broken up a conference of Northern Methodists that had convened a conference at Timber Creek; five months later Dallasites had flogged and driven out of town two ministers of that same denomination.[5]

It was not surprising that the outbreak of fires on the same afternoon in three towns not forty miles apart seemed too much of a coincidence to many of the citizens of Dallas, and soon, according to the recollection of one witness, men were gathering in small groups on the ash-strewn streets, "grim-faced, and speaking in hushed tones," making certain that "nothing was said in the presence of anybody who was not known to be with them."[6] A few days after the Dallas fire a local farmer suspected one of his slaves of setting fire to his barn. He reportedly forced a confession from a young black boy by threatening him with death and warning him that "the devil would get him sure." The young slave apparently implicated others, and when these were interrogated an incredible story of an extensive abolitionist plot unfolded. The details were revealed in a series of letters written by Charles R. Pryor, twenty-eight-year-old editor of the *Dallas Herald*, whose press had been destroyed in the fire. Pryor sent his letters to three prominent Texas editors, all of whom shared their young correspondent's southern-rights views and all of whom were strong supporters of John C. Breckinridge, the Southern Democrats' candidate for president. In his first missive, written to John Marshall, editor of the *Austin State Gazette* and secretary of the state Democratic Party, Pryor laid out the essentials of the plot.

Inspired by the two Methodist ministers who had been expelled the previous year, selected blacks were "to devastate, with fire and assassination, the whole of Northern Texas," and after the region was reduced to helplessness there was to be a general revolt of the slaves on August 6, the date of the state elections. In subsequent letters to L. C. De Lisle, editor of the *Bonham Era*, and E. H. Cushing, editor of the *Houston Telegraph*, Pryor further embellished his first report, adding horrors often featured in the classic, stereotypical southern slave insurrection panic. Egged on by their white sponsors, the blacks would set fire to towns and private dwellings, plant poison in food and water supplies, and after having disposed of the white males and older females, ravish the younger, prettier women. "They have even gone so far as to designate their choice," wrote Pryor, "and certain ladies had already been selected as the victims of these misguided monsters."[7]

The publication and reprinting of Pryor's letters in newspapers around the state quickly spread the panic. Although the Dallas editor's version had depicted a plan to abolitionize only northern Texas, reports of new fires in other areas of the state convinced most communities that they might be targeted as well. Although nearly all of the subsequent reports of fires later proved false, a state of alarm consumed Texas from late July until mid-September. Towns and counties from the Red River to the Gulf coast organized vigilance committees that launched intensive investigations. In the time-honored way of southern vigilantism, law-enforcement officials and judges stood aside so that popular justice could have its way. Vigilantes relentlessly interrogated suspected blacks—often beating and frightening confessions from them—and "waited on" white strangers, especially those with northern accents. After holding hasty "trials," these committees collectively hanged at least thirty alleged white and black insurrectionists, although the actual number of deaths was probably much higher. Many suspicious whites whose guilt was apparently uncertain were expelled from the state; large numbers of others, apparently fearing that their northern backgrounds might invite suspicion, left voluntarily.[8]

Political newspapers all over the South reprinted one or more of the Pryor letters and warned their readers that similar horrors might await them if watchfulness was not maintained.[9] In August and September, as if in confirmation of these admonitions, new plots were reported throughout the South, notably in Virginia, Georgia, Alabama, Mississippi, Louisiana, and Arkansas. Although these later scares were more localized than the "Texas Troubles," they were made to appear to be a part of a vast, concerted abolitionist scheme to destroy slavery and, with it, southern civilization. Thus, the Texas slave panic became, by extension, a great southern panic.

It could not have come at a worse time for those who loved the Union, nor at a better time for those who wished to destroy it. The breathtakingly rapid spread of fear across the whole South was due in large measure to the efforts of pro-Breckinridge Democratic newspapers, which gave credence, it seemed, to every report of incendiarism and which saw to it that the political lessons to be learned were not lost on their readers. Editor Pryor and those to whom he wrote his oft-quoted letters were all staunch sup-porters of Breckinridge, as were most of the journalistic publicists of the plot in the other southern states. Their first objective was to use the "Texas troubles" to help elect their candidate for president, largely by depicting Breckinridge as the only candidate who had a realistic chance of defeating the incendiary Republican candidate. Failing that increasingly elusive goal, many Democratic editors and politicians clearly wanted to convince their readers and constituents that the South had no alternative but to secede.

Most southerners had long equated Republican free-soilism with aboli-tionism; nevertheless, the northern party's opposition to slavery's expan-sion and its alleged determination, at some point in the future, to abolish slavery in the southern states hardly posed an immediate threat to the average white person in the South. As Unionist papers were fond of reiterating, the Republicans probably would not control both houses of the Congress, and the Supreme Court, which likely would have a decidedly Democratic majority for some time to come, would block any efforts to strike a blow at slavery. Since Abraham Lincoln, as president, would be unable to damage slavery even if he wanted to, the South should be willing to accept his election and give him a chance to show evenhandedness toward the slaveholding states. If he were to commit an "overt act" against the South's constitutional rights, there would be plenty of time for the slave states to join together and go out cooperatively, as a unit.[10]

The fire-eaters knew that the "cooperationist" approach advocated by southern conservatives was a sure formula for defeating their dream of a southern confederacy. They had traveled the road in 1849–1850, only to have their hopes dashed when the Nashville Convention failed to create southern solidarity. It was essential from the secessionists' point of view that one or more of the more radical slave states of the Lower South act unilaterally to leave the Union. Such a bold step would undoubtedly lead to a confrontation with the federal government, which in turn would force the more timid slave states to support the seceded state or states. This strategy was worked out by William Lowndes Yancey, Robert Barnwell Rhett, and other like-minded radicals at the Southern Commercial Conven-tion, which convened at Montgomery, Alabama, on May 10, 1858. Although they admitted that the southern people as a whole were unready for secession, the Montgomery radicals were hardly discouraged, for they recognized that revolutions are carried out by small groups of dedicated men, not by the masses.[11] A few weeks after the convention finished its deliberations, Yancey summed up the new strategy in a letter to James S. Slaughter of Atlanta. Secessionists should emulate their revolutionary fore-fathers by forming "committees of public safety" all over the Deep South. Yancey was convinced that through the activities of such small cadres, "we shall fire the Southern heart—instruct the Southern mind—give courage to each other, and at the proper moment, by organized concerted action, we can precipitate the Cotton States into a revolution."[12]

The "proper moment," most secessionists had long proclaimed, would be the election of a "Black Republican" as president. Yet, although most southern whites probably agreed with the fire-eaters that the fledgling northern party posed a threat to slavery—the word *abolitionist* had become virtually a synonym for *Republican* in the southern lexicon—it is far from clear that, outside South Carolina, a majority in any state believed that the election of a Republican president would warrant such a drastic step as secession. Given the checks and balances provided by the other branches of government, even a hostile chief executive would be limited in the damage he could do to southern interests.

Clearly, southern revolutionaries needed an emotional issue to drive their secession engine. They thought they had found one in the person of John Brown, the bearded fanatic whose abortive raid on Harper's Ferry in October 1859 sent a shiver of horror throughout the South. However, they were soon disappointed, for the excitement quickly subsided after Brown's execution. Brown's incursion had failed, after all, and southerners could point to the old abolitionist's failure to arouse the local slaves to his cause as proof of their contention that their chattels were generally a docile and loyal lot. The *Charleston Mercury* later theorized that Brown's failure, "like a strong opiate, first excited, and then put Virginia to sleep; whilst it spread over the whole South a corresponding apathy."[13] Although Brown was hardly forgotten by southerners, the press soon found other issues to discuss, and by the spring of 1860 relatively little newspaper space was being given to new reports of slave violence.[14] In April, the *Montgomery Mail*, Yancey's sounding board in Alabama, expressed its disgust over the South's lack of concern over reports of abolitionist activity in the region, complaining that the South had become "comatose."[15]

The "Texas troubles" not only revived the South from its "coma," it enabled the Breckinridge camp and the secessionists to seize the initiative from the conservatives who had been minimizing the effect of a possible Republican victory in the presidential election. Ignoring the denunciation of Brown's raid by leading Republican newspapers and politicians, includ-ing Lincoln, southern-rights men now alleged that the Republican Party was tied both to Brown and to the perpetrators of the latest insurrectionist conspiracy. A correspondent of the *New York Day Book*, writing from Fort Worth, said that the people of his community "believe that Lincoln is the head and the representative of this *Abolition Aid Society*, which sent John

Brown to Virginia, and which is now giving us so much trouble here."[16] The *Austin State Gazette* called Lincoln "the wicked sympathizer of John Brown, [and] the apostle of murder, arson and servile war. . . ."[17] The *Fayetteville Arkansian* even hinted at a direct connection between the Brown raid and the Texas conspiracy, asserting that some of Brown's lieutenants had escaped and, having learned from the Harper's Ferry fiasco to use more surreptitious techniques, were now employing fire and poison and operating under cover of darkness.[18]

The southern-rights press everywhere picked up the theme of Republican culpability for the alleged insurrectionary plot, and many editors dropped all restraint in their efforts to stir their readers' fear and hatred against a party that allegedly had as its goal nothing less than the total destruction of southern society. The efforts of the press to demonize Lincoln, which had begun after his nomination, seemed to grow in irresponsibility and intensity in the aftermath of the "Texas troubles." In a long editorial on the Texas "plot," the *Washington Constitution* stated: "The flag of Lincoln and [Hannibal] Hamlin proclaims everywhere the principles of [Hinton] Helper, and tells to every slave that he has the right to cut his master's throat!"[19] Lincoln and his cohorts "would hail a servile insurrection as 'the dawn of a political millennium,' " warned the *Natchez Mississippi Free Trader*, for the "Black Republicans pant for the hour to arrive when the black man . . . will 'wage a war of extermination against the white man.' "[20] The *Montgomery Mail* called the alleged plot in Texas *"practical Lincoln-ism"* and argued that there could be no possible compromise if the Republican candidate was elected: "If with blazing Texas in full view, the North puts LINCOLN upon us, all will admit that our duty is plain."[21] Moreover, pro-Breckinridge editors were fond of pointing out that the arsonists in Texas had done their dastardly work while an administration friendly to the South had been in office. What could be expected once Lincoln succeeded James Buchanan? The *Athens* (Ga.) *Southern Banner* echoed the thoughts of many when it wrote, "If such things come upon us with only the *prospect* of an Abolition ruler, what will be our condition when he is *actually in power*?"[22]

The Unionist press fought back as best it could. The *Austin Southern Intelligencer*, Governor Sam Houston's organ in Texas, accused the "secessionist crew" of deliberately distorting and exaggerating the reports of fires and insurrectionary plots. These distortions, opined the *Southern Intelligencer*, had led the people to believe that "they are in imminent danger of the torch, the knife and the lust of an infuriate servile insurrection," when in fact no such danger existed.[23] Nevertheless, although conservative journals often expressed a measure of skepticism and thought that the stories of conspiracies in Texas and elsewhere were exaggerated, many conservative editors seemed to believe that the reports were at least partially true. Some expressed as much alarm as their radical counterparts. For example, the *Alexandria* (Va.) *Gazette*, which supported John Bell of Tennessee, nominee of the Constitutional Union Party, declared: "The news from Texas is startling. If it is true, if not greatly exaggerated, it will raise a flame in the South fiercer than the fires which the emissaries of the traitorous villains who concoct such schemes have raised. Politics, and Presidential elections, and party movements—who shall be elected to high office, and what is to be done if one man should be elected—all sink into insignificance, when placed in comparison with the preservation of men's families, their homes, their property and their institutions."[24] Even though they often deplored the exploitation of the conspiracy reports by Breckinridge advocates and secessionists, conservative editors were still shaken by the sensational accounts of alleged slave tampering. After noting that some reports had been exaggerated, the *New Orleans Picayune* still concluded: "Incendiarism is surely at its diabolical work," and it warned its readers that the recent experience in Texas was proof that there were "many strangers" in the South who were prepared to carry out "the most atrocious deeds." The *Picayune* urged the local citizenry to exercise the greatest vigilance, since some of those "abolitionists" who had been exiled from Texas "are known to have sailed for this city."[25]

Southern whites, regardless of their political persuasions, hardly needed the reminders to be vigilant. In Texas, where the panic was greatest, the terror reached almost pathological proportions. On August 12 a resident of Marshall reported: "Women and children have been so frightened by these burnings and threatened rebellion of the negroes, that in several instances they have left their homes in their fright, and when found were almost confirmed maniacs!"[26] A citizen of Henderson sounded a similar note when he wrote: "All is alarm and excitement with our women and children."[27] On the day after the state elections, a young resident of Marshall told his father in Houston that every man had been on watch the previous day, thus preventing the "cowardly cutthroats" from carrying out their bloody plans. "I would like to tell you all about this insurrection," he concluded, "but I am too nervous to write anymore."[28] S. B. Barron, who had recently moved to Texas from Alabama, later wrote: "The excitement, apprehension, unrest, and the vague fear of the unseen danger pervading the minds of the people of Texas cannot be understood by persons who were not in the State at that time."[29]

The pro-Breckinridge press's apparent success in implicating the Republicans in the alleged plots had a palpable effect on the politics of secession. Understandably, the impact was most immediately apparent in Texas. A San Antonio correspondent of the *New York Herald* exaggerated only in degree when he wrote: "The excitement growing out of these matters has killed off all conservative feeling in Texas. You may now note down every Texan as a disunionist. They do not care what you all do in the North. We believe that this state of things will continue so long as the Union lasts; therefore the great majority of us do not care how soon the crisis comes."[30]

Citizens in the other southern states were scarcely less affected by the stories of fires and planned murder than those in the Lone Star State. Those who had relatives in Texas naturally experienced the greatest anxiety. In a letter to her kin, one North Carolina woman wrote: "I hardly no what more to say for I dont know whether you will ever get this or not for the negros may kill you if they have not all ready done it[.] from what we heare it scares me all most to death[.] report ses evry town in Texas is burnt[.] write to us an tell us all you no about it."[31] Since the "Texas troubles" had reportedly spread to other slave states, southerners everywhere apparently believed their own domiciles were in as much peril as those on the western frontier. By transporting the distant horrors of which they had heard to their own doorsteps and by blaming them directly on the Republicans, southerners could easily justify in their own minds the necessity for leaving the Union. Sarah Lois Wadley, a resident of Vicksburg whose father had just returned from a business trip to Texas, confided to her diary that there could no longer exist a union between the North and the South because the abolitionists "have burnt our homesteads, killed our citizens and incited our servants to poison us. . . ." Although her family roots lay in New England, whose soil was still dear to her, "never can I claim Friendship with those who have contemplated my country's ruin. Better far for us would be civil war than this dreadful incubus which hangs over us now. . . ."[32] In Louisiana, a correspondent identifying himself only as a "Henry Clay Whig" still professed to love the Union, but said that it would be folly to submit to "this vile Black Republican party. . . . Is it that we are to live under the presidency of a man who will permit his Abolition hordes to incite our slaves to the work of applying the midnight torch to our homes and murdering our parents, our wives, our children and ourselves, in cold blood? O Power Supreme, forbid!"[33] Those without a direct economic stake in the slave system appear to have been no less concerned about slavery's defense from the alleged abolitionist assaults than were slaveholders. At the height of the secession crisis a nonslaveholding farmer in Tennessee expressed his anger and anxiety in a letter to Senator Andrew Johnson. The Constitution and the law were on the side of slavery and the South, the letter writer said, but "Higher Law Republicans" had resorted to "John Brown spikes and murder in the first degree" to override legalities. By instigating "murder in Virginue and in Texas stricnine[,] fire and blood," the Republicans apparently meant "God's law" when they used the phrase "higher law." But asked the farmer, "Does God require them to use stricnine[,] powder[,] lead[,] fire[,] and every means of distruction [to take] the life of innocent Women and children to fulfill his Law[?] God forbid any such hypocracy[.]"[34]

The leaders of the secession movement quickly saw that the fearful reactions of southerners of all classes to the conflagration in Texas and to the brushfires it had spawned in other states could be put to good use in the cause of southern nationalism. They often emphasized the alleged horrors to dramatize their contention that the South could not afford to remain in the Union under a "Black Republican" president.[35] Henry A. Wise, former governor of Virginia, admonished a correspondent in Texas: "Fight all invaders of your state, and hang all you can catch. It is time that the slave States were ready for the revolution which is coming inevitably. . . ."[36] Lawrence M. Keitt, South Carolina secessionist whose own brother had been murdered by slaves the previous February, cited Lincoln's "house divided" speech as proof that the South must sacrifice its peculiar institution or expect more John Brown raids, "more torches to her dwellings, and more poison in her fountains. He means that the South must be abolitionized, or she must be lighted with the blaze of the incendiary, and harried with the steel of the assassin."[37] A Lincoln victory, Keitt wrote on another occasion, would usher in the "wildest democracy" since the Reign of Terror during the French Revolution. "What of conservativism? What of order? What of social security or financial prosperity can withstand Northern Republican license? A drunken and licentious soldiery would hardly be as bad."[38]

Edmund Ruffin of Virginia first heard of the events in the Lone Star State on September 5, 1860, while traveling in Tennessee. Although he thought that the reports probably were greatly exaggerated and that many innocent persons would suffer along with the guilty, he nevertheless was convinced that a conspiracy existed. Even if only one-tenth of the reports were true, he wrote in his diary, added to the Brown raid "it would be alone sufficient for a separation of the Union to exclude northern emissaries & incendiaries from southern territories." Until secession was accomplished, argued Ruffin, such Republican-sponsored incursions were bound to continue, "while, after separation, we may more securely defy the whole power of northern abolitionism."[39] The Virginia secessionist was cheered by a report from the Lone Star State that he had seen in a northern newspaper declaring that Texans had been converted to secession by the alleged abolitionist plot there, and he clearly wished that the same physic would cure the disease of unionism elsewhere. Although such conspiracies were "deplorable," Ruffin nevertheless concluded that if another such plot were to be uncovered, "I earnestly hope that it will be in Georgia. If the dull and lethargic body of that great central southern state could be thus thoroughly aroused to self-defense against the north & would take the step of secession, every adjoining state (except N.C.) would immediately follow, & the movement would be secure & effective—& necessarily soon to be followed by all the more northern slaveholding states."[40] Ruffin's wish was soon granted; within the next two months, allegations of local conspiracies would be reported in several Georgia communities.[41]

The secessionist who made the most extensive use of the slave insurrection panic during the presidential campaign was William Lowndes Yancey of Alabama, whom historian Clement Eaton has aptly called "the orator of secession."[42] Yancey made a speaking tour of the Upper South and portions of the North during the campaign. In a much-reported speech in New York City, the Alabama ultra began moderately enough, telling his audience that the South wanted only to maintain its social system, which had been ordained by geography and the Constitution. Before long, however, he reverted to his usual harangue about the northern antislavery men who, he said, were determined to destroy the South. Asserting the orthodox southern view that the Republicans "are the same as the abolitionists," Yancey alleged that if the government were to come under the control of a Republican president, "the emissaries of the Abolitionists would be found everywhere through the South with strychnia to put in their wells as they are now found in Texas." The *New York Times*, which printed the speech in its entirety, reported that this statement was greeted with a mixture of applause, hisses, and "cries of 'Put him out!' "[43] Undaunted by the catcalls, Yancey forged on:

In Texas, it was proven beyond all doubt, men calling themselves Reverend had been arrested with strychnia upon their persons, and arms had been found stored away. How came they there? They were there for the purpose of carrying on the "irrepressible conflict." The emissaries of the Abolitionists there crawled about at midnight with their incendiary torches, poison and incitements to insurrection. Those things were there and they were traced to the Abolitionists. Now, if the Black Republicans were in power, would not the institution be in danger of being blown up at any time by some insignificant being—capable of little good but able to do a great deal of mischief? With the emissaries of the North among them, with the offices of the Government in the hands of their enemies, their property would be deteriorated; there would be general desolation and the North would share in the universal ruin.[44]

The pro-Republican *Times* not surprisingly thought Yancey was out-of-bounds in equating abolitionism with Republicanism, but so did the *New York World*, which said: "The designs he imputed to the republican party are not the thoughts of the majority of that party. If they were, and it was so understood, that party could not stand a day." Thus, secession on account of Lincoln's election was, in the view of the *World*, unjustified.[45] Yancey delivered another speech in Cincinnati in late October and aroused much the same criticism in the press there. The *Cincinnati Daily Commercial* said that the southern orator seemed to be under the impression that his audience was made up of "New Englanders and Abolitionists." Moreover, complained the editor, "He did not in any sentence recognize a possibility that Republicans are not Abolitionist," nor did he seem to comprehend that a party could gain majority status in one section of the country "without an assault being made upon the constitutional rights of the minority."[46]

Yancey's numerous speeches in the South naturally played to a much more receptive press and to more appreciative audiences. In Washington, much of his address dwelled upon the dangers of submission to Lincoln.

He played heavily upon the theme that had been stressed by other secessionists: Given the assaults of Brown and the Texas conspirators under a
friendly administration, southerners must expect even worse under Lincoln. "Why, gentlemen, if Texas is now in flames, and the peace of Virginia
is invaded now under this administration . . . tell me what it will be when
a higher law government reigns in the city of Washington?" His listeners,
when asked if "any brave and heroic people" could sacrifice their constitutional principles and betray their "families and firesides" by submitting,
shouted "Never, never."[47] In New Orleans, on October 29, Yancey was even
more eloquent in describing what might happen after Republicans had
taken over and the South had been overrun by abolitionists:

When you call on one of them [Republican authorities] to arrest an incendiary who
is prowling about in your neighborhood, he will tell you that he is sleepy; that he
will attend to it in the morning; and by that time your house will have been burned,
and the incendiary will be at a safe distance. You call one of them in the daytime,
and he will tell you it will take him some time to find his horse, and some time to
get ready, and a long time to find the offender; and when he starts, he will find a
cold track; for you know how easy it is for a man to appear to do something, even
when he is doing nothing.[48]

The Texas inferno and its satellite brushfires in the other states had
subsided well before the election, but the issue did not die. Secessionists
continued to stir the embers in their effort to play on the fears of southerners. Indeed, the afterglow of the "Texas troubles" was a powerful weapon
against those conservatives who argued that the South had little to lose by
adopting a wait-and-see policy. After Lincoln's election, the battle shifted
to the state houses, where legislators debated whether a Black Republican's
elevation to the presidency required the convocation of a secession convention. The cotton states all decided this question in the affirmative, and a key
issue was the specter of race violence that secessionists raised time and
again. For example, in Georgia, the pivotal state of the Deep South, Governor Joseph E. Brown set the tone by warning that "a hungry swarm of
abolition emissaries" was set to sweep over the South in the wake of
Lincoln's election, flooding "the country with inflammatory abolition documents" and probably instigating violence.[49] More graphic was the speech
of Thomas R. R. Cobb, who solemnly asked his colleagues to

Recur with me to the parting moment when you left your firesides, to attend upon
your public duties at the Capitol. Remember the trembling hand of a loved wife, as
she whispered her fears from the incendiary and the assassin. Recall the look of
indefinable dread with which the little daughter inquired when your returning
footsteps should be heard. And if there be manhood in you, tell me if this is the
domestic tranquility which this "glorious Union" has achieved. Notice the anxious
look when the travelling pedlar lingers too long in conversation at the door with
the servant who turns the bolt—the watchful gaze when the slave tarries long with

the wandering artist who professes merely to furnish him with a picture—the suspicion aroused by a Northern man conversing in private with the most faithful of your negroes, and tell me if peace and tranquility are the heritage which this Union has brought to your firesides. Take up your daily papers, and see reports of insurrections in every direction. Hear the telegram read which announces another John Brown raid.

Cobb expressed confidence in the loyalty of a great majority of southern slaves.

But a discontented few here and there, will become the incendiary or the poisoner, when instigated by the unscrupulous emissaries of Northern Abolitionists, and you and I cannot say but that your home or your family may be the first to greet your returning footsteps in ashes or in death.—What has given impulse to these fears, and aid and comfort to those outbreaks now, but the success of the Black Republicans—the election of Abraham Lincoln![50]

While the legislatures of the Lower South went about the business of laying the groundwork for secession, the eyes of the nation focused on Washington. The thirty-sixth Congress convened for its second session on December 3, 1860, and when its members took their seats to hear President Buchanan's opening address, the unionists among them listened anxiously for some indication that the nation's chief executive would use his powers to discourage wavering slave states of the Lower South from following rash South Carolina, which everyone agreed would surely secede. The friends of the Union were quickly disappointed. Buchanan, the doughface from Pennsylvania, had demonstrated throughout his presidency his belief that sectional peace could be maintained only by being concessionary to the South. Although he now reaffirmed his devotion to the Union and denied that a southern state had the constitutional right to secede, Buchanan made it clear that he would not attempt to coerce a state that might take such action. Moreover, in analyzing the reasons why the Union was in jeopardy, he placed the blame not on the effort to exclude slavery from the territories, or even the attempts by some northern states to subvert the Fugitive Slave Law, but upon the "incessant and violent agitation of the slavery question throughout the North for the last quarter of a century." This ceaseless bombardment had "produced its malign influence on the slaves, and inspired them with vague notions of freedom. Hence a sense of security no longer exists around the family altar. This feeling of peace at home has given place to apprehensions of servile insurrections." Evoking imagery much like that of T.R.R. Cobb in the Georgia legislature, Buchanan said: "Many a matron throughout the South retires at night in dread of what may befall herself and her children before morning. Should this apprehension of domestic danger, whether real or imaginary, extend and intensify itself, until it pervade the masses of the southern people, then disunion will become inevitable." The president went on to assert his view that the fear had not yet become all-pervasive in the slave states and to express the hope that it would not. Unfortunately, he was wrong; the Texas terror had indeed spread a malaise over the whole South. On the eve of the presidential election, one newspaper had said that "the minds of the people are aroused to a pitch of excitement probably unparalleled in the history of the country. . . ."[51] Lincoln's election, far from alleviating the frenzy, raised it to new heights, since the party that allegedly had sponsored the purported insurrectionary conspiracies would now possess the presidency.

Southern members of Congress clearly demonstrated the anxieties of their constituents in the early days of the session, especially in the Senate, where a brisk debate broke out over whether to establish a committee of thirteen to consider possible compromise measures. During the course of the debate, extended references to the alleged abolitionist slave insurrection conspiracy by southern senators and the incredulous reactions by their Republican counterparts highlighted the credibility gap that had developed between the sections. Several southern solons alluded to the insurrectionary allegations as "evidence" that the Republicans were planning to rid the nation of slavery.[52] Not surprisingly, the Texas fire-eater Louis T. Wigfall went to the greatest lengths in detailing the alleged conspiracy in the Lone Star State. Solemnly recounting his own harrowing experience of the previous summer, Wigfall said: "I returned home, sir, after the fatigues of the last session; I went there for peace and for quiet and consultation with my neighbors; and from the day I reached my home until I left—between six weeks and two months—there was a guard of twenty-four men every night in a small village of between two and three thousand inhabitants. I myself had to shoulder my gun, and stand guard." After describing the fear that had gripped his own community and state, the senator went on to blame the Republican Party for the outrages in Texas, even alleging at one point that Senator William H. Seward had alerted "his John-Brown, Wide-Awake Praetorians" to remain organized following the election so that the fruits of victory could be ensured. "One half million of men uniformed and drilled, and the purpose of their organization to sweep the country in which I live with fire and sword. . . ." At this point, with Wigfall in mid-sentence, Seward interrupted, strongly denying that he had said any such thing. Wigfall politely accepted the senator's denial, but did not abandon his main point that somehow the Republicans and their ancillary organizations were involved in a plot to destroy the South. "I would not misrepresent him [Seward]. But that this praetorian band is organized; that its members do undergo military drill; that it is a military organization, no man who has looked upon them, *as I did this last summer*, and heard their regular military tramp, does or can doubt."[53]

Republican Senator Benjamin Wade, like Seward, reacted to the charges of northern aggression with disbelief. Saying that he had listened patiently to the complaints of his southern colleagues, the Ohioan confessed that "I am now totally unable to understand precisely what it is of which they complain." He pointed out that the Republicans had never done harm to the South, and he suggested that southerners' fears over future abuses were "mere apprehensions—a bare suspicion; arising, I fear, out of their unwarrantable prejudices, and nothing else." Then he addressed the question of insurrectionary violence to which Wigfall and others had alluded.

Why, sir, I can hardly take up a paper—and I rely, too, upon southern papers— which does not give an account of the cruel treatment of some man who is traveling for pleasure or business in your quarter; and the lightest thing you do is to visit him with a vigilance committee, and compel him to return: "We give you so long to make your way out of our coast." "What is the accusation?" "Why, sir, you are from Ohio." They do not inquire what party he belongs to, or what standard he has followed. I say this is the case, if I may rely on the statements of your own papers; and many of these outrages occur under circumstances of cruelty that would disgrace a savage; and we have no security now in traveling in nearly one half of the Union, and especially the gulf States of this Confederacy. I care not what a man's character may be; he may be perfectly innocent of every charge; he may be a man who never has violated any law under heaven; and yet if he goes down into those States, and it is ascertained that he is from the North, and especially if he differs from them in the exercise of his political rights, if he has voted for Lincoln instead of for somebody else, it is a mortal offense, punishable by indignity, by tar and feathers, by stripes, and even by death; and yet you, whose constituents are guilty of all these things, can stand forth, and accuse us of being unfaithful to the Constitution of the United States! Gentlemen had better look at home.[54]

Answering the charge by southern ultras like Wigfall and much of the southern press that all members of his party were "John Brown men," Wade said the encouragement of racial violence in the South was "a thing no Republican ever dreamed of or ever thought about." Still, in spite of denials by all of the party's leaders, the exasperated Ohioan continued, the southerners still believed the irresponsible charges: "No doubt they believe it because of a terrible excitement and reign of terror that prevails there. No doubt, they think so, but it arises from false information, or the want of information—that is all. Their prejudices have been appealed to until they have become uncontrolled and incontrollable."[55]

Senator Alfred O. P. Nicholson of Tennessee replied that Wade was correct in stating that there was a "deep and wide-spread conviction that the Republican party is the mortal enemy of the institutions and rights of the South." He denied, however, that this conviction rested upon misapprehension or misinformation, arguing instead that it was based upon "stubborn facts," derived from "authentic and reliable sources." Although he did not contend that the Republican Party had actually supported the Brown raid or the recent "insurrection plot" in the South, Nicholson nevertheless argued that Wade's party represented social opinions that, if applied, would

"involve our final destruction." Since Republicans allegedly regarded slavery as a "social, moral, and political evil," they would undoubtedly use their
control of the government, once gained, to bring about the ultimate destruction of the South's peculiar institution. Although they might not endorse
violence, what assurance could southern families take, knowing that "some
misguided fanatic or monomaniac, who, feeling restive and unwilling to
await the slow process of the Republican mode of liberating the slaves,
chooses to resort to the torch and to insurrection? . . . Repose is the great
object desired by the South."[56]

Southern radicals were not the only members of Congress to accept as
true the allegations that Republicans had instigated race violence in the
South. On December 10, amid debate on proposed concessions that might
prevent the South's secession, Jefferson Davis, perhaps the most moderate
of senators from the "Gulf squadron," criticized the proposals that had been
made because they attacked the symptom, not the disease. "What though
all the 'personal liberty bills' were repealed," he asked, "would that secure
our rights? Would that give us the Union our fathers made? Would that
renew good offices, or restrain raids and incendiarism, or prevent schools
being founded to prepare missionaries to go into lands where they are to
sow the seeds of insurrection, and, wearing the livery of heaven, to serve
the Devil by poisoning wells and burning towns?" The real remedy was in
"mutual affection" between the people of the sections, and if that no longer
existed, then it was better, "instead of attempting to preserve a forced and
fruitless Union," that the South should secede. The Founding Fathers had
created the Union "for domestic tranquillity," Davis argued, "not to organize within one State lawless bands to commit raids on another. . . . Who
would keep a flower which had lost its beauty and its fragrance, and in their
stead had formed a seed-vessel containing the deadliest poison?"[57] Representative John H. Reagan of Texas, who had been reelected on a Unionist
platform in 1859, similarly blamed the South's feeling of insecurity upon
the alleged conspiracy in his district. Stopping just short of directly implicating the party of Lincoln in the affair, Reagan nevertheless asserted that
"These things . . . were the results of abolition teachings; a part of the
irrepressible conflict; a part of the legitimate fruits of Republicanism."[58]

Events soon made all of the oratory in Congress irrelevant. South Carolina
seceded on December 20, and most of the Lower South quickly joined the
Palmetto State in forming the Confederacy on February 4, 1861. Texas added
a seventh star to the Confederate flag on March 2 after its voters ratified that
state's secession. The other eight slave states hung in the balance until the
bombardment of Fort Sumter forced them to choose allegiances.

It is likely that had there been no slave panic of 1860, the course of
secession at least would have been altered, although the end result might
have been the same. The one state that definitely would *not* have acted
differently was South Carolina, which was already determined to leave the

Union upon the election of Lincoln. Florida and Mississippi probably would have followed, just as they did in actuality. Beyond those states, however, the slave panic looms increasingly as the key force that pushed the cause of secession over the top. Texas was understandably the most immediately affected of the other Gulf states. Unionist candidates in the Lone Star State had virtually swept the state in August 1859; a year and a half later the state voted to secede by a three-to-one margin. Although there were other issues that aided secessionists in Texas, notably Commanche raids on the frontier and banditry on the Mexican border, the slave panic was by far the dominant issue in the minds of the voters.[59]

Texas aside, it is easy to forget that several states of the Deep South seceded only after fiercely contested battles in the legislatures and secession conventions. In the key states of Louisiana, Alabama, and Georgia, there was significant opposition. John Bell and Stephen A. Douglas combined polled more votes than Breckinridge in both Louisiana and Georgia, and in Alabama the southern-rights Democrat edged the other two by only eight thousand votes. Moreover, although secessionists won majorities in the conventions of all three states, the vote for delegates was significantly lighter in each case than it had been in the recent presidential election, indicating that many conservatives may have stayed at home.[60] There is no question that the great slave panic of 1860 had a dramatic impact upon the decisions of these states. Not only was the Texas panic used to great effect by secessionist editors and politicians in Louisiana, Alabama, and Georgia, but each of those states also had its own smaller panic that served to dramatize and make even more immediate the danger of submitting to a Republican president. Those who wished to preserve the Union or at least to delay its destruction were generally cowed by the avalanche of fear and emotion; indeed, many of them were also affected by the horror stories that secessionist papers and politicians told. Those who challenged the wild accounts of conspiracy ran the risk of being branded as traitors who would put their own people in harm's way by counseling submission to an incendiary Black Republican president. Few could withstand such pressure.

Suppose only Mississippi and Florida had immediately followed South Carolina out of the Union. What then might have happened? First, it seems unlikely that these three noncontiguous states could have formed the Confederacy; they would surely have waited until other states could be persuaded to join them. This would have bought time for the new administration, and time was its most pressing need. The cooperationists of the Deep South had argued that Lincoln had been constitutionally elected and should be allowed to demonstrate that his administration would not harm the South. Given the caution with which Lincoln approached the South in general and South Carolina in particular after his inauguration, it seems probable that he would have been even more circumspect had only three states seceded. If this were the case, the conservative position would have been vindicated, and it is even possible that the crisis would have passed without its bloody dénouement.

Of course, any scenario outside the actual chain of events may be dismissed as groundless speculation. Even without a Confederate government to give it support, South Carolina undoubtedly would have tried to precipitate a crisis over Fort Sumter, in the hope of bringing all the slave states to its side. Without a central government to support it, however, the Palmetto State's task would have been more difficult. Lincoln could more easily have agreed to abandon the fort, as his cabinet wanted him to do anyway. Such a step would have sealed South Carolina's isolation. In time, the seceded states would have been forced by economic and political pressures to make an accommodation with the federal government that would bring them back into the Union.

This hypothesis admittedly accords well with the old-fashioned view that the Civil War was avoidable. Two generations ago, the "revisionists" argued that the Civil War was precipitated by a failure of leadership on both sides. Generally speaking, they asserted that demagogues on both sides—especially northern abolitionists—practiced the politics of extremism, exaggerating sectional differences and distorting events and issues for the purpose of inflaming the public and advancing their own agendas. After World War II the revisionist argument faded from popularity as most Civil War historians generally came to accept the view that America's greatest conflict arose from fundamental issues.

While conceding that irresponsible extremists had deliberately stirred emotions to the breaking point, most scholars of the late twentieth century have contended that it was the issues themselves, not the "heat" which they created, that caused the war. Looked at in this way, the emotional frenzy whipped up by southern fire-eaters in the aftermath of the Texas fires may have been based on false information, but it reflected a solid understanding that the Republicans posed a very real threat to slavery in the long run. Thus, the hobgoblins in the fevered southern mind represented a metaphor for what *could* happen in the future. Steven A. Channing neatly summed up this view: "Secession was the product of logical reasoning within a framework of irrational perception."[61] Even if Lincoln's election were to have no immediate effect upon slavery, the disapproval by his party of the "peculiar institution"—clearly shown in the rhetoric of Republican leaders and in their determination to keep slavery from spreading—portended ultimate extinction for the South's labor system. This in turn, at least from the white southerners' perspective, would mean the loss of social control of blacks and, consequently, a bloody race war. In effect, the "Texas troubles" constituted a preview of what such a struggle might entail. This view that southerners were right in assuming Republican action against slavery ignores both the racial and constitutional conservatism of that party and, indeed, that of the North in general. Moreover, for all their differences, the southern and northern wings of the Democratic Party would have continued to act as a powerful deterrent to any antislavery action by the Republicans; and, in addition, the Supreme Court, with its strong Democratic majority, promised to act as a bulwark in the defense of southern rights for some time to come. Although slavery was becoming a worldwide anachronism, its end would have come slowly in America, and it may be assumed, the longer a resolution of the problem could be deferred, the less would be the likelihood that it would be achieved through violence.

Some have at least partly agreed with Herbert Aptheker that a seething slave population was a real menace to the South and that determined abolitionists, like John Brown, constituted a bona fide threat to set off another Santo Domingo.[62] Whether this is true of earlier incidents may be debated, but it does not apply to the panic of 1860. Although the press reported that numerous towns had burned, that poison had been hidden for use in wells and cisterns, that guns had been cached to murder unsuspecting whites, that blacks had laid plans to rape white women, and that the correspondence of abolitionist ringleaders had revealed the whole bloody plan, it is important to note that no credible evidence was ever produced to prove any of the allegations. That several disastrous fires occurred was the only undeniable fact, but no one saw an arsonist at work nor found suspicious combustibles at the sites. On the other hand, there was strong circumstantial evidence to indicate that the fires were due to natural causes. The only "poison" actually tested turned out to be snake root in one case and paregoric in another. Mysteriously, the guns that had reportedly been imported from the North never were publicly displayed. Although some white women were driven out of their minds by anxiety, no rapes were reported. And a letter from an alleged abolitionist ringleader of the "Mystic Red" was clearly forged.[63] Most important of all, there was no evidence at all of Republican involvement in a scheme to attack slavery from within. Yet, even though the exaggerations and the paucity of evidence had become glaringly obvious before the presidential election and were publicized by conservatives in Texas and elsewhere, secessionists persisted in making the "desolation" of the Lone Star State the exhibit number one in their litany of charges against the Republicans. This seemingly cynical use of propaganda to achieve secession—a goal which most southerners had not previously desired—lends substance to the old revisionist assertion that secession and the war resulted in large measure from an excess of emotionalism, fostered at least in part by the irresponsibility of secessionist editors and political leaders. On the other hand, there is little indication in the private correspondence of these fire-eaters that they doubted the existence of a plot, although several admitted that its extent had been exaggerated. Thus, it is entirely possible that they had deluded themselves into believing their own propaganda.[64]

Even without the great southern slave panic of 1860, of course, sectional hatred and fear would have remained on both sides, and it is impossible to say that secession and war would not have occurred at some future point. But as C. Vann Woodward has reminded us, southerners have never been much influenced by abstractions;[65] therefore, a fear of what the Republicans might do at some point in the distant future was insufficient to induce most southerners to leave the Union of their fathers. The slave insurrection panic of 1860 provided a needed concrete example of the horrors that allegedly awaited the South under a Republican administration, and this, in turn, gave the secessionists of the Lower South the momentum they needed to put their cause over the top.

NOTES

1. Herbert Aptheker, *American Negro Slave Revolts* (New York, 1969). Aptheker lists scores of alleged insurrections. Although the validity of his work as history is gravely weakened by his all-too-evident readiness to accept unsubstantiated reports from suspect sources, Aptheker nevertheless provides a valuable survey of the numerous panics that from time to time swept various regions of the South. For other uncritical accounts of slave insurrections, see Joseph C. Carroll, *Slave Insurrections in the United States, 1800–1865* (Boston, 1938), and Harvey Wish, "American Slave Insurrections Before 1861," *Journal of Negro History*, 22 (1937):299–320.

2. Bertram Wyatt-Brown, *Southern Honor: Ethics and Behavior in the Old South* (New York, 1982), 402–34.

3. Nat Turner led an insurrection in Southampton County, Virginia, in 1831, killing some sixty whites. L'Ouverture led the great uprising on the island of Santo Domingo between 1791 and 1803, which killed thousands of whites and overthrew the French colonial regime there. During the secession crisis, southern newspapers and politicians cited the Santo Domingo insurrection much more frequently than the Turner insurrection, probably because the latter was much more limited in scope, while the former had decimated the white population.

4. All three fires of July 8 started on the site of stores that stocked such matches. Donald E. Reynolds, *Editors Make War: Southern Newspapers in the Secession Crisis* (Nashville, 1970), 97–98, 109.

5. Wesley Norton, "The Methodist Episcopal Church and the Civil Disturbances in North Texas in 1859 and 1860," *Southwestern Historical Quarterly*, 68 (1965):317–41; Frank H. Smyrl, "Unionism, Abolitionism, and Vigilantism in Texas, 1856–1865" (Master's thesis, University of Texas, 1961), 37–38; *Dallas Herald*, August 17, 31, 1859.

6. "Judge Nat M. Burford's Version," *Dallas Morning News*, July 10, 1892.

7. Reynolds, *Editors Make War*, 98–100.

8. Donald E. Reynolds, "Vigilante Law during the Texas Slave Panic of 1860," *Locus*, 2 (1990):173–86. Vigilantes sometimes went to great lengths to punish those who had been accused of abolitionist activities. Anthony Bewley, a Northern Methodist minister who had previously attended the Timber Creek Conference and had served a pastorate in Johnson County, fled with his family when the panic began in mid-July. A posse, inspired no doubt by the offer of a $1,000 reward by

the Fort Worth vigilance committee, tracked the minister to southern Missouri, captured him, and brought him back to Texas, where he was hanged. See Reynolds, "Reluctant Martyr: Anthony Bewley and the Texas Slave Insurrection Panic of 1860," *Southwestern Historical Quarterly*, 96 (1993):344–61.

9. The reports from Texas were carried in the vast majority of southern political papers. For a sampling of these see Reynolds, *Editors Make War*, 251, n.9.

10. Avery Craven, *The Growth of Southern Nationalism, 1848–1861* (Baton Rouge, LA, 1953), 350–51.

11. Laura A. White, *Robert Barnwell Rhett: Father of Secession* (New York, 1931), 144–45.

12. Quoted in Allan Nevins, *The Emergence of Lincoln*, vol. 3, *Ordeal of the Union* (New York, 1950), 406.

13. *Charleston Mercury*, August 29, 1860.

14. Ollinger Crenshaw, *The Slave States in the Presidential Election of 1860* (Baltimore, 1945), 91–92.

15. *Montgomery Mail*, April 20, 1860.

16. *New York Day Book*, September 8, 1860.

17. *Austin State Gazette*, November 3, 1860.

18. *Fayetteville Arkansian*, August 31, 1860.

19. *Washington Constitution*, August 3, 1860.

20. *Natchez Mississippi Free Trader* (weekly ed.), August 13, 1860.

21. *Montgomery Weekly Mail*, August 3, 1860. For some examples of similarly dire predictions of a regional bloodletting under a Lincoln administration, see *Opelousas Courier*, August 25, 1860; *Marshall Texas Republican*, August 25, 1860; *Fayetteville Arkansian*, August 17, 1860; *Athens* (Ga.) *Southern Banner*, November 1, 1860.

22. *Athens* (Ga.) *Southern Banner*, September 6, 1860. See also *New Orleans Bulletin*, n.d., quoted in *Houston Weekly Telegraph*, July 31, 1860; *Clayton* (Ala.) *Banner*, August 9, 1860; *New Orleans Daily Delta*, July 31, 1860; *Charleston Mercury*, October 11, 1860.

23. *Austin Southern Intelligencer*, August 15, 1860.

24. *Alexandria Gazette*, July 27, 1860. For examples of other conservative papers that expressed alarm, see *McKinney* (Tex.) *Messenger*, July 27, 1860; *New Orleans L'Abeille de la Nouvelle-Orleans*, August 8, 1860; *Raleigh* (N.C.) *Register*, September 12, 1860; *Talladega Alabama Reporter*, August 2, 1860; *Wadesborough* (N.C.) *Argus*, September 13, 1860; *Seguin* (Tex.) *Union Democrat*, August 6, 1860.

25. *New Orleans Daily Picayune*, September 20, 23, 1860.

26. Letter of "W.R.D.W.," *New York Day Book*, August 12, September 8, 1860, clipped in *Austin Southern Intelligencer*, October 10, 1860.

27. M. D. Ector, Henderson, to C. A. Frazier, Marshall, *Marshall Texas Republican*, August 11, 1860.

28. James L. Craig to A. K. Craig, quoted in *Cincinnati Daily Commercial*, September 1, 1860.

29. S. B. Barron, *The Lone Star Defenders* (New York, 1908), 16–17.

30. Anonymous letter dated August 20, clipped in *Charleston Mercury*, September 8, 1860.

31. Violet C. Delling, Lincoln County, North Carolina, to B. F. Shelton [no address given], September 4, 1860, Miscellaneous Letters, Archives, James G. Gee Library, Texas A&M University, Commerce.

32. Entry for October 26, 1860, Sarah Lois Wadley Diary, 77. Typescript in Southern Historical Collection, University of North Carolina Library, Chapel Hill.

33. *Baton Rouge Daily Advocate*, November 14, 1860.

34. J.H.C. Basham, Union City, Tennessee, to Andrew Johnson, December 1, 1860, in LeRoy P. Graf and Ralph W. Haskins, *The Papers of Andrew Johnson* (Knoxville, 1972), 3:676.

35. For the reactions of some of these leaders, see Crenshaw, *The Slave States in the Presidential Election of 1860*, 89–111.

36. Wise to T. D. Murray, Paris, Texas, August 16, quoted in *Richmond Enquirer*, September 7, 1860.

37. Keitt to William Murray, Orangeburg Court House, September 22, quoted in *Charleston Mercury*, September 27, 1860.

38. Keitt to William Porcher Miles, October 3, 1860, William Porcher Miles Papers, Southern Historical Collection.

39. William K. Scarborough, ed., *The Diary of Edmund Ruffin*, 3 vols. (Baton Rouge, 1972), 1:455–56, 470. After the Brown raid, Ruffin became almost obsessed with the idea that secession was the only way to prevent slave tampering by abolitionists. In spring 1860 he published a strange, futurist novel, set in the years 1864 to 1870, in which new Republican President William H. Seward (Lincoln having served only one term) sponsored a massive abolitionist crusade against a separate southern nation with the intention of raising a Santo Domingo–like insurrection. In Ruffin's apocalyptic vision, the sturdy South, with the help of its loyal slaves, crushed the invasion, thus maintaining its independence. Ruffin's argument was that the South had been able to repel the Northern army and maintain the viability of slavery only because it had created a government that could resist such violations. See Edmund Ruffin, *Anticipations of the Future to Serve as Lessons for the Present Time* (Richmond, 1860).

40. Ibid., 463–64.

41. Crenshaw, *The Slave States in the Presidential Election of 1860*, 103–4.

42. Clement Eaton, *The Freedom-of-Thought Struggle in the Old South* (New York, 1964), 51.

43. *New York Times*, October 11, 1860.

44. Ibid.

45. *New York World*, October 11, 1860.

46. *Cincinnati Daily Commercial*, October 27, 1860.

47. *Richmond Enquirer*, September 25, 1860.

48. *New Orleans Daily Delta*, October 30, 1860.

49. William W. Freehling and Craig M. Simpson, eds., *Secession Debated: Georgia's Showdown in 1860* (New York, 1992), xi–xii.

50. Ibid., 11–12.

51. *Natchez Daily Free Trader*, November 2, 1860.

52. For example, see the speeches of Robert Toombs and Thomas L. Clingman, *Congressional Globe*, 36th Cong., 2d sess., 4, 267.

53. Ibid., 74–75. Representative John H. Reagan, of Palestine, later gave a similar speech in the House, in which he alleged that no fewer than a dozen towns in his district lay in ashes and that the poisoning of wells was only prevented "by information, which came to light before the plan could be carried into execution." Ibid., 389. Yet Reagan, once an ardent Unionist, had to know that the number of

towns he cited was a wild exaggeration. He also must have known that no poison had ever been discovered; in fact, when a substance purported to be strychnine turned out to be a harmless substance, the chairman of the vigilantes in nearby Athens, Texas, reported in disgust that the committee had dissolved itself, apparently concluding that there was no insurrection conspiracy. Reynolds, *Editors Make War*, 109–10.

54. *Congressional Globe*, 36th Cong., 2d sess., 99–100.

55. Ibid., 104.

56. Ibid., 184–87.

57. Ibid., 29.

58. Ibid., 393.

59. Walter L. Buenger, *Secession and the Union in Texas* (Austin, 1984), 37–39, 55–58, 75–77.

60. For a brief survey of the postelection secession campaigns in the Lower South, see Craven, *The Growth of Southern Nationalism*, 349–90.

61. Steven A. Channing, *Crisis of Fear: Secession in South Carolina* (New York, 1974), 286.

62. For example, in addressing Herbert Aptheker's account of numerous southern slave insurrection panics, William W. Freehling has suggested that although most were based upon unsubstantiated allegations, there were enough actual incidents to warrant the seemingly unreasonable fears that whites felt. Freehling, *The Road to Disunion: Secessionists at Bay, 1776–1854* (New York, 1990), 579, n.6.

63. Reynolds, *Editors Make War*, 97–117; Reynolds, "Vigilante Law During the Texas Slave Panic of 1860," 173–86. On the forged letter see Reynolds, "Reluctant Martyr: Anthony Bewley and the Texas Slave Insurrection Panic of 1860," 344–61.

64. The susceptibility of southerners to racial fears was not ended when the South seceded. Panics of a less general nature continued to plague certain areas even after the war began. For one notable example, see Winthrop D. Jordan, *Tumult and Silence at Second Creek: An Inquiry into a Civil War Slave Conspiracy* (Baton Rouge, 1993).

65. C. Vann Woodward, *The Burden of Southern History*, 3d ed. (Baton Rouge, 1993), 22–24.

6

Lessons in Generalship: Robert E. Lee's Military Legacy for the Twenty-First Century

Carol Reardon

Over three decades ago, during the Civil War Centennial and at the height of the cold war, Charles P. Roland posited that Confederate General Robert E. Lee still could teach twentieth-century American military leaders important lessons about the art of war. If the world avoided "the fiery bolts of extinction" by nuclear conflagration, he wrote, then "Lee's strategic and tactical concepts will again prove useful in the employment of conventional military forces."[1]

When Roland first made this suggestion in 1964, the notion that the generalship and campaigns of Robert E. Lee might serve as a source of insight to modern soldiers may well have seemed empty of promise. To cold-war combatants with huge arsenals of weapons of mass destruction at their command, the accomplishments of the great southern chieftain no doubt seemed entirely irrelevant. Still, Roland had made an important point. Implicitly embracing Napoleon's timeless injunction to "peruse again and again the campaigns of Alexander, Hannibal, Caesar, Gustavus Adolphus, Turenne, Eugene, and Frederick" as "the only means for becoming a great captain, and of acquiring the secret to the art of war," Roland added Robert E. Lee to the list of history's most outstanding soldiers whose accomplishments still might inform consideration of modern doctrinal and strategic issues.[2]

In the last thirty years, American officers from newly commissioned second lieutenants to senior generals indeed have applied lessons from the military career of the great Confederate commander to modern professional concerns. They did not respond directly to Roland's challenge alone, and they did not turn to Lee alone—even among Civil War generals—for useful lessons. Moreover, they did not always study Lee's career particularly systematically or with deep intellectual rigor; few of these soldiers could be called trained historians, and seldom have they attracted the attention of a scholarly community that has tended to dismiss much of their work as hopelessly subjective. No matter what inspired them or what conclusions they reached, however, they still proved Roland right: fully a century after his own time, Robert E. Lee could continue to serve as a useful model to the soldiers of an army whose uniform he himself once wore.

When Roland first made his case, not long after the Cuban Missile Crisis and on the eve of escalated involvement in Vietnam, he echoed contemporary calls for a national defense policy that offered more options for relieving international tensions than the heavy-handed threats of nuclear brinksmanship and massive retaliation of the Eisenhower years. He saw a need to "again learn the skills of swift maneuver and the delivery of paralyzing blows by highly mobile forces upon lines of communication and points of decision" by conventional American forces "composed of semi-independent, self-contained units." In encouraging the Army officer corps of the 1960s to look to Lee for some of the timeless lessons of the art of war that technology had not rendered obsolete, Roland asked much of them.[3]

Three factors rendered it unlikely that military officers of that era would see much point in a history-based inquiry into contemporary strategic or doctrinal issues. First, World War II and the cold war that followed shaped the professional mindset of most senior American officers. The global scope of recent conflicts seemed to offer a range of challenges quite different from those the United States had faced during the American Civil War. Even those commanders who studied military science during the interwar years, when military history held an important place in officer education, seldom looked for relevant links between past and present. As a result, they eliminated historical context as an element in decision making. This came back to haunt them when they deployed American forces to Southeast Asia and elsewhere in the cold-war years.

A second factor that turned American officers away from the historical foundations of their profession stemmed from the first. With the dawn of the atomic era, many military professionals believed that the new technology stripped almost all pre-1945 military history of its practical utility. Moreover, with the growing specialization demanded by increasingly sophisticated technology and weapons systems, many ambitious senior officers became managers and analysts of warfare—technocrats of the worst kind, some have argued—and, in so doing, they compromised, or lost entirely, their primary identity as war fighters. For such soldiers, traditional military history seemed to belong only to the hazy realm of institutional heritage. Presumably no lessons from military history—Robert E. Lee's ideas included—could penetrate the narrowly focused intellectual fortress into which much of the senior officer corps had retreated in the decades after 1945.

The intellectual blinders on junior officers were even worse. As technology claimed a more important place in military education, history found itself bumped out of the curriculum of most of the U.S. Army's Basic Schools for newly commissioned officers in nearly all its branches. Indeed, by 1954, only the Chemical School still required military history as part of its course offerings. Most American officers commissioned after World War II possessed only the shallowest of historical foundations from which to understand their profession, their army, their opponents, or their wars.

The third factor, of course, that held back the Army from taking Roland's suggestions seriously was the growing war in Southeast Asia. The harsh realities of combat in a hostile physical environment fighting an enemy whose aims and tactics they did not entirely understand consumed all the time and imagination the officer corps possessed. Most used history for little more than the celebration of branch birthdays, enhancement of unit pride, and other morale-building programs. If soldiers looked to the lessons of the past at all, they mostly sought immediately useful, practical expedients to resolve field problems. One example must suffice. When he fought in the Mekong Delta as a junior officer, future general William G. Pagonis, American logistical chief for Operation Desert Storm, tried to figure out how to build a stable firing platform for mortars and artillery in that swampy terrain. He turned to the Office of the Center of Military History in Washington, D.C., to find out how Union engineers around Charleston, South Carolina, had built their "water batteries" during the Civil War. Armed with century-old sketches by Union army engineers, Pagonis found a history-based answer to his tactical problem in Vietnam.[4]

Even in 1964, Roland believed that the Civil War's military leaders could offer more to modern soldiers than practical answers to immediate concerns. Not until the early 1970s, however, did the U.S. Army take steps to inculcate a new spirit of historical awareness into its officer corps. As the United States withdrew from the jungles of Southeast Asia, military leaders searched for ways to resolve the crisis of confidence that threatened the morale and competence of the officer corps and to assure both themselves and the nation that defeat would never again be their lot. An intellectual reawakening of sorts became a key element in its revitalization, and a renewed reliance on military history became a core element of the officer corps' reeducation.

In 1971, a panel of academic military historians and serving officers, designated the Department of the Army Ad Hoc Committee on the Army Need to Study Military History, met at the U.S. Military Academy. Its members discussed how the study of history might help the officer corps to combat its lost sense of esprit de corps and to stimulate innovative thinking about strategy, tactics, logistics, and other professional concerns.

This, they hoped, would right the Army's post-World War II misdirection away "from its traditional reliance upon the experience of history" that contributed to the unhappy results of the war in Vietnam.[5]

Army leadership endorsed the board's recommendations. All levels of the Army officer education system, from ROTC for officer candidates through the senior service schools for colonels, introduced, reintroduced, or improved their history curricula. Conventional nonnuclear wars again commanded study for their many potentially useful insights. Karl von Clausewitz's nineteenth-century classic *On War*—a work that rested on a solid foundation of historical examples from the Napoleonic era—firmly established itself for the first time as the intellectual guiding light in U.S. Army classrooms. History-based teaching techniques, most notably the "staff ride" to actual battle sites where real soldiers had commanded troops in armed conflict, became standard elements in military classrooms and filtered down to troop units as well. The lessons of history found their way into the making and writing of doctrine, and the introduction of historical vignettes in the Army's training and field manuals encouraged soldiers of all ranks to use history—and not merely personal experience—to think seriously about their profession and their role in it. None of these changes occurred overnight, but as Roland surmised, the lessons of even a century-old American conflict and its greatest leaders, such as Robert E. Lee, found new disciples.

What have late-twentieth-century soldiers found in Lee and his generalship to command their close attention? They have discovered a rich legacy indeed.

Probably reflecting concerns about low morale and career worries in the post-Vietnam officer corps, the timeless qualities of Lee's "military character" quickly drew their special interest. Long enamored of Lee's "nobler qualities," Roland already had asserted that the general possessed "the imperatives of leadership for national survival." These he described as: "intellect to divine and cope with enemy capabilities and intentions; boldness to strike when the occasion demands, however grave the risk; and above all, character to inspire purpose and sacrifice in the midst of supreme stress, hardship, and danger."[6] Officers grounded in modern fundamentals of military leadership could recognize immediately that Roland's delineation of the qualities of Lee's professional mien sounded familiar. General Matthew B. Ridgway, for instance, had already outlined the fundamental traits of successful commanders that Roland described and did it in only three words: courage, character, and competence.[7] Roland took the general's prescription a step further: he applied a generally understood ideal to a real individual. His assessment of Lee's generalship has provided a number of American soldiers in the post-Vietnam era with a starting point for developing their own thoughts on military professionalism.

Modern soldiers embrace Roland's positive commentary on Lee's physical and moral courage. On this point, indeed, both soldiers and civilian scholars tend to agree. Lee "set the moral tone for his forces. His personality reached to the individual soldier and that strength was reflected back to its leader," wrote one Army War College student who chose to study Lee as an example of a strategic leader.[8] Lee's appearances at or near the front lines inspired his men to greater efforts, and they often responded splendidly as they did at the Wilderness and again at Spotsylvania. Both military professionals and academic scholars can understand the impact of Lee's personal example and personal risk on the morale of his Army of Northern Virginia. Only soldiers, however, using today's military parlance, consider how Lee's reliance on the high morale of his men could become a key combat multiplier that "added to his offensive strength and often proved decisive in the face of overwhelming odds."[9] Lee's bravery, both physical and moral, still withstands challenge.

In similar fashion, modern soldiers continue to validate Roland's commentary on Lee's personal and professional character. In sharp contrast to such civilian writers as Alan T. Nolan, who has criticized Lee for occasional unethical conduct, the Confederate leader remains both an admirable man and a good soldier in the eyes of his modern comrades in arms.[10] His sense of professional ethics provided such a positive example for modern soldiers that one veteran of the Gulf War felt compelled to declare that "the U.S. was fortunate that both Gen. Schwarzkopf and the forces under his command *actually* emulated the tactics of the Confederate general" and rejected those of the modern general's own admitted hero, William T. Sherman.[11] Lee remains so well respected as a flawless professional role model that one Army War College student recently noted that "It is difficult for any mere student to study the campaigns of Robert E. Lee and to remain objective for long," adding that "Lee's leadership is legend, and rightfully so."[12] Indeed, asserted researchers who sought potential lessons for the retired officer in the general's last year, "Lee was a thoroughbred even in utter defeat."[13]

The specific elements of Lee's professional and personal character that still touch modern officers vary widely. What is clear is that Lee helps many soldiers explain their thoughts about the prerequisites of a superior commander. To one colonel, Lee's greatest strength came from a "mental agility and spirit" that thrived "even when times were most difficult," noting that, at bottom, "Agility is, above all, mental."[14] To another officer, Lee's "simplicity, devotion and humility" in the performance of his great responsibilities rubbed off on his army and inspired in his men both respect for their commander and confidence in their own ability to succeed against increasingly substantial odds.[15]

But Lee offers more than a laundry list of positive character traits to the modern U.S. Army officer corps. This is not always apparent; too often, the absence of systematic analysis of Lee's generalship and a tendency to pick and choose from the vast number of lessons his career offers prevents complete consensus on what the general can teach modern soldiers. Nowhere is this made more clear than considering the negative consequences of Lee's positive personal traits when misapplied by a combat commander. Lee's "boundless courtesy and humility," taken to excess, could be the chief flaw in his generalship, Roland argued, adding that "deep religious convictions united with the chivalric tradition of Virginia aristocracy to endow Lee with remarkable serenity and nobility of nature."[16] Much of the confidence Lee displayed in his men and in his senior subordinates in the field rested on a strong, deeply personal, religious faith. Readers of *Parameters*, the professional military journal of the Army War College, recently learned that Lee's spiritual strength continues to be an example of professional character that can be considered an appropriate "individual choice . . . that can help one transcend difficult circumstances," guided as it is "by a core set of unwavering beliefs."[17] But, some soldiers have argued, Lee's trust in his men and his God could instill an overconfidence that might translate into a flaw in Lee's military character. "Confidence in one's plans is not a fault but it must be balanced with an honest acceptance of capabilities," an Army War College student noted, remarking that Lee's trust in his men sometimes blinded him against recognizing weaknesses in his own force or strength in his opponents.[18] Even a Naval officer conceded that Lee's overconfidence may have led him to lapses in judgment at Gettysburg, when he accepted and then remained engaged in battle despite insufficient information from his cavalry.[19]

Among military men, even such objective criticism tends to get lost in the legacy of Lee's image as the Confederacy's flawless "marble man." Just as one colonel identified Lee's unquestioning faith in his men as dangerous, another believed entirely and without much evidence that "Lee was aware of both the hard, killing quality or potential of his army and he was equally aware of the army's softer, weaker points. He knew how much he could demand and what would hurt the Army the most."[20]

Interestingly, modern soldiers and recent civilian scholarship have found common ground in their tendency to consider Lee's strength of character beyond his military life alone. Both Thomas L. Connelly and Emory M. Thomas, in very different ways and to very different conclusions, work from the premise that Lee should be considered fundamentally as a complex human being; as Thomas notes, "history needs Robert E. Lee whole" and not merely as some artificially constructed martial icon.[21] Similarly, in today's U.S. Army, where "quality of life" issues have become a high priority, Lee offers one model to illustrate the benefits of caring for the "total" person and, by extension, for those who are important to him. Even before the Civil War ended, Lee had "become a prototype of intergenerational caregiving, familial responsibility, and social support" to his invalid wife and daughters, to his sons in the service, and to their wives and children at home, all while enduring "the traumas of war and his cumulative losses." Still, as noted in a study in *Parameters*, he maintained a "personal sense of control and autonomy" and took steps to protect or restore his fiscal, physical, and spiritual assets, all signs of a strong character guaranteed "to have an uncommon influence in all spheres of his life and decisionmaking."[22]

Far more contentious than any discussion of Lee's courage and appropriate personality for a professional military man in the minds of modern soldiers, however, are their concerns about Ridgway's third pillar of martial proficiency: professional competence. Even today, most academic students of the Civil War and, at least until the 1970s, most modern soldiers as well, understood military science as divided into two levels—tactics and strategy. Now a bit dated, these two classifications still provide a starting point for evaluating Lee's soldierly abilities, where "tactics" refers to his conduct of battles and "strategy" considers his planning and execution of campaigns in Virginia or his insights on military matters outside the Old Dominion.

The Army's current war-fighting manual, *FM 100-5: Operations*, defines tactics as the "art by which corps and smaller unit commanders translate potential combat power into victorious battles and engagements."[23] Lee never found himself comfortable in the role of tactical commander in battle. An engineer most of his professional life, he never led troops in battle until he took army command in West Virginia in 1861. Lee's skill as a tactician has impressed few objective Civil War scholars, and most soldiers agree with their assessment.

Perhaps, however, it is entirely unfair to look to Lee for tactical lessons. After all, Donald A. Carter argued, tactics was not Lee's most important responsibility as the commander of an army. As an instructor of junior officers, Carter found himself in a bind. He wanted to persuade the junior officers to study military history seriously, but at the same time he admitted that Lee's successful employment of cavalry in a particular battle would not likely help a lieutenant or captain with small-unit troop leading, especially because the "more specifically we try to remove useful lessons from their historical context," the more vulnerable to misuse they become. So he urged junior officers to look to Lee and other senior officers instead for insights about the higher arts of war or for clues to effective leadership that remained relevant at all levels of command.[24]

Did this soldier mean to argue that Lee offers modern officers no useful insights on tactics? Not really. Evidence of Lee's tactical weakness in fact presents many useful lessons. For instance, Lee failed to reassert tactical control over his forces on the morning of July 1, 1863, west of Gettysburg, a step he likely should have taken when his subordinates brought on a battle he did not wish to fight. One infantry captain who examined different elements of the fight on McPherson's Ridge described a series of tactical problems that circumscribed a classic meeting engagement in which "reconnaissance, cavalry screening, hasty attacks, defensive fighting, command and control, withdrawals under fire, and subordinate initiative were all present in abundance." Despite the day's results—apparently a victory for Lee—the junior officer argued persuasively that the most useful lessons for the modern soldier do not emerge from the study of Lee's successful offensive. Rather, they result from an examination of Union General John Buford's response to the tactical challenges Lee presented him. The way in which the Northern officer used his cavalry to accomplish his missions is familiar to late-twentieth-century armored cavalrymen and aviators: "to find the enemy and develop the situation; and . . . to provide reaction time and maneuver space" for the main body. Lee's ultimate success on July 1 did not impress this modern soldier. Instead, he admired the competence, aggressiveness, and initiative shown by experienced "quick-thinking officers" in blue, especially Generals Buford, James Wadsworth, Lysander Cutler, and Solomon Meredith.[25] Lee's inaction on the tactical level early on the first day at Gettysburg demonstrated an important concept: a defender can steal away the initiative from an attacker.[26]

What might have happened if Lee had exerted appropriate tactical control early on July 1? Could he have prevented any further development of a battle he did not want? Might nagging historical controversies about General Richard S. Ewell's inability to take Cemetery or Culp's Hill, or General James Longstreet's failure to take the Round Tops, or Pickett's Charge be rendered moot if Lee had decided to disengage? Perhaps so, but it was not Lee's style of tactical leadership. Jay Luvaas of the Army War College faculty has argued that Lee proved to be an uncertain tactical leader, one who "appeared unsure how much latitude to give his principal subordinates—he gave operational latitude to Ewell, a new corps commander, and issued specific tactical orders to Longstreet, his most experienced subordinate. On July 2, he sent only one message and received only one report, despite the fact that two of his three corps commanders were new at the job."[27]

Lee's command and control efforts on that single battlefield offer many lessons for tactical leaders on all levels, and few reflect well on him. On this point, soldiers and civilian scholars tend to agree. What separates their perspectives, however, is the soldiers' tendency to find more than antiquarian interest in the study of old battles; they use the battle to illuminate, validate, or challenge contemporary tactical issues.

At least among his admirers, Lee performed far better as a strategist than he did as a tactician. Roland certainly thought well of Lee's understanding on the strategic level of war. He quoted in evidence a Michigan soldier who suggested that Lee *must* be a great strategist because everywhere the Northern army went, the rebels were already there, concluding that "To friend and foe alike, Lee's skill seemed miraculous."[28] Roland's views represent only one side of a rich debate in academic circles over the quality of the general's strategic skills. Richard M. McMurry and Gary W. Gallagher both tend to agree with Roland that Lee showed glimpses of brilliance as a strategic thinker.[29] Virulent detractors, including Thomas L. Connelly and Alan T. Nolan, argue equally strongly against such notions.[30]

Post-Vietnam American officers, even those who admire Lee on other grounds, find little to debate here. Indeed, they remain fairly united in asserting that Lee's understanding of strategy shone only a tiny bit brighter than his tactical abilities. Much of their criticism stems from their embrace of today's military lexicon, which gives "strategy" a far more comprehensive definition than most civilian Civil War generals or civilian scholars have given it. Now the concept has evolved into a study of the way that all elements of national power—political, economic, social, and diplomatic and not simply the utilization of its armed forces—might help to obtain "national and alliance political aims at the lowest possible cost in lives and treasure."[31]

Fairly or not, today's soldiers usually use this broader concept in their evaluations of Lee, and they tend to chop away at his reputation. In 1990, Colonel John J. Meyers, a student at the Army War College, posed an interesting question: "Robert E. Lee: Great Captain of History?" To earn the title of great captain, Meyers argued, a general must be "capable of strategic and operational planning for an entire campaign as well as an individual battle." The colonel concluded that Lee most decisively failed these tests on the strategic level. The general understood when, where, and how to strike aggressively and showed no qualms about taking acceptable risks in tactical situations. He had done so most successfully both at Second Manassas and at Chancellorsville. The colonel argued, however, that in the summer of 1863 Lee proved unable to transfer that same aggressiveness to the strategic level. To keep the Confederacy from being cut in two by the fall of Vicksburg and the capture of the Mississippi River, Lee "should have taken the same desperate chances" he had taken in his battles in Virginia. He should have considered sending or taking part of his army into the western theater, but he did not do so because of his "loyalty and devotion to Virginia." His sentiments toward his home state led Lee to Pennsylvania and to Gettysburg. "Ultimately," Colonel Meyers declared, Lee's "loyalty to his state doomed the Confederacy."[32]

Criticism of Lee's devotion to Virginia is nothing new to most students of the Civil War. Nolan even argued that the appearance of the general's allegiance to Virginia provided a cover for choosing personal courses of action that otherwise might be considered highly self-interested.[33] But Meyers's emphasis on the capacity of great captains to "demonstrate their ability to organize their forces to best accomplish their mission utilizing the best leaders available" recasts the argument into military terms, not parochial political or cultural ones. He concluded starkly: "Robert E. Lee is clearly a man loved by all within his native Virginia and the Confederacy— yet, his overall performance falls short of what is expected of a great captain of history and 'Master in the Art of War.' "[34]

An important reason for such harsh assessment stems from a growing appreciation of Clausewitz's description of war as an extension of politics. War is an instrument of policy, not an end in itself. No senior military leader of the Confederacy, Lee included, had particularly clear notions of the government's strategic objectives. The generals could not have such vision, it seems at least in part, because Jefferson Davis and the Confederate Congress reached no political consensus on the war's goals. Did the South seek independence? Or could some substantial concession from the North, such as a constitutional amendment protecting slavery, serve as the foundation for ending the fighting and resolving the sectional crisis peacefully? Until recently, by the way, despite a spate of literature addressing the nature of Southern nationalism and Confederate war aims, few civilian scholars linked those issues to the actual conduct of the war itself.[35]

Neither Roland nor many of Lee's modern critics entirely appreciate the problems that stemmed from the hazy guidance the general's civilian superiors provided. Roland insisted that Lee did understand the relationship between strategy and statecraft, especially in his "adaptation of abstract military theory to the exigencies of Southern politics, economics, and logistics," without really coming to grips with the lack of consensus on war aims among members of the Davis administration and the South's legislative leaders.[36] Taking the opposite position, Meyers stated forthrightly that Lee's "military objectives did not support the political strategy of the Confederacy," but the colonel did not explain the South's goals either.[37] As a result, whether forced by the absence of such guidance or in the rejection of what little insight the Davis administration gave him, it seems easy to cast Lee as an old-fashioned general who sought out "the climactic battle[,] and his obsession to annihilate the Army of the Potomac cost him the very life blood he was so determined to preserve."[38]

Even if this one scholar and this one soldier do not agree on this issue, at least they both remember the fundamental premise of civilian control over the military that guides the making of strategy. Not all Civil War students do. Alan Nolan argued hotly that Lee should have surrendered in 1864 to save lives when it became clear that he could not win. Roland recently has noted that "objective students of the ethics of command will exonerate him of this charge. He was obligated to fight as long as the civil authorities chose to do so, and as long as his army had the capacity to do so."[39] On at least this strategic issue, Roland and modern soldiers agree.

Still, the recent conduct of a standard Army War College class assignment suggests that Meyers is far from alone in his reservations about Lee's status as a strategic leader. Early in the academic year, each student chooses one key figure in world military history from a list of so-called strategic leaders. Although the exercise is designed primarily to assess each officer's ability to give effective oral reports, it still requires each student to explain why— and, occasionally, if—his subject belongs on that list. Robert E. Lee did not even make the assignment designers' list of eight names presented to the class of 1994. The general did claim a spot on the list during the next academic year, but most student evaluations concluded that Lee did not meet the War College's ideal of a strategic leader. Perhaps it is unfair to judge Lee's capacity for strategic leadership by measuring him against a concept he would not have understood entirely. Still, if today's professional soldier can separate the complexities of the person he studies from the concept he seeks to understand, even the shortcomings of a subject such as Robert E. Lee may prove useful.

In the thirty years since Roland offered his challenge, the most enlightening professional discussion of Lee's military competence has come through examinations of his performance in Virginia, in what is often called theater command. Although he did not use the phrase "operational art," a concept articulated most clearly by the Army's doctrine makers only after the Vietnam years, Roland clearly understood this important concept that now is an integral part of the professional soldier's vocabulary.

Since its initial inclusion in *FM 100-5* in 1982, the operational art now is recognized as a third level of modern war, nestled between tactics and strategy. Formally, the operational art is "the employment of military force to attain strategic goals in a theater of war or theater of operations through the design, organization, and conduct of campaigns and major operations." Likewise, soldiers come to understand that a campaign is a "series of joint actions designed to attain a strategic objective in a theater of war."[40]

As with most new ideas, this innovative concept has required considerable explanation and elaboration. In the hands of the Army's military historians who tried to explicate the inner workings of the new notion, Robert E. Lee's campaigns have become most useful models. According to Jay Luvaas, Lee clearly grasped the basic principles of the operational art and could make the all-important "fundamental decisions about when and where to fight and whether to accept or decline battle" to further larger goals. His most important obligation rested with "the identification of the enemy's operational center-of-gravity and the concentration of superior combat power against that point to achieve a decisive success." Robert E. Lee, Luvaas concluded, had mastered that concept and incorporated it into the command philosophy the general himself had described to Prussian military observer Justus Scheibert: "I think and work with all my powers to bring my troops to the right place at the right time," then "I leave the matter up to God and the subordinate officers."[41]

Sometimes, such a command arrangement worked. For example, Lee resisted the urge to recall "Stonewall" Jackson from the Shenandoah Valley in the spring of 1862 to strengthen the Richmond defenses against the advance of General George B. McClellan's Army of the Potomac. Instead, he allowed Jackson to continue his independent actions, throwing his support to "a daring maneuver—a deep attack by the Valley Army" that affected the way military leaders in Washington allotted manpower within the entire Virginia theater, including those facing Lee near Richmond.[42] On other occasions, such as the first day at Gettysburg, July 1, 1863, Lee's command arrangement failed him. If the first Southern troops to advance down the Chambersburg Road that morning had been cavalry carrying out its traditional mission of scouting, intelligence gathering, and, once in contact with the enemy, forcing them to reveal their intentions, Lee likely would have retained operational control of the day. The Southern chieftain could have decided whether this was the time and the place for a battle, and he could have rendered moot all criticism of his failure to exert tactical control over the fight. In advancing with neither a cavalry screen nor senior officers of appropriate rank to control the advance, subordinates leading the Third Corps's infantry divisions stole that choice from him. He had to throw out the grand scheme around which he had planned his offensive operation—to fight only if attacked—and redirect his thinking toward tactical combinations, a level on which, as we have seen, he did not feel at ease. Early success on the field and his own combative nature allowed Lee to report later that "A battle had, therefore, become in a measure unavoidable," but it seemed clear from what followed, argues Luvaas, that "Lee's theory of command and his conduct at Gettysburg suggest that he felt more comfortable at the operational than the tactical level."[43]

Unfortunately, such a rapidly changing operational scenario such as occurred at Gettysburg robbed Lee of a chance to think through his actions. As one modern officer wrote, Lee failed because he "found it impossible, through all the ebb and flow, to choose and accomplish a clear objective. This, the first principle of war, is often the last to reveal itself."[44]

It is not always easy or useful to separate the three levels of war in any truly insightful examination of the military art. Among the most useful and most frequently utilized instructional techniques now employed to encourage soldiers to think about Lee's abilities as a tactical, operational, and strategic leader is the "staff ride." A Prussian practice developed in the early nineteenth century and introduced in the United States early in the twentieth, a fully developed staff ride, according to one of its top practitioners in the army schools, "brings to life, on the very terrain where historic encounters took place, examples, applicable today as in the past, of leadership, tactics and strategy, communications, use of terrain, and above all, the psychology of men in battle." The greatest benefit of such exercises comes from the realization that while technological changes might render lessons in minor tactics obsolete, "other lessons are timeless because they spring either from universal operational principles or from universal human characteristics," and these universalities are useful to every officer who aspires to master his profession. The well-executed staff ride can introduce soldiers to important concepts on all levels of war without resorting to dry lists of maxims.[45]

Although military instructors have led staff rides to battle sites around the world, Civil War battlefields still host the greatest number of these trips. Gettysburg, Fredericksburg, Antietam, Chancellorsville, The Wilderness, Spotsylvania, and Petersburg—all battles in which Lee held command— have drawn the greatest share of professional students. Gettysburg has become especially popular, fueled at least in part by the popularity of Michael Shaara's Pulitzer Prize-winning novel *The Killer Angels* (1974). The novel's movie version entitled *Gettysburg* has added to that battlefield's appeal for military audiences. Secretaries of defense, chiefs of staff and their deputies from all the armed services, numerous congressmen, and senior officers from foreign armies have traced Lee's battles and campaigns, as have hundreds of cadets from West Point, Marine Corps officers from their schools at Quantico, and ROTC cadets from many civilian universities.

Its innate flexibility makes the staff ride amazingly useful in military education. Imaginative instructors tailor trips to meet specific teaching goals or to suit the experience level of the audience. If Robert E. Lee's decision-making process for a two-division assault on the Union left on July 2 cannot hold many immediately useful lessons for a junior officer who leads only a platoon, he still can be made to understand how the general's decision shapes the way in which he prepares and leads his men in the accomplishment of their mission. There is quite some intellectual distance from Lee's army-level decision making and the important discovery made by a group of ROTC cadets from St. Bonaventure University as they struggled to the summit of Big Round Top: "The highest peak is not always the best to defend. Too steep a rise may fatigue troops and isolate a unit from the rest of the army."[46] Still, later in their careers, these cadets may well remember their physical discomfort that day and begin to understand that it resulted directly from a military decision made at the higher levels of command to which they aspire.

Similarly, members of the staff of a Reserve Component military police brigade visited Lee's Maryland battlefields for a professional development exercise. Initially unconvinced that staff rides might prove to be useful training tools for combat support and service support units, the soldiers found that the early battles of Lee's 1862 incursion into the North held lessons entirely relevant to their branch mission. Since "the military police are the primary combat force on today's rear area battlefield," one member wrote, Lee's handling of the battles for Turner's Gap, Fox's Gap, and Crampton's Gap that "turned into a critical Confederate delaying action with a modest force of infantry and cavalry" seemed quite similar to the military police rear-area security mission. When the students had mastered the historical case, the instructors created a simulation in which a Soviet airborne regiment dropped in the vicinity of Washington, D.C., and then advanced westward—as Union forces had done in September 1862—toward an airfield and logistical center located where Lee had positioned his trains and reserves. The military policemen then had to apply their new appreciation of terrain, the way a previous generation of soldiers had defended it, and modern doctrine to design a defense of the threatened position.[47]

Army engineers who visited the same field considered not just the historical event but also how modern techniques in their specialty could be used on that same ground today. As combat support troops, they, too, came to "a much better understanding of the reactions of leaders and soldiers in the crucible of combat."[48]

Military instructors who use staff rides and in-depth campaign studies to address key concepts can use Robert E. Lee's decisions to inform discussion on a variety of important elements in operational planning. Lee's handling of the Chancellorsville campaign, for example, suggested to a number of officers the successful execution of a mobile defense, a necessary skill for an outnumbered commander defending a large geographical area against a stronger enemy force. This became a subject of some interest to American officers during the cold-war era who trained to defend against numerically superior communist-bloc aggressors. The Army of Northern Virginia's primary vulnerability in the spring of 1863 as it lay in winter camps around Fredericksburg resulted from a similar scenario: "its lack of sufficient forces to defend an extended front." Lee had to destroy or damage severely a larger enemy force along the Rappahannock River both to retake the initiative for his future operational plans and to secure Richmond from the north. A mobile defense did not require him to deplete his strength to protect to the death any specific terrain that lacked military usefulness. Moreover, such a scheme allowed him to exploit opportunities, such as his approval of Stonewall Jackson's assault on the unprotected Union right flank in the woods west of Chancellorsville. Lee's aggressiveness in this essentially defensive operation—which most civilian scholars usually ascribe to Lee's *offensive*-mindedness—when combined with Jackson's tactical strokes and flawed Union intelligence operations, brought him stunning success. Lee then shifted troops back toward Fredericksburg to contain a potentially crushing blow at Marye's Heights. "With a highly mobile reserve and the permissive nature of the mission," Lee "oriented his forces on the destruction of the enemy within the penetration." In this way, one officer concluded, "General Lee employed [operational] doctrine that was one hundred years ahead of his day."[49] A Marine Corps officer deduced the same lessons from his visit to those fields: "It was a classic exhibition of the philosophy of defensive maneuver."[50]

One of the most contentious Clausewitzian concepts applied to all levels of war concerns the determination of the "culminating point" of a military operation, and Lee's campaigns have proved useful in elucidating this point, too. According to modern Army doctrine, the culminating point is "that time in every operation, unless it is strategically decisive and ends the [tactical] fighting, where the strength of the attacker no longer significantly

exceeds that of the defender, and beyond which continued offensive operations therefore risk over-extension, counterattack, and defeat."[51]

Lee's conduct of the Gettysburg campaign again provides a laboratory
in which to examine that confusing concept on tactical, operational, and
strategic levels. One of the most important things a commander must be
able to do is to recognize the advent of the culminating point for his own
forces or those of the enemy and be prepared to take action to remedy or
exploit it. Following *FM 100-5* as his guide, an Army War College student
identified a number of factors facing Lee that might well have brought his
own operational plan for Pennsylvania to an early culminating point. "Lee
entered the battle outnumbered, fighting on ground and with tactics not of
his choosing, faced with supply vulnerabilities if he remained static, on
exterior lines compared to the Union forces, and with many of the same
command, control, communications, and intelligence problems his army
had experienced in previous battles." None of these problems proved
inconsiderable, but to the best of his ability Lee tried to lessen the effects of
those within his control, even though, the officer admitted, most still
"worked against Lee to prevent the success he expected to achieve." One
additional point merited special attention: the commander's own perception of the enemy. The most telling consideration over which Lee had
control and apparently made no effort to alter was "the assumption that the
Union army would not put up a creditable fight."[52]

This military student's conclusions are important, if somewhat akin to an
exercise in hair-splitting. They challenge the traditional notion—one seemingly apparent only in retrospect—that Gettysburg and the Pennsylvania
campaign were necessarily the "high water mark of the Confederacy." A
culminating point is a relative thing, he observed. It did not exist absolutely
and could not be understood on one level of war in isolation from the others.
On the tactical level, for instance, Lee never exceeded his culminating point
"since the [Union] counterattack and follow-on decisive battle never took
place."[53] Not all modern soldiers reached that same conclusion, however.
Another officer, after describing Pickett's Charge on July 3, argued that Lee's
army indeed reached a tactical culminating point at Gettysburg, and it did
so "on the *approach* to the ridge" where the Union defenders waited.[54]

On the operational level, the Army War College student argued, Lee
"was neither defeated nor destroyed. Even during his withdrawal to Virginia he had made plans for a defense in the hope that Meade might attack
at a disadvantage to give Lee an operational victory." Lee's actions in
Maryland between July 5 and July 14, when he finally recrossed the Potomac, "indicate that he did not believe he had reached his culminating
point." Perhaps. Or maybe the high water that prevented an earlier crossing
made the whole issue moot.[55]

Does the fact that his army was not destroyed reflect well on Lee? Not
really. An army can reach its culminating point in two ways: through

self-imposed problems or through those imposed by the enemy. The Army War College student insisted that even if Lee's army had not reached its culminating point in any way, his generalship on the tactical and operational levels still left much to be desired. His "unwarranted overconfidence, poor command, control, and coordination, unrealistic expectations of decisive results, limited tactical options, forcing an attack, assuming a weak and broken enemy, unfavorable force actions, inadequate intelligence, logistical shortages/dependence on uncertain supply sources, tactical miscalculations, over-reliance on morale as a combat multiplier, failure to think through possible branches and sequels to the campaign plan, and poor battlefield communications" all contributed to his defeat even before his army had reached its culminating point. Of the self-imposed and enemy-imposed factors that might lead one's force to that point, "Lee hastened his own defeat more than did Meade" defeat him.[56] A brother officer rendered the student's entire question irrelevant, however, when he argued that the South had already passed its culminating point on the more important national strategic level well before Gettysburg. The Confederacy continued to exist only by using up a rapidly dwindling supply of irreplaceable military, economic, and political resources.[57]

Even more contentious a concept for military students and planners is the Clausewitzian notion of "center of gravity." Like discussions of culminating points, considerations about centers of gravity may take into account tactical, operational, and strategic components. In a generalized fashion, Clausewitz defined it as "the hub of all power and movement, on which everything depends." On a tactical level, a command post or the capture of a key terrain feature can be the center of gravity. On the operational level, it may be the opposing force itself (or key individual elements) or its logistical base or lines of communication. On the strategic level, a key economic resource, the center of government, or even some intangible such as political and popular will may be centers of gravity.[58] Recognizing the enemy's weakest point and exploiting its vulnerability at the right time can lead to decisive victory, and identifying it is more difficult than it seems.

As with so many other elements of the military art, Lee's campaigns can help soldiers understand this concept. The general understood that Northern public opinion was the critical element to continuation of the war effort. As an Army War College student wrote, Lee "attacked that center with his invasion of Pennsylvania, support of the war in the Valley of the Tennessee, and by his constant maneuvers near Washington, D.C. He connected the political objectives with the operational and tactical plans" of his army. Conversely, another officer pointed out that the Confederacy began irretrievably to fall apart politically in the fall of 1863, and that this weakness truly marked the South's center of gravity. "At the very moment the South needed to stiffen its will to compensate for an overall decline in military fortunes" after the defeats at Gettysburg, Vicksburg, and Port Hudson, "that will became less reliable. Reunion and peace began to have attractive features," as substantial numbers of antiadministration candidates won seats in the Confederate Congress in the fall elections.[59] Roland always had placed the importance of popular will high on his list of factors that contributed to Southern defeat, and he did so before most other students of the war.[60] It is interesting to note that recently both soldiers and scholars have taken so well to this important theme.[61]

In 1964, Roland added yet another important dimension to the analysis of military leadership in general—and Civil War leadership specifically—with this insightful comment: "success and failure in war demonstrate that generalship alone does not always prevail, however good it may be. Victory requires that one side overmatch the opposite in the sum of its generalship plus all other capabilities for waging war. Hence, judged fairly, a general's record must be weighed against the resources at his command."[62] He considered Lee a master of accomplishing much with little. In so concluding, Roland foreshadowed the way modern senior leaders learn to conceptualize military planning, especially on the operational and strategic levels.

The study of logistics never has drawn much interest from the civilian Civil War student. Even professional soldiers, until fairly well into their career, rarely embrace such a study in more than a restrictive "bullets-and-beans" manner. Army instructors now demand that resources be considered an integral part of the strategic planning process. Students at the Army War College, for instance, learn early in the academic year that strategy making can best be understood as a three-legged stool: the first considers the "ends," or the objective to be accomplished; the second considers the "ways," or the methods to be employed to obtain the ends; finally, and most recently added, the third considers the "means," the resources available to carry out the ways to accomplish the desired ends. Omitting consideration of any one of the three leaves the stool precariously balanced and introduces a degree of risk that strategic planners may or may not decide is acceptable.

Lee's actions have suggested to modern soldiers that Roland was right to stress the general's awareness of logistical concerns on the higher levels of war. Lieutenant Colonel C. R. Shrader, an officer in the Transportation Corps, noted that Lee's operational plan for the Maryland campaign, for one example, offered at least six reasons that justified an invasion of the North in the fall of 1862. Of the six, two were essentially logistical in nature: a desire to obtain supplies from a Maryland countryside as yet unvisited by the destruction of war, and an intention to cut important east-west raillines to disrupt the movement and supply of Union troops. Shrader found equally important evidence of Lee's understanding of logistical influences on operational planning in the general's awareness that his own force was ill suited to the task at hand. Lee wrote to Jefferson Davis that the Army of Northern Virginia "lacks much of the material of war, is feeble in transport, the animals being much reduced, and the men are poorly provided with clothing, and, in thousands of instances, are destitute of shoes."[63] Some soldiers have argued that Lee also knew that he could sustain a campaign of any length in Pennsylvania in the summer of 1863 only by capturing Union stores; the unpredictability and unreliability of logistical support—and a shortage of artillery ammunition for the pre-assault cannonade before Pickett's Charge is only the most well known piece of evidence here—shaped Lee's operational flexibility. This is a useful lesson for all senior officers.[64]

Even in 1964, Roland did not idealize the Southern leader. He took on, and occasionally agreed with, the criticisms offered by Lee's detractors and even his strongest supporters. But he drew the line when it came to a charge made by Lee's own adjutant Walter Taylor, who blamed the South's defeat in part on his own general's deference to President Davis. No professional soldier of Lee's generation could have perceived his role any differently than the general did, Roland understood. Lee's unwillingness to test the boundaries of his authority robbed the general "of the qualities of a revolutionary leader." But this was a good thing. According to Roland, "Lee was too American to play Napoleon."[65] He has never wavered from this conclusion, most recently noting that Lee suffered "from a lack of an implacable revolutionary purpose."[66]

In the turbulent 1960s, it was important for Roland to consider Lee as a revolutionary leader, even if he be an unlikely one. But the primary benefactors of such insights would not have been found among American soldiers. In some ways, Roland spoke to issues that more fundamentally concerned the enemies of the United States during the cold war. Indeed, Lee might well have understood their problems even better than did many American military leaders a century later. Nor was Roland alone in discovering such links. As Edward K. Eckert, a civilian historian who occasionally taught in army schools, pointed out, the Civil War produced two kinds of generals: McClellans and Grants. Eckert advised against McClellan-style generalship that rested too closely on the theory of some "school solution" such as those propounded by Napoleonic-era military thinker Henri Jomini, West Point professor Dennis Hart Mahan, or even Union general and acknowledged soldier-scholar Henry W. "Old Brains" Halleck. "Book strategy could only be successful when the opponent agreed to adhere to the same book," Eckert warned, and unfortunately for the first Union generals in Virginia, "their principal adversary was Lee who had not only read their book, but had prepared his own, and he could check every move they planned almost before they had begun to march."[67] Lee understood a simple reality that American enemies of the cold-war years learned, too. As Roland had argued in his study of Lee, "when one lacks the resources to destroy the enemy's armed forces, he must resort to other means; he must then attempt to destroy the enemy's will through measures short of the destruction of military power." These might include traditional approaches such as the capture of his capital or something more, such as "the inflicting of casualties beyond the enemy's expectations."[68] Such a strategy, especially continued over a long period of time, required a linking of military and political goals, and Roland's discussion of the strategic challenges facing Lee—and indeed the entire Confederacy—soon found real-world parallels during the Vietnam War. Unfortunately for thousands of American soldiers, sapping of the enemy's will to continue the struggle claimed a far more prominent place in the "people's war" revolutionary rhetoric and political writings of North Vietnamese leaders Ho Chi Minh and Vo Nguyen Giap, Mao Tse-tung, and Che Guevara than in American military literature.

More than thirty years later, then, we can see that Roland had been correct when he asserted that the great Southern leader's career still held relevant lessons for modern soldiers. Lee's professional life, even when reduced to bits and pieces, could provide something of value for nearly any military professional who sought insights into his own career. Even Lee's postwar years offered retiring soldiers reentering the civilian world a model worthy of emulation. A study of the five years of Lee's life after Appomattox suggested ways to "assist contemporary veterans in negotiating their own responses to the events of their lives and in planning successful futures" outside the military. Lee's postarmy life suggests that retirees needed to evaluate their attitudes toward lifelong learning and to examine their willingness to assume new roles, take risks, and find ways to make use of their talents and experiences. Moreover, just as Lee had supported his family for years, he now learned to look to them as a positive source of support, affection, information, advice, and assistance. After hanging up his uniform, Lee expanded his social network to expose himself to new things while enjoying the greater stability of life at home among old friends and family. Moreover, he "made every effort to maintain regular physical activity, even when it was likely that the discomfort he was experiencing would have made a sedentary lifestyle tempting." The researchers concluded that, even today, "the quality of each veteran's life will be affected by the investment he or she makes in examining and assessing the life themes that were so successfully addressed by Robert E. Lee."[69]

Noted military historian S.L.A. Marshall once offered three elements as the best foundation for officer education: "a continuous study, first of the nature of men, second the techniques that produce unified action, and last, of the history of past operations."[70] In positing that modern soldiers still could learn much from the study of a great captain such as Robert E. Lee, Charles Roland reminded the U.S. Army not to ignore valuable professional role models from any era in American military history. Soldiers of the nineteenth century still have much to teach the military leaders of the twenty-first century.

NOTES

1. Charles P. Roland, "The Generalship of Robert E. Lee," in Grady McWhiney, ed. *Grant, Lee, Lincoln and the Radicals: Essays on Civil War Leadership* (Chicago, 1964), 68.

2. Quoted in Peter G. Tsouras, *Warriors' Words: A Quotation Book from Sesostris III to Schwarzkopf, 1871 B.C. to A.D. 1991* (London, 1992), 199.

3. Roland, "The Generalship of Robert E. Lee," 68.

4. William G. Pagonis, with Jeffrey L. Cruikshank, *Moving Mountains: Lessons in Leadership and Logistics from the Gulf War* (Boston, 1992), 36–37.

5. Memorandum of Maj. Gen. Kenneth C. Wickham, January 18, 1971, printed in *Department of the Army Ad Hoc Committee Report on the Army Need for the Study of Military History*, 4 vols. (West Point, 1971), 1:Annex A, p. A–1.

6. Roland, "The Generalship of Robert E. Lee," 69.

7. Matthew B. Ridgway, "Leadership," in Robert L. Taylor and William E. Rosenbach, eds., *Military Leadership: In Pursuit of Excellence* (Boulder, CO, 1984), 22–32.

8. Lt. Col. Thomas A. Green, "A Comparison of the Operational Art of George Gordon Meade and Robert Edward Lee during the Period July 1863, to March 1864," Army War College Military Studies Paper, 1988, p. 25. Copy in U.S. Army War College Library, Carlisle Barracks, PA.

9. Col. John J. Meyers, "Robert E. Lee: Great Captain of History?" Army War College Military Studies Paper, 1990, p. 57. Copy in U.S. Army War College Library.

10. See Alan T. Nolan, *Lee Considered: General Robert E. Lee and Civil War History* (Chapel Hill, 1991), 30–58, for instance, for accusations that Lee resigned from the U.S. Army only after making sure that he already had secured himself a more senior appointment in Richmond. Nolan, an attorney, argues more from a presentist, legalistic foundation than from the tenets of American military professionalism.

11. Maj. Jeffrey F. Addicott, "Desert Storm: Robert E. Lee or William Tecumseh Sherman," *Command*, issue 17 (July/August 1992):38.

12. Green, "A Comparison of the Operational Art of George Gordon Meade and Robert Edward Lee," 25.

13. M. W. Parker, W. A. Achenbaum, G. F. Fuller, and W. P. Fay, "Aging Successfully: The Example of Robert E. Lee," *Parameters*, 24 (Winter 1994–95):102.

14. Green, "A Comparison of the Operational Art of George Gordon Meade and Robert Edward Lee," 26.

15. Maj. Don T. Riley, "Serve Your Soldiers to Win," *Military Review*, 66 (November 1986):14.

16. Roland, "The Generalship of Robert E. Lee," 65, 67.

17. Parker et al., "Aging Successfully," 108–10.

18. Lt. Col. James D. Coomler, "Clausewitz's Concept of the Culminating Point and its Application to the Gettysburg Campaign," Army War College Military Studies Paper, 1993, p. 31. Copy in U.S. Army War College Library.

19. Capt. Robert C. Rubel, USN, "Gettysburg and Midway: Historical Parallels in Operational Command," *Naval War College Review*, 48 (Winter 1995):102.

20. Green, "A Comparison of the Operation Art of George Gordon Meade and Robert Edward Lee," 25.

21. See Thomas L. Connelly, *The Marble Man: Robert E. Lee and His Image in American Society* (New York, 1977), chap. 1, for a discussion of Lee as a decidedly flawed individual. See also a more objectively human Lee in Emory M. Thomas, *Robert E. Lee: A Biography* (New York, 1995); quotation comes from p. 20.

22. Parker et al., "Aging Successfully," 101–3.

23. Headquarters, Department of the Army, *FM 100-5: Operations* (Washington, DC, 1986), 10. No significant changes in this definition appear in the updated *FM 100-5* issued in 1993.

24. Donald A. Carter, "Military History: A View from the Schoolhouse," *Army History*, 17 (Winter 1990–91):18–19.

25. Capt. Michael A. Phipps, "McPherson's Ridge: A Study of a Meeting Engagement," *Infantry*, 74 (January–February 1984):26.

26. An evaluation of Buford's action, compared to Admiral Raymond A. Spruance's proactive air strike on Japanese carriers at Midway, can be found in Rubel, "Gettysburg and Midway: Historical Parallels in Operational Command," 99.

27. Jay Luvaas, "Lee and the Operational Art: The Right Place, the Right Time," *Parameters*, 22 (Autumn 1992):6–7.

28. Roland, "The Generalship of Robert E. Lee," 53.

29. See Richard M. McMurry, *Two Great Rebel Armies: An Essay in Confederate Military History* (Chapel Hill, 1989), 141–55; and Gary W. Gallagher, "'Upon Their Success Hang Momentous Interests': Generals," in Gabor S. Boritt, ed., *Why The Confederacy Lost* (New York, 1992), 101–8.

30. See, for instance, Thomas L. Connelly, "Robert E. Lee and the Western Confederacy: A Criticism of Lee's Strategic Abilities," *Civil War History*, 15 (1969):50–64; and Nolan, *Lee Considered*, esp. chap. 4, "General Lee."

31. *FM 100-5: Operations*, 9.

32. Meyers, "Robert E. Lee: Great Captain of History?" 1, 48.

33. Nolan, *Lee Considered*, 31.

34. Meyers, "Robert E. Lee: Great Captain of History?" 60.

35. For two good examples that show keen insights, see George C. Rable, *The Confederate Republic: A Revolution against Politics* (Chapel Hill, 1994), esp. chap. 8; and Gallagher, " 'Upon Their Success Hang Momentous Interests,' " 98–99, 101–4.

36. Roland, "The Generalship of Robert E. Lee," 63.

37. Meyers, "Robert E. Lee: Great Captain of History?" 58.

38. Ibid., 59.

39. See Nolan, *Lee Considered*, 121–22, 129–30, 180–84. For a rebuttal, see Charles P. Roland, *Reflections on Lee: A Historian's Assessment* (Harrisburg, 1995), 99.

40. *FM 100-5: Operations*, 10.

41. Luvaas, "Lee and the Operational Art," 2.

42. Walter P. Lang, Jr., J. Frank Hennessee, and William E. Bush, Jr., "Jackson's Valley Campaign and the Operational Level of War," *Parameters*, 15 (1985):54.

43. Luvaas, "Lee and the Operational Art," 7.

44. Col. Daniel K. Malone, "The Stars and Bars and the Corsican Eagle," *Military Review*, 67 (June 1987):57.

45. William G. Robertson, *The Staff Ride* (Washington, DC, 1987), 3–4. For more on the evolution of the staff ride in the U.S. Army, see Carol Reardon, *Soldiers and*

Scholars: The U.S. Army and the Uses of Military History, 1865–1920 (Lawrence, KS, 1990), chap. 4.

46. Edward K. Eckert, "St. Bonaventure Cadets Visit Gettysburg," *Army History*, 13 (Fall 1989):11.

47. Raymond E. Bell, Jr., "Reserve MP Brigade Studies Antietam," *Army History*, 13 (Fall 1989):12–14.

48. Donald D. Jacobovitz, "Engineers Analyze Antietam," *Army Historian*, 12 (October 1988):18.

49. Maj. Robert D. Yearout, "Chancellorsville: The Mobile Defense," *Infantry*, 63 (November–December 1973):29, 32.

50. Maj. Terrence P. Murray, "The Merits of Military History," *Marine Corps Gazette*, 65 (November 1981):40.

51. *FM 100-5: Operations*, 109.

52. Coomler, "Clausewitz's Concept of the Culminating Point and its Applications in the Gettysburg Campaign," 22–23.

53. Ibid., 28.

54. Col. George M. Hall, "Culminating Points," *Military Review*, 69 (July 1989):81.

55. Coomler, "Clausewitz's Concept of the Culminating Point and its Applications in the Gettysburg Campaign," 24.

56. Ibid., 24–25.

57. Hall, "Culminating Points," 82.

58. *FM 100-5: Operations*, 110, 179.

59. Coomler, "Clausewitz's Concept of the Culminating Point and its Applications in the Gettysburg Campaign," 24–25.

60. This theme is apparent throughout Roland's *The Confederacy* (Chicago, 1960) and is sustained in his later work. In *An American Iliad: The Story of the Civil War* (New York, 1991), Roland expanded his study of the homefront to include the North as well.

61. For one of the best recent works by a civilian on the interrelationships of popular will and military strategy, see Rable, *The Confederate Republic*.

62. Roland, "The Generalship of Robert E. Lee," 31.

63. Lt. Col. C. R. Shrader, "Field Logistics in the Civil War," in Jay Luvaas and Harold W. Nelson, comps., *The U.S. Army War College Guide to the Battle of Antietam: The Maryland Campaign of 1862* (Carlisle, PA, 1987), 277–78.

64. Malone, "The Stars and Bars and the Corsican Eagle," 47.

65. Roland, "The Generalship of Robert E. Lee," 59.

66. Roland, *Reflections on Lee*, 98.

67. Edward K. Eckert, "The McClellans and the Grants: Generalship and Strategy in the Civil War," *Military Review*, 55 (June 1975):60, 62.

68. Roland, "The Generalship of Robert E. Lee," 69.

69. Parker et al., "Aging Successfully," 112.

70. Quoted in Murray, "The Merits of Military History," 41.

7

"No negro is upon the program": Blacks and the Montgomery Race Conference of 1900

John David Smith

By 1900 white southerners, ironically, had won much of what they had fought for, and lost, in the Civil War. The dismantling of the Reconstruction governments in the 1870s and 1880s left the region firmly in the grasp of white Bourbon Democrats. While a few southern black Republicans continued to occupy minor political offices until the eve of World War I, they held little power within the South or influence within Republican ranks. Despite the lure of northern capital, the postwar South remained an agrarian land much as before, with native southerners strongly in control of the region's land and labor. The systems of sharecropping and farm tenantry that became the norm during Reconstruction reached maturity by the turn of the century. In 1900 over 75 percent of black southerners worked as farm tenants. Only 24.5 percent owned their own farms. Though chattel slavery never again would serve as the South's labor system, during the 1890s whites took legal steps—Jim Crow and peonage laws—to proscribe, segregate, and discipline the former slaves and their children. When political, legal, and economic mechanisms failed to control the blacks, whites resorted to violence to enforce "white supremacy." Between 1897 and 1906 whites lynched at least 884 blacks. It was, according to historian Rayford W. Logan, the "nadir" of American race relations. By 1900, then, the vast majority of black southerners belonged to a landless peasant class. They were denied the "promise" of the "New" South.[1]

Despite their overwhelming control over the black southerners, turn-of-the-century whites nonetheless had a seemingly insatiable need to discuss what they called the "Negro problem." In newspapers, magazines, books, and on stage and screen, what historian Joel Williamson has labeled white Conservatives and Radicals repeated endlessly the story of the Negro's alleged degeneration since emancipation. While both groups believed steadfastly in the Negro's inferiority, Conservatives "sought to preserve him by defining and fixing his place in American society." Radicals, however, held out no hope for the Negro and predicted his "ultimate demise."[2]

Ignoring significant black achievements during the postwar years, whites emphasized the blacks' supposed decreased agricultural productivity, increased immorality and mortality, and whole-scale propensity for crime. Black participation in politics, white polemicists alleged, had resulted in the "excesses" of Reconstruction and, later, corruption. Describing blacks not only as inferior but also in some cases as brutal, barbaric, and even as subhuman, Radicals commonly wrote of the threat that black men posed to the safety of white women. Convinced that state and local Jim Crow laws were insufficient to control blacks, white southerners clamored for the repeal of the Fifteenth Amendment. Though the nexus between voting and raping always remained vague and illogical, whites considered the removal of blacks from politics a cure-all for the South's problems. According to historian Dewey W. Grantham, whites "undoubtedly believed that removing blacks from politics would end the political corruption of the 1890s and enable whites to deal constructively with substantive issues." White southerners considered disfranchisement an essential "reform."[3]

The Montgomery, Alabama, Race Conference of May 1900 provides an insightful forum to analyze Progressive-era southern racial "reforms." Occurring at a moment of intense interest in racial questions, it was, according to historian Hines H. Hall III, the "focal point" of racial discourse at the fin de siècle. Progressives of both races, and on both sides of the Mason-Dixon Line, believed that conferences offered open, systematic, and "scientific" means of discussing issues, testing ideas, and formulating solutions to contemporary problems. In 1890 and 1891, for example, northerners and southerners met at Lake Mohonk, New York, to begin to resolve racial and sectional issues. While, according to historian Leslie H. Fishel, Jr., the two Mohonk Conferences on the Negro Question "may not have elicited anything new, they were measurably significant in the cycle of American race relations." They "were the first meetings of any consequence where Northerners and Southerners sat down together for serious discussion of black-white issues." They were important, too, because of their "underlying ambiguity of purpose" and because blacks were excluded from their proceedings.[4]

Influenced by the "conference idea," twenty-five influential whites in Montgomery organized in January 1900 the Southern Society for the Promotion of the Study of Race Conditions and Problems in the South and began plans for an annual conference. The organization's executive committee outlined several basic assumptions and goals. First, it believed

steadfastly that the South's race problem was best solved by white southerners. "Suggestions from the North," the organizers concluded, "offered
with the best motives, have frequently been based upon inadequate acquaintance with our conditions." Second, the Southern Society was formed
to "create a perfectly free arena for the expression of every serious phase of
Southern opinion. We shall not expect the speakers in this conference to
agree, for we are not agreed ourselves, on the various questions to be
presented." The committee concurred, however, on a third point: the cen-
trality of blacks "for the prosperity and happiness of our Southern country."
A final issue framed the Southern Society's agenda: Should black voting
rights be limited? And if so, how? The organization scheduled the first
conference for May 8–10, 1900.[5]

Episcopal priest Edgar Gardner Murphy (1869–1913) was the driving
force behind the Montgomery Conference. A native Arkansan, he had
studied at the University of the South, General Theological Seminary in
New York, and Columbia University. After his ordination in 1890, Murphy
served several congregations before becoming rector of St. John's Church
in Montgomery in 1899. He gained national exposure that year by publishing a rejoinder to northern press accounts following the double lynching of
two black Georgians. While forcefully condemning lynchings, Murphy
blamed them on irresponsible whites, not on the entire society. Such outrages would decrease dramatically, he added, if the "better" class of white
southerners was allowed to formulate its own solutions to racial problems.
Though sincerely opposed to racial violence and committed to black uplift,
Murphy was an elite Conservative who subscribed firmly to racial inequality and endorsed segregation. Historian Ralph Luker describes him as "one
of segregation's most sophisticated apologists." By organizing the Southern
Society and opposing lynching, Murphy "was a moderating influence
among Southern whites." But his "inclination to think in terms of racial
self-fulfillment" masked "at best, a benign racism."[6]

Speaking in Philadelphia in March 1900, Murphy set the tone for the
upcoming Montgomery Conference. Though he courted northern money
to develop the South, Murphy urged northerners not to interfere with racial
questions in the region. In his opinion, upper-class whites—"the forces of
intelligence and property"—must control the South. Lower-class whites
were responsible for lynchings, which could be prevented by leadership
from the "better" class. Murphy considered blacks childlike, but believed
they could be nurtured along by the class that understood them best—the
ex-slaveholders. He favored industrial education for common blacks and
whites on the model of Tuskegee Institute. Legalized segregation would
encourage black economic and social progress, diminish racial friction,
disarm extreme racists, and prevent lawlessness. Property and literacy tests
for blacks *and* whites would disfranchise "the shiftless and the illiterate of
both races" and enable qualified blacks like Booker T. Washington to vote.

The capstone of Murphy's reform agenda was "modification," a euphemism for repeal of the Fifteenth Amendment. Local disfranchisement was a realistic, honorable resolution of the franchise problem, Murphy said, one that might reduce southern representation in the House of Representatives yet ultimately eliminate the threat of federal coercion. No longer would the southern states have to use subterfuge to "count the Negro out in the election" but "count him in for representation." According to Murphy's sympathetic biographer, in his lecture he "overvalued" the southerner's "sense of justice and reflected his tendency, most becoming in a cleric, to always see the best in others." George A. Mebane, a contemporary black North Carolinian, viewed Murphy's Philadelphia speech differently. Labeling Murphy "the advance agent of the [Montgomery] conference," Mebane said that "no human ingenuity could have contrived a more thorough defense of a 'lost cause' or a discreditable purpose."[7]

Though white southern Conservatives and Radicals would control the Montgomery Conference, organizers realized the importance of inviting a few sympathetic northerners to speak. One organizer proposed that an entire day be reserved for black speakers—"the best representatives of the negro element in Southern life." Clearly, Booker T. Washington, from nearby Tuskegee and the foremost black leader of the day, would speak. The inclusion of northern and black spokesmen would demonstrate to the nation that the Southern Society was open to various views. Murphy achieved a minor coup by lining up both New York publisher Walter Hines Page, originally a North Carolinian, and William Bourke Cockran, a well-known Irish immigrant and New York Democratic politician. Murphy failed, however, when the executive committee refused to allow blacks, even Washington, to speak. "The speakers at this Conference," Murphy assured Alabama Governor Joseph F. Johnston, "will be made up entirely of white men." Montgomery minister Robert C. Bedford, a close Washington ally, concluded that "ultra conservatives do not want any colored people invited to the first conference." Though Murphy allegedly fought "to the last" to include black speakers, he later judged that their absence from the program was advantageous. In his opinion blacks lacked the "self-control" necessary to withstand the racist assaults of whites. He also believed that whites made better advocates for their cause than blacks. In the end the committee agreed to a "compromise" whereby blacks would not speak but would be allowed to attend the sessions in segregated galleries.[8]

Although the executive committee denied Washington a place on the program, he played an active behind-the-scenes role in selecting speakers. Determined to have some influence, Washington mentioned as possible speakers such prominent black clergymen as Henry H. Proctor, Wesley J. Gaines, and Henry McNeal Turner, who shared his commitment to black suffrage. To add a national perspective, Washington suggested that the executive committee invite U.S. Senator Chauncey M. Depew of New York.

None of these men appeared on the program, however. In mid-February Murphy sought Washington's opinion regarding inviting William A. Mac-Corkle, ex-governor of West Virginia, to speak. Like Murphy, MacCorkle favored disfranchising persons of both races. Murphy assured Washington "that I regard you as the best able to select a man to present . . . your side of the case." When Washington recommended other speakers, Murphy invited MacCorkle anyway. In Murphy's view, however, the executive committee included Washington "most frankly and fully into our confidence in relation to the discussion upon the franchise." According to Murphy, "the Committee was so anxious to be fair to the Negroes" regarding the franchise "that we summoned Booker T. Washington . . . to pick his man from the whole South in order that the closing speech might represent the contention that any suffrage test should be evenly applicable to both races." Washington, however, had a different perspective. Excluded from the program, his recommendations ignored, and concerned that Murphy's disfranchisement plan might become the cause célèbre of the conference, Washington "began to waver and was sustained only by tactful explanations." He nonetheless remained guardedly optimistic about the upcoming conference.[9]

In early February, Washington explained to Francis J. Garrison, son of William Lloyd Garrison, that conference organizers were eager to reach "the element in the South that has always opposed everything tending towards the elevation of the Negro." In order to do so, however, the meeting, by necessity, would have to be "managed on very conservative lines." Otherwise, the sponsors would alienate "the very element that now gives the greatest trouble." Washington informed Garrison that holding the event in Montgomery, "perhaps one of the most conservative towns in the South," was significant. Not only had the Confederacy established itself there thirty-nine years earlier, but the race conference was supported enthusiastically by Montgomery's business community. "You must not expect too much from this first conference," Washington warned Garrison. "In order not to get itself in bad odor with the fire eating element of the South the Conference is going to give the anti-Negro element the opportunity to state their case at the first conference." Friends of the Negro would be there too, Washington assured Garrison. He explained: "Almost nothing in the last dozen years has served to give me so much hope and encouragement as this movement." Two days later Washington wrote one of the speakers, the Reverend Hollis B. Frissell of Hampton Institute, that he did "not believe that any movement that has ever been started in the South is so pregnant of good as this one." Washington added:

Of course the whole effort of the convention at first especially is going to be very conservative but I think the very conservatism of the people who have it in charge constitute[s] its greatest hopefulness. After further discussion and consideration it has been decided wise not to place any colored man on the public programme in May though colored people will attend private conferences.[10]

Assessing Washington's strategy regarding the conference, historian Louis R. Harlan commented that Washington's response illustrated his "almost limitless capacity for accommodation." Black editor T. Thomas Fortune of the *New York Age* was less willing to accept the whites' terms. In March, he remarked that by its exclusion of black speakers, the Montgomery Conference had "already killed itself by a false start." Selection of the other speakers, virtually all elite white southerners, proved less controversial. But the process confirmed the conference's southern, Conservative, and, in the case of three speakers, Radical ideological bent.[11]

By April, Washington's role as a member of what Harlan has termed the Southern Society's "kitchen cabinet" was virtually nil. The executive committee experienced a crisis when Walter Hines Page withdrew from his commitment to speak after learning that in his address Cockran would advocate repeal of the Fifteenth Amendment. Page considered such a move "retrogressive" and declared that "I should as soon undertake to turn the course of the Mississippi River into the Pacific ocean as to secure the repeal of the Amendment. . . ." He described Cockran as "one who has neither character, nor principles, nor any standing" in the North. Murphy, who also favored disfranchisement, backed Cockran, predicting that Cockran's support of disfranchisement "will be of great aid to our whole Southern country." Murphy condemned Page for removing himself from the program, arguing that his absence resulted from "pressure . . . brought to bear upon him from several different directions at the East." He predicted that Page's position ultimately would injure "the cause of the Negro." In order to fill the hole in the program left by Page's departure, Murphy, without consulting Washington, selected Paul B. Barringer, a North Carolina physician, chairman of the faculty of the University of Virginia, and a leading Radical racist. Murphy presented Barringer's invitation to Washington as a fait accompli.[12]

Barringer's appointment to the program discomforted Washington. He would have much preferred a Conservative in place of a Radical. As the conference approached Washington confided to Garrison his increasing concerns. "I hope it will accomplish some good but I confess my faith has been somewhat shaken in it recently." Page's withdrawal from the panel unnerved Washington. "He says he cannot afford to speak on the same platform on the same night as Bourke Cochran [*sic*]." Three days before the opening session, Washington informed Fortune: "We shall have to be prepared for some very radical and I think unwise things in connection with the race conference at Montgomery." "I hope, however, that some good may come from the move."[13]

Publicly, as usual, Washington masked the depth of his worries and expressed cautious optimism in May, when he publicized the conference in the black press. "I have no connection with this conference," he explained in three leading black publications, thus making abundantly clear that he had serious reservations about the meeting. First, some of the speeches probably would offend blacks. Second, blacks should expect few specific results from the conference. Third, while all phases of the race question would be addressed, only whites would be permitted to speak. Finally, some of the speakers might propose disfranchising blacks. Despite his caveat, though, Washington insisted that a truly open discussion on race in the Deep South would represent, no matter how distasteful some of the speeches might be, a symbolic victory. He also assured blacks that they would be represented by "true and tried friends of our cause," including Frissell, Page, MacCorkle, and J.L.M. Curry. "Let us not be alarmed," Washington said, "if some of the speakers favor taking away from the Negro some of the rights which he now possesses. . . . Our cause is just and can stand the light of open, free discussion."[14]

Privately, Washington worried most about one of the speakers—Barringer. In February 1900, Barringer delivered a widely publicized lecture in Charleston, South Carolina, defending slavery and declaring that "the phylogeny of the negro is carrying him back to barbarism." The slaveholder, Barringer explained, trained the Negro to "be a respectful and respectable, obedient and faithful servant. But he knew him well enough to know that underneath this thin veneer of decent life and manners was the nature of a savage, which had to be shaped aright while the cells were still soft in youth, or it was useless to try."[15]

The *Richmond Times*, committed to disfranchisement, praised Barringer's lecture as "scholarly" and complimented his "scientific reason." Barringer convinced the *Richmond Central Presbyterian* that sections of the South would either "be forsaken by the whites, or there will come a race war that can only end in the extermination of the blacks." The *New York Sun* judged Barringer's perspective "gloomy, practically hopeless." Black journalist John E. Bruce considered his "pessimistic wail" utterly "ridiculous," typical of efforts "to read the negro out of human society . . . by an appeal to science." Bruce, in fact, found race-baiting South Carolina Senator Benjamin Tillman "more dangerous to society than all the 'black savages' whom he [Barringer] pretends to fear." Murphy congratulated Barringer on his lecture, but hoped that in Montgomery he would offer a more "*constructive* contribution to the problem," one emphasizing industrial education for blacks.[16]

Barringer never was comfortable with the fact that blacks would attend the Montgomery Conference. A month before the meeting he expressed reservations about even appearing on the program because he feared that blacks would serve on the Southern Society's "counsel board." Writing on behalf of the executive committee to calm Barringer, the Reverend Neal L. Anderson assured him that "No negro is upon the program, or a member of the Society, and those who may be present will be assigned separate seats in the gallery of the auditorium." In a postscript, Anderson explained to Barringer that the executive committee had elected "to issue not more than

200 tickets of admission to the auditorium to respectable negroes who may desire to hear the discussions. . . . These will be seated in the *upper gallery* of the auditorium. No negro will be allowed upon the floor of the conference."[17]

Determined to temper what he feared would be Barringer's antiblack comments, Washington invited him to visit Tuskegee while en route to the conference. Explaining that his trip would be too rushed to enable him to stop there, Barringer sent his regrets and explained:

> You are doubtless aware that, as regards your people, I am a pessimist, but this does not prevent my profound admiration for those of you who are standing bravely against the current. I wish all of your people could understand that in dealing with racial matters I speak of the *race* and not of individuals. The very generic tendencies which you have to combat makes the assumption of the position of worth and prominence among men the more to be appreciated. I am of the South, for the South, and primarily for the white people of the South—my own people—but as a native of that section of which your people form so essential a part, I can take interest and pride in all that they do to rise above the condition in which their brother man, regardless of motive, has placed them.

As Washington feared, Barringer would be the most reactionary of the white Conservatives and Radicals who addressed the overflow audience in Montgomery's new city auditorium.[18]

Despite Murphy's hopes and optimistic preconference news releases, none of the speakers added anything fresh to the discussion of the "Negro problem." Though Frissell and Curry acknowledged educational progress among blacks, most of the panelists restated well-known, hackneyed expressions of white supremacy. References to black suffrage served as the conference's rhetorical lightning rod—what Booker T. Washington's ghostwriter Max B. Thrasher termed the meeting's "real storm-center." A New Yorker noted perceptively that "the burning question is that of the franchise." He warned that "the Southern white men had as well cease calling conventions for the purpose of taking the Fifteenth Amendment from the Constitution. It took rivers of blood to put it there, and it will take oceans to wash it away." Nevertheless, in 1900 state legislators throughout the South debated why, how, and when to disfranchise blacks. Speakers at the Montgomery Race Conference did their part, rehashing dog-eared justifications for the limitation of black suffrage.[19]

Governor Johnston, for example, described universal black suffrage as a "grave and fundamental mistake" and drew a connection between voting and the rising tide of black criminality. "If we go back to the days of slavery," he said, "we find that the Negro was not disposed to commit crime. . . ." Johnston hoped that industrial education would "[divert] his attention from politics" and free blacks from "political agitators and . . . irresponsible and corrupt legislation." Hilary A. Herbert similarly declared that "Negro suffrage has failed . . . It has not bettered the condition of the black man or the white." Herbert, too, concluded that black participation in politics led to increases in crime, "idleness," illegitimacy, and rape of white women. "Never was there such a blunder as in the theory that suffrage would help educate the Negro," he said. "What the Negro did want above all things, was to know how to take care of himself so that he might develop. This he might have had from his old master, on terms which would have been advantageous to both. . . . It was the carpet-bagger that drew the color line."[20]

Alfred M. Waddell, mayor of Wilmington, North Carolina, labeled the Fifteenth Amendment "the greatest political crime . . . perpetrated in the history of this country." It was a punishment forced upon the vanquished South, he said, and the results were disastrous. Waddell recalled how blacks, led by "unprincipled white demagogues," grasped power and transformed coastal North Carolina into "a Negro paradise." According to Waddell,

Idle and drunken Negroes infested the streets of Wilmington day and night, and grew more and more insolent and aggressive. Ladies were frequently and grossly insulted and citizens assaulted and robbed in broad daylight. Burglaries were of almost nightly occurrence, and no arrest followed. A Negro newspaper was established, and crowned a series of offensive articles by an attack upon the virtue of white women in general.

Conveniently omitting Wilmington's 1898 race riot that drove the blacks from office, and his central role in instigating it, Waddell explained that the blacks' rule ended when their white supporters no longer could tolerate their conduct. Waddell applauded the proposed North Carolina constitutional amendment—imposing a literacy test for black voters immediately and for white voters by 1908—as the type of legal action that would "eliminate the ignorant Negro vote, and assure the supremacy of the whites." He justified the differing standards for whites and blacks by asserting that "the very basis of our problem is the inequality of the races. . . . It is stupid and criminal to force them to live together with equal rights and privileges. . . ." The Reverend R. T. Pollard, a black minister from Selma, Alabama, listened to Waddell's paper and described it as "the most bitter and seemingly prejudicial in the conference."[21]

Cockran and MacCorkle had the least local political capital at stake and, not surprisingly, were the most forthright speakers on the topic of black suffrage. George T. Downing, a black from Newport, Rhode Island, expected Cockran to venture to Montgomery "in the midst of the enemy to chastise them." The New York politico, however, shocked his northern supporters when he toed the southern white line, brazenly advocating repeal of the Fifteenth Amendment. Like Murphy, Cockran argued that suffrage should be determined by the states, not the federal government. Disfranchisement would restore law and order, he said, establish tranquility between the races, and "improve the condition of the weaker race." White voters would "protect" disfranchised blacks. Practically, Cockran added, the South already had virtually nullified the Fifteenth Amendment, making it unenforceable except by military rule. Not surprisingly, Cockran's speech unleashed an avalanche of criticism against him in the North. William Lloyd Garrison, Jr., for example, branded him a hypocrite. To disfranchise blacks would deny them the same "weapon of defence and their salvation" that protected Cockran's Irish immigrant forebears. Others accused Cockran of currying votes for the Democratic Party in the November 1900 election.[22]

MacCorkle, determined "to make a right vigorous discussion down at Montgomery," took the most pro-black stand of all the panelists. He argued that the Negro's "privilege of franchise is as sacred as ours, and should be as sacredly guarded." Assuring the audience that educational and property requirements would prevent blacks ever from establishing "domination," he identified hidden benefits for whites in black suffrage. First, it would provide an incentive to blacks for self-improvement. Second, qualified black voters ultimately could align politically with whites and, ironically, strengthen the South in its economic struggles with the North. According to Henry B. Blackwell, a black who followed the proceedings from Massachusetts, MacCorkle was the only speaker who "rose above the semi-barbaric level of race proscription." MacCorkle, who "told" Thrasher to have Washington "come and see me" from the gallery, regretted that "every human being in the sound of my voice seemed to be opposed to my idea." Even so, the West Virginia politician felt compelled to endorse the South's racial mores by declaring, "I adhere to social and racial separation as earnestly as any one to whom I speak."[23]

Not more so than John Temple Graves, who was a well-known race baiter and proponent of black colonization. At Montgomery, Graves declared that immutable racial differences prevented blacks and whites from living in harmony. Suffrage or not, he said, whites never would allow blacks to advance. "Take Booker Washington," for example, Graves said.

He is the type and embodiment of all worth and of all achievement in his race. His linen is as clean as yours. His fame is broader than the repute of any statesman in this hall. His character, stainless and unimpeachable, defies criticism. His patriotism is clear, his courtesy unfailing. What attribute of worthiness could you add to his equipment? And yet I challenge this Conference with a proposition:

What man of you . . . would install this great and blameless Negro in your guest chamber tonight? If he were unmarried, what man of you would receive with equanimity his addresses to your daughter or your ward? What man of you would vote for this proven statesman for governor of Alabama? . . .

Search through all your logic for a reason. . . . And when you fail to find in reason, in religion, or knowledge or justice, anywhere an answer, you will find at last the answer—*in his skin!* Bleach that to the whiteness of your own, and you have solved the problem by a chemical solution. But until this leopard shall remove his spots, until this Ethiopian shall have changed his skin, you may tug in vain to draw out this leviathan of problems with a hook.

Ironically, Graves proposed *"separation"* as his solution to the problem that left Washington relegated to the Jim Crow gallery. Graves feared for the future unless the blacks emigrated. "We can make it peaceably now," he concluded. "We may be forced to accomplish it in blood hereafter."[24]

Only Barringer surpassed Graves's pessimism and open antagonism toward blacks. Convinced that they belonged on the lowest rung of a natural racial hierarchy, Barringer had little hope that blacks would climb far. The slave, in Barringer's opinion, exhibited "the simple intelligence of a child . . . with the instincts of a veritable savage." Emancipation was a fatal mistake, he added, because the bondsmen "were happy and did not wish to be free." Once freed, Barringer explained, the Negro retrogressed into "an unalloyed pagan in a tropical jungle, savage, brutal and ignorant, a cannibal." Since emancipation, blacks had become an unsufferable burden on whites. Citing statistics from Prudential Insurance Company actuary Frederick L. Hoffman and others, Barringer identified declining birthrates among blacks but dramatic increases in violent crimes, arrests, poverty, disease, and mortality. "In my opinion," he concluded, "nothing is more certain than that the Negro will go as the Tasmanian and the Carib have gone, but till then he is our problem." It was only a matter of time, he predicted, before blacks would inevitably become extinct. Sitting in the audience, Mississippi planter Alfred Holt Stone nodded approvingly. He informed Barringer that his daily contact "with the true negro type . . . not your half-educated graduate of Hampton and Tuskegee," confirmed "that slow but certain process which is tending toward the final destruction of the negro race."[25]

Cockran disagreed, however, with Barringer's extinction theory. In his opinion, "the capacity of the Negro for work completely refutes the theory advanced by Dr. Barringer that the Negro is essentially a barbarian, incapable of civilization, and certain in a state of freedom to develop irresistible tendencies to savagery." Cockran pointed to the blacks in the gallery as proof of their "capacity for civilization," regardless of "whatever theories to the contrary scientific men may have formulated." As the session concluded, Barringer, incensed by Cockran's public rebuke, reportedly "shouted above all the confusion that he wished Mr. Cochran [*sic*] would cross the ocean and present his ideas to the disfranchised peasants of Ireland!" Murphy, who considered Barringer's speech "odious in spirit" and "without largeness of mind or of heart," welcomed Cockran's challenge to Barringer's "philosophy of pessimism." "No man was ever more thoroughly *smashed*" than Barringer, he said, "and how much better that this result should have been attained . . . right here in the South. . . ." A week later Murphy distanced himself totally from Barringer, informing a Boston newspaper "that I wholly regret Dr. Barringer's spirit and . . . largely dissent from his conclusions. Such a coupling of [our] names is unjust, both to Dr. Barringer and myself."[26]

Washington attended most of the sessions of the conference, perched in the Jim Crow gallery along with his private secretary, Emmett J. Scott; William H. Councill, president of Alabama Agricultural and Mechanical College; and roughly one hundred other Montgomery blacks. Following the conference the Reverend Neal Anderson said that "several hundred" blacks "were in constant attendance" at the three days of meetings. He found them "orderly and attentive listeners." Murphy informed Washington that when Cockran spoke, between three and four hundred blacks occupied gallery "seats that were *wanted* by some of the best *white* people of Montgomery, for the gallery accommodations were shared by our white people as well as by the Negroes. The rights of the Negroes, however, were respected without disturbance or complaint." Editor A. N. McEwen, black editor of the *Mobile Watchman*, acknowledged that blacks attended the conference, but quipped that "any discussion of the negro problem with the negro not a party to the discussion is the play of *Hamlet* with Hamlet left out."[27]

Following Cockran's speech, Washington proved Anderson wrong and no doubt shocked Barringer: he descended from the gallery to shake Cockran's hand. Though black columnist John E. Bruce reprimanded Washington for ingratiating himself to a speaker who had just demanded repeal of the Fifteenth Amendment, Washington, as always, had his own agenda. He scored a symbolic victory by standing face-to-face in public with the likes of Bourke Cockran and, in the process, netted a small endowment for Tuskegee to assist black agriculturists. More important, by violating southern white racial etiquette, Washington reminded whites on the floor, and blacks in the gallery, that he still was a force to be reckoned with.[28]

Though Washington may have been seated in the gallery during the conference, his presence permeated its entire proceedings. Again and again the speakers mentioned Washington's accomplishments. Cockran, for example, endorsed industrial education and said: "Let the Negro be prepared for life as Booker Washington prepares him. . . . Let there be a Tuskegee in every community, and I promise you that the next generation, instead of troubling about the Negroes, will be celebrating a glorious success in settling a question graver than any presented to a nation in the history of the human race." Barringer, on the other end of the ideological spectrum, worried publicly about Washington's influence. In a newspaper report of his speech, absent from the official conference report, Barringer remarked: "Carry every theory of Booker Washington to its full and perfect consummation, and you only make a new and deadlier competition between antagonistic races. The conflict heretofore has been social and political. You will carry it then to the material things. . . ." In keeping with his pseudoscientific racism, Barringer predicted smugly that Washington's black followers ultimately would lose the "battle of the loaf" and be destroyed.[29]

Such comments confirmed Washington's deepest fears. But despite the conference's paternalistic, if not hostile, attitude toward blacks in general, and the condescending manner with which its organizers treated him, Washington surveyed the impact of the Montgomery Conference and tried to make the best of a bad situation. During the summer, for example, responding to Murphy's request, he used his influence to block plans by some disgruntled Montgomery blacks to sponsor their own race conference, which Washington feared might inflame whites. Writing to Emily Howland, a white philanthropist and Tuskegee supporter, he explained that more good than bad actually had come from the Montgomery Conference. "There was some very mean things said at this conference about the Negro," Washington confessed, but "at the same time there was some good and brave things said." He explained:

Now that some of these people have said the very worst they can say I feel that future meetings are going to be more encouraging. It is a great thing to have a meeting in the midst of the Southern white people where the women could be present. I am quite sure that many Southern white women for the first time in their lives heard a colored man called "Mister," and providentially it seems that almost every speaker who referred to an individual negro called him "Mister."

Washington then admitted his deeper concerns. "These are rather serious and in some respects trying days for our people, and I have to give a great deal of my time and sympathy to correspondence with the different elements throughout the country." He watched efforts to disfranchise Virginia's blacks with deep concern.[30]

Publicly, however, Washington was more upbeat. In *Century Magazine* he applauded the conference and underscored its potential for solving the race problem. Though he disagreed with many of the speakers, Washington nevertheless approved of the conference's goals. He opposed, for instance, Cockran's plan to repeal the Fifteenth Amendment but complimented the New Yorker's "plea for the highest justice to the negro." All polemics aside, Washington judged the conference a success simply because it proved that white southerners would allow free speech on the "Negro question." "If this first session was not all that might be desired by some," Washington added, "it should be borne in mind that no great movement can reach perfection at once." Accommodating to a fault, Washington informed *Century*'s national audience that blacks sat quietly and listened politely while one white speaker after another insulted and degraded them. The most "note-worthy and most encouraging fact," he said, was "that every speaker, no matter what his views, was received with the greatest respect and consideration."[31]

Straining to emphasize the conference's positive side, Washington stressed that only four of the nineteen speakers were in any sense antagonistic to blacks. None openly endorsed lynching. Graves alone advocated deportation. MacCorkle, "a Southern man and Democrat," insisted that all property and education tests be applied to both races equally. And except for just one speaker, all favored educating and exposing the blacks to Christianity. With his characteristic disarming humor, Washington added: "Every one is in favor of salvation for the negro in the future world; it is only the salvation of his mind and body in this world that causes disagreement."[32]

Barringer's vicious remarks, however, tested Washington's magnanimity. "I would say of Dr. Barringer's expressions as I would of others," Washington remarked, "that if persons have feelings that are antagonistic to what we should consider the best interests of the negro it is better that these views be expressed than repressed; and herein again, is shown the value of these conferences." Though he professed to welcome Barringer's candor, Washington felt compelled to respond to what he termed the influential Virginian's "misleading statements." According to Washington,

In Dr. Barringer's speech of over an hour he gave the most discouraging views I have ever listened to regarding the present and the future of the negro, industrially, physically, mentally, and morally, and as I sat through it I wondered what would be its effect on the Southern audience.

Washington was encouraged when Hilary Herbert, a former slaveholder who delivered the conference's closing remarks, disagreed openly with Barringer's direful conclusions. Here was evidence that thoughtful white southerners, "who have known and lived with the negro for three centuries," would defend blacks from unfair and extreme criticism.[33]

To disprove Barringer, Washington then cited examples of Tuskegee graduates whose accomplishments overturned Barringer's statistics. Determined to end his analysis of the conference on an optimistic note, Washington said that he hoped future meetings would investigate "the negro's real condition." Americans "must come to judge the negro much as they do other races—by the best types, and not by the worst." Infuriated by Washington's public attack against him, Barringer prepared a press release in which he charged that his critic misquoted him. "It is perfectly natural and right that Booker Washington should speak up for his people," Barringer wrote, "but he has a large job of white-washing on his hands." The two men finally appeared together on a program several months later in Chicago, where they took diametrically opposite positions on the race problem and established an icy rapprochement. With typical diplomacy, Washington informed Barringer "that on the vital points connected with the elevation of our race there is not so much difference between us as I feared there was."[34]

Other blacks were less conciliatory. Most expressed a sense of outrage and betrayal at the Montgomery Race Conference. The Reverend E. M. Jones, a black Methodist from Montgomery who attended the sessions, complained that the whites offered no new solution to the race problem. "I never heard of a problem that had so many salvations as the Negro problem," he quipped. "No wonder it is not yet solved." What irked Jones most was the whites' assumption that they must control the government and public policy. "The sad feature about this was they [the white speakers] said this must be done at all hazards, and by whatever method it takes." Jones added that "this is no new opinion, for it has been both preached and practiced," and the race problem remained unsolved.[35]

For months after the Montgomery Conference, the black press hammered away at the meeting's negative influence. Former North Carolina black congressman George A. Mebane compiled a forty-page pamphlet, composed largely of northern newspaper accounts, that generally praised Mac-Corkle but ridiculed Cockran and the other speakers. Mebane considered the conference an assembly of "the unreconciled, to revive and resuscitate the 'lost cause.' " Despite Washington's plea that blacks suspend a priori judgment of the conference, Mebane said that most viewed it with suspicion from the start because of the exclusion of blacks and northerners. The panelists were, he noted with cynicism, "an able body of men, composed principally of ex-Confederate Generals, Colonels and Congressmen." Their determination to strip constitutional rights from blacks, Mebane concluded, was enough "to condemn the object of the Conference, and to make all liberty-loving Americans despair of benefit from its future gatherings." He warned whites that if they "disfranchise and goad the negro to despera-tion . . . it may take a standing army . . . and bloodhounds to keep him repressed; that it will cost more than 'white supremacy' will be worth."[36]

Black humorist John E. Bruce, "Bruce Grit," reminded readers in the *Washington Colored American* that no matter what "the staid and solemn white men" in Montgomery said, whites—not blacks—caused the "Negro problem." After noting their "inconsistency," their "jackassical persistency," and how they were "conscience-stricken," he then quoted a fictitious speech by Herbert in which the Alabamian admitted a century's worth of sins perpetrated against the Negro. In Bruce's imaginary scenario, Herbert confessed that whites raped, exploited, and projected blame onto their victims. Unfortunately, Bruce concluded, in 1900 such a speech was pure fantasy. "The South must confess its faults," he said, "and begin to make restitution to the negro for its hell-black crimes. . . . Every one of the men who spoke against us at Montgomery should put his red hand over his mouth and hang his head in shame."[37]

George L. Knox, the erratic editor of the *Indianapolis Freeman*, blasted those speakers at the Montgomery Conference who advocated the repeal of the few constitutional protections afforded blacks. In his opinion, "The attack made on the 14th and 15th Amendments to the Constitution while in . . . the name of free speech, was a bold departure from . . . conventions in the past no matter how radical." He added sarcastically: "Notwithstand-ing the very timely advice, the race could scarcely help from growing fretful when an invasion of the very citadel of their liberties seemed imminent." It was hard to admire candor, Knox observed, as one's constitutional rights were being stripped away.[38]

Despite these words of caution, Knox seemed reconciled to the inevitability of educational tests and property qualifications for voting in the South. Mississippi already had led the way in such "legalized infamy," he acknowledged, and Virginia seemed poised to disfranchise the Negro as well. Citing similar tests in England's African colonies as precedents, Knox argued that "the tendency to acquiesce in educational and property qualifications is not an alarming position since it seems to be the universal rule for similar conditions." He insisted, however, that the U.S. Constitution should not be altered. "If the Southern states are secure in their privilege to abridge or deny the rights of its citizens; they should be content to let the case rest there." After all, Knox said, northern states had no plans to restrict their black voters. "To speak against the amended sections of the Constitution that refer to Negroes, is a privilege [of each sovereign state]. But it should not be abused. . . . To carry the case further is racial persecution." Knox warned that if whites launched "a color war under the guise of educational and property qualifications," such conflict ultimately would backfire. He explained that "just as some states outwit the intent of the federal Constitution, just so will this invention be outwitted. It will hasten the day of amalgamation that seems to have dawned." Knox, a former Tennessee slave, knew that the mere mention of miscegenation—the great fear of white supremacists—would capture their attention.[39]

Other black journalists were even more critical of the proceedings in Montgomery and the speakers' open support of disfranchisement. Contemporaneous with the Montgomery meeting, John Mitchell, Jr., editor of the *Richmond Planet*, blamed its white rival, the *Richmond Times*, for printing scurrilous, antiblack comments to incite its white readers. The timing was ripe for anti-Negro propaganda because Virginians readied themselves for a constitutional convention to decide disfranchisement. According to Mitchell, the *Times* fueled the fires of race antipathy. He reminded whites

> For our part, we are a citizen of the United States: we pay taxes, both real and personal: we are intelligent: we have rights guaranteed to us by constitutions, both state and national and color forms no basis in either instrument. Why should we be denied our rights? This is the question the *Times* must answer.
>
> You can hold your constitutional convention. You can take away from one freeman his rights, but it will not be long before the other freemen on the white side of the contention will meet a similar fate. . . .
>
> Both in sacred and profane history the record is spread to be read of all men and we insist that all of our rights be given us and all of the privileges accorded which are guaranteed under our laws.

In another editorial Mitchell wrote sarcastically of the *Times'* alleged benevolence toward blacks. "Oh, yes," he wrote, "the Indian was a friend to the bear,—he wanted both his meat and his hide. . . . So is the *Times*, a friend to the colored men,—it wants their taxes without representation and their labor without just compensation."[40]

The *Planet* particularly delighted in lampooning Barringer, whom Mitchell dubbed "that prince of vilifiers." In his Charleston speech, the Charlottesville professor asserted that blacks born since emancipation exhibited lower morals than their slave-born ancestors. Mitchell noted, however, that those blacks with questionable morals simply imitated their supposed white role models. "The only difference," he insisted, between the morals of the races "is that the white man in this country has become past-master in the art of deception." Whites often times financed black-run "gambling dens" and "whiskey resorts." Willing to concede that blacks could improve by observing whites, Mitchell admonished them nonetheless "to imitate the virtues of the white people and ignore their vices. This will bring prosperity and will lift us in the scale of human civilization."[41]

Mitchell found little, however, in the Montgomery Conference worth emulating. In fact, the *Planet* judged the conference a conspiracy against black Americans and labeled the meeting regrettably as "one of the most remarkable events in this country." Although the focus of the conference, blacks were excluded from the program. Specifically, the *Planet* identified two especially egregious aspects: the selection of Waddell as opening speaker and the relegation of Washington, "the foremost Afro-American in this country," to the segregated gallery.[42]

Waddell, the *Planet* reminded its readers, had masterminded Wilmington, North Carolina's, notoriously bloody race riot two years earlier. In their senseless rage whites ousted the mayor and took control of the city, leaving in their wake scores of casualties. How, then, could anyone consider Waddell a dispassionate, fair-minded spokesman on the race question? The slap against Washington, according to Mitchell, symbolized an utter disregard by the conference organizers for a balanced, representative, and constructive program. The *Planet* also took aim at Cockran, whom Mitchell described as a wolf in sheep's clothes—a New York "Democrat who has accepted the views of the bourbon wing of the Southern Democracy."[43]

Quoting passages of Cockran's speech from wire reports, the *Planet* challenged his argument that the blacks' legal status should equal their social status. Instead of encouraging blacks to improve, to strive for more accomplishment, Montgomery's speakers sought to keep them suppressed by denying their basic constitutional rights. "To take away the elective franchise from the Negro," Mitchell complained, "will be to crush out ambition, to make him careless of governments and pay no attention to the affairs of state." "This," Mitchell said, "was a startling declaration. It was an absolute yielding to the siren voice of the tempter. It was the ignoring of great principles, an expression of contempt for ethics and a casting aside of the teachings of the Saviour." If the government followed such a distorted policy, the *Planet* insisted, the black man would "become in law what he may now be in fact—a pariah in his native land."[44]

The *A.M.E. Church Review* reiterated many of the criticisms leveled earlier by the black press. The Reverend Hightower T. Kealing, editor of the *Review*, scoffed "that it was a Southern man's convention and upon a Southern man's question." Cockran, he explained, was invited as a token northerner and "was so mindful of the courtesies due a sensitive host that he made the very address expected and desired." According to Kealing, "As a piece of special pleading and specious argument," Cockran's speech "is entitled to all that eloquence without logic and catering without conscience can claim of the fair-minded."[45]

Kealing then exposed the shallowness of Cockran's logic. According to the New York politician, the U.S. Constitution should be amended because certain states refused to abide by its provisions. In the case at hand, the Reconstruction Amendments should be scrapped because whites in the southern states objected to them and were determined to proscribe their black citizens. This, Kealing warned, might establish dangerous precedents. Looking backward and forward, he contemplated the absurdity of it all.

That is to say, the right way to have cured the evils of slavery was to have yielded to the wishes of the slave-holder and made it national; the way to have dealt with secession was to have passed a law making it legal; the way to remove the moral stain of lynching is to pass laws allowing mobs to burn and flay suspected Negroes.

Cockran obviously had surrendered himself to the purposes of white southerners. "It will be seen," Kealing said, "that this great New Yorker who went South to show gratitude for the invitation by saying the words put into his mouth by . . . Murphy favored legalizing lawlessness to make it righteousness. He knows no standard of morality. . . ." Following Cockran's logic, each region could define the Constitution in terms of its own "preponderant interest." White southerners could "lynch, burn and hang Negroes accused of rape" and be spared "reproach of the barbarism." This, Kealing feared, would be the legacy of the Montgomery Conference.[46]

As late as January 1901, the black press fired away at Barringer. Responding negatively to a revised version of his Montgomery talk, editor E. E. Cooper of the *Washington* (D.C.) *Colored American* turned the tables on Barringer and placed blame for the "Negro problem" on Barringer's slave-holding forebears. According to Cooper, "as to his moral depravity, the Negro brought no vice to these shores—he learned them all right here and from the Anglo-Saxon whose duty it now is, according to Barringer, to teach the Negro morality." Real reform, Cooper insisted, would come only when whites reimbursed their former slaves for years of unpaid labor. In the meantime, Cooper said, blacks should "be spared the painful infliction of such drivelling rot . . . from such nincompoops as Barringer."[47]

Ironically, such rancor played little role in the Southern Society's decision not to host another race conference. While publicly Murphy proclaimed the Montgomery meeting a success, privately he confessed to Washington that it "did some harm" but fortunately "attained no national importance or significance." Should there be another conference, he said, "There will be no speeches like those of Barringer and Graves; and perhaps no such strong advocacy of your cause as the speech of Dr. Curry; the whole discussion will be more 'even' in temper." Many white southerners, however, considered the Montgomery Conference a triumph.[48]

After all, the speakers had reaffirmed white supremacy and, with the exception of MacCorkle, agreed on disfranchisement. Influenced by the endorsement of disfranchisement at the Montgomery Conference, Alabamians in November 1901 revised their state constitution to disfranchise most blacks and some poor and illiterate whites. They employed the poll tax, literacy and property tests, and a grandfather clause to do so. Within five years, only 2 percent of Alabama's adult black men were registered to vote. In contrast, 83 percent of the state's adult white males were registered. By 1903 all of the southern states had one or more devices in place to disfranchise blacks. While Murphy objected to the politics of the disfranchisement process, he nevertheless remained committed to "white supremacy," insisting only that it be attained "under purer conditions." With disfranchisement achieved, Murphy turned to other reforms, including child labor and education. Passage of disfranchisement "reform" legislation throughout the South rendered the race "conference idea" unnecessary.[49]

Yet others occurred. A week after the Montgomery Conference the Southern Industrial Convention met in Chattanooga, Tennessee. This meeting focused principally on economic development but included one session on race. Though most of the speakers were white, William H. Councill of Alabama A & M and Hightower T. Kealing of the *A.M.E. Church Review* appeared on the program. According to historian August Meier, Councill radiated "unctuous sycophancy" and was a "notorious accommodator." In Alabama he was Washington's foremost black rival for influence among whites. At Chattanooga, not surprisingly, Councill endorsed disfranchisement and opposed labor unions. Regarding black suffrage, he argued "that the time has come for its restriction on some fair and equitable basis. . . ."[50]

Blacks in New York City disagreed. They rented Carnegie Hall on May 27 to express their anger at the Montgomery Conference and similar attacks on their civil rights. The Reverend C. T. Walker, pastor of New York's Mt. Olivet Baptist Church, was outraged by the exclusion of black speakers from the meeting and by Cockran's assumption that white southerners could circumvent the Fifteenth Amendment simply because they "had made up their minds not to submit to it." Defending his race, Walker declared:

the negro is a member of the body politic. The colored man is the American of Americans; he has been here almost as long as any one else. Our emancipation did not make us men; the amendment to the Constitution gave us Constitutional liberty. God made us men long before men made us citizens.

According to the *New York Tribune*, Walker's impassioned speech "incited" the blacks in attendance "to a frenzy of approval at times." A few days later, other black New Yorkers, led by T. Thomas Fortune, met in Brooklyn to denounce the Montgomery Conference. Imploring blacks to resist disfranchisement, Fortune argued:

It cost tons of blood to put the fifteenth amendment in the Constitution, and it will cost tens of tons to cut it out. You must organize and keep your powder dry in order to demand an eye for an eye and a tooth for a tooth in the great crisis which will soon be upon the negro, in which much blood may be spilled. The first gun of the fight was fired at the Montgomery conference.

Shocked by this threat, a Montgomery editor warned organizers of the city's next proposed race conference "to steer clear of an invitation to such dangerous agitators as Thomas Fortune." There was no need to worry.[51]

Though southern white Progressives deemed the Montgomery Race Conference a success, from the perspective of blacks the meeting was a dismal failure because it excluded their voices from the discussion. Defining blacks as the source of the "Negro problem," white Conservatives and Radicals treated them as passive agenda items. According to historian Williamson, the "conference idea" fitted "the Conservative style of leadership" to a tee. In organizing the conference, Murphy "loaded the dice" with a preponderance of Conservatives. He expected the northern white "friends of the Negro" to speak for them and, in the process, excluded blacks from the conversation. Blacks thus never were seriously considered active participants in the discourse.[52]

Washington, ever cautious yet politically astute, was caught perilously in the middle between white Conservatives and blacks. Though spurned by Montgomery's Conservatives, he was forced to cooperate with them to ensure that Radicals did not dominate the conference. Painfully aware that disfranchisement was enveloping the South, Washington realized that his sole option was to lobby for the equal application of educational and property tests for blacks and whites. Historian Sheldon Hackney argues that "it was naive of Washington to think registrars would apply suffrage tests fairly to both races." But in 1901 it was Washington's only hope. Even though Conservatives denied Washington a voice at the Montgomery Conference, his influence among blacks guaranteed that Conservatives would at least lend him their ear. Though Washington worked tirelessly behind the scenes to defeat proscription, he also needed to maintain dialogue with Conservatives and prevent Radicals like Barringer from gaining influence.[53]

Aside from providing them with yet another example of white racism to rally around, blacks correctly judged the Montgomery Race Conference a disaster. But Washington's experience with the meeting may in fact have taught him the limitations of the "conference idea." In November 1903, he reluctantly spoke at the Washington Conference on the Race Problem, an integrated program sponsored by the National Sociological Society, in the nation's capital. Preoccupied with new Jim Crow railroad laws in Tennessee and an upcoming meeting in Chicago concerning their enforcement, Washington supposed he might "accomplish more good in the private conference than by public utterance." Given the racial dynamics of the New South, he no doubt was correct.[54]

ACKNOWLEDGMENTS

The author wishes to thank Beth L. Calamia, Steven D. Lisk, and Daniel J. Salemson, graduate students in the Department of History, North Carolina State University, for research assistance with this article.

NOTES

1. Eric Foner, *Freedom's Lawmakers: A Directory of Black Officeholders During Reconstruction* (New York, 1993), xxix; *Negro Year Book: An Annual Encyclopedia of the Negro, 1925–1926* (Tuskegee, 1925), 369; *Negro Year Book: A Review of Events Affecting Negro Life, 1941–1946* (Tuskegee, 1946), 308; Rayford W. Logan, *The Negro in American Life and Thought: The Nadir, 1877–1901* (London, 1954); Jay R. Mandle, *Not Slave, Not Free: The African American Economic Experience Since the Civil War* (Durham, 1992); Edward L. Ayers, *The Promise of the New South: Life After Reconstruction* (New York, 1992), 409.

2. Joel Williamson, *The Crucible of Race: Black-White Relations in the American South Since Emancipation* (New York, 1984), 6.

3. C. Vann Woodward, *The Origins of the New South, 1877–1913* (1951; Baton Rouge, 1971), 350–53; Dewey W. Grantham, *The South in Modern America: A Region at Odds* (New York, 1994), 21. For a broad sampling of writings on the "race question," see John David Smith, ed., *Anti-Black Thought, 1863–1925: "The Negro Problem,"* 11 vols. (New York, 1993).

4. Hines H. Hall III, "The Montgomery Race Conference of 1900: Focal Point of Racial Attitudes at the Turn of the Century" (Master's thesis, Auburn University, 1965), 1–2, 27, 29; Leslie H. Fishel, Jr., "The 'Negro Question' and Mohonk: Microcosm, Mirage, and Message," *New York History*, 74 (1993):277, 282, 293; James M. McPherson, *The Abolitionist Legacy: From Reconstruction to the NAACP* (Princeton, 1975), 137n–138n. Tuskegee and Hampton Institutes began a series of annual conferences, respectively, in 1890 and 1897. Atlanta University did so as well in 1896. While "distinguished" whites attended these conferences, they were aimed

largely at black audiences. See August Meier, *Negro Thought in America, 1880–1915* (1963; Ann Arbor, MI, 1971), 122–23.

5. "The Race Problem," *Montgomery Advertiser*, January 9, 1900, reprint in Governors' Records (Joseph F. Johnston, 1900), Alabama Department of Archives and History; "Our Conference on Race Problems," *Montgomery Advertiser*, April 1, 1900; *Constitution of a Southern Society for the Promotion of the Study of Race Conditions and Problems in the South* (n.p., n.d.); *A Southern Conference for the Discussion of Race Problems in Relation to the Welfare of the South. A Great Inter-State Meeting to be Held in Montgomery, Ala., May 8, 9, 10—A.D. 1900 and Annually Thereafter* (n.p., n.d.), in Edgar Gardner Murphy Papers, Southern Historical Collection, University of North Carolina at Chapel Hill; *Race Problems of the South: Report of the Proceedings of the First Annual Conference Held Under the Auspices of The Southern Society for the Promotion of the Study of Race Conditions and Problems in the South* (Richmond, 1900), 7–11 (hereafter cited as *Race Problems of the South*).

6. Hugh C. Bailey, *Edgar Gardner Murphy: Gentle Progressive* (Coral Gables, 1968); Murphy, "The Georgia Atrocity and Southern Opinion," *Outlook*, 62 (May 20, 1899), 179–80; Allen J. Going, "The Reverend Edgar Gardner Murphy: His Ideas and Influence," *Historical Magazine of the Protestant Episcopal Church*, 25 (1956):400; Murphy to Booker T. Washington, January 1, 1902, in *The Booker T. Washington Papers*, Louis R. Harlan, ed., 14 vols. (Urbana, IL, 1972–1989), 6:367–68; Ralph Luker, "Liberal Theology and Social Conservatism: A Southern Tradition, 1840–1920," *Church History*, 50 (1981):200.

7. "Race Problems," *Montgomery Journal*, n.d., Murphy Papers; Edgar Gardner Murphy, *The White Man and the Negro at the South: An Address Delivered Under Invitation of the American Academy of Political and Social Science, the American Society for the Extension of University Teaching, and the Civic Club of Philadelphia, in the Church of the Holy Trinity, Philadelphia, on the Evening of March 8th, A.D. 1900* (n.p. [1900]), 27, 28, and passim; Murphy to Washington, March 28, 1900, Booker T. Washington Papers, Manuscript Division, Library of Congress; Bailey, *Edgar Gardner Murphy*, 40–41; George A. Mebane, *"The Negro Problem" as Seen and Discussed by Southern White Men in Conference, at Montgomery, Alabama* (New York, 1900), 1.

8. "The Race Problem," *Montgomery Advertiser*, January 9, 1900, Governors' Records; "The Race Problem. Conference Called at Montgomery in May to Exchange Ideas," *Philadelphia Public Ledger*, January 17, 1900, Murphy Papers; John Joel Culley, "Muted Trumpets: Four Efforts to Better Southern Race Relations, 1900–1919" (Ph.D. diss., University of Virginia, 1967), 40, 48–50; Murphy to Johnston, March 19, 1900, Governors' Records; Louis R. Harlan, *Booker T. Washington: The Making of a Black Leader, 1856–1901* (New York, 1972), 293; Murphy to Washington, May 30, 1900, Washington Papers; George Sale, "The Montgomery Conference," *Chicago Standard*, May 26, 1900, Southern Education Board Papers, Southern Historical Collection, University of North Carolina at Chapel Hill.

In his account of a January 1900, meeting between Murphy, Tuskegee's Trustees, Washington, and other influential blacks, New York philanthropist Robert C. Ogden stated that "the colored men advised their Northern friends to assist the conference when requested, but to leave the direction of it entirely to Southern men." See "Negro Progress," *New York Evening Post*, April 21, 1900, Southern Education Board Papers.

Hugh Bailey explains the exclusion of black speakers as the result of "Murphy's own timidity. . . . He acceded to the majority and came to feel his action was wise; to have Negroes on the regular program would have aroused prejudice and defeated the purpose of the conference." See *Edgar Gardner Murphy*, 37.

9. Washington to Murphy, February 3, 1900, Murphy to Washington, February 17, 1900, Murphy to Washington, February 23, 1900, Murphy to Washington, March 28, 1900, Washington Papers; Murphy to Walter Hines Page, April 14, 1900, Walter Hines Page Papers, Houghton Library, Harvard University; Bailey, *Edgar Gardner Murphy*, 43.

10. Washington to Garrison, February 3, 1900, Miscellaneous American Letters and Papers, Schomburg Center for Research in Black Culture, New York Public Library; Harlan, *Booker T. Washington*, 293.

11. Harlan, *Booker T. Washington*, 294. The final program consisted of Cockran, Frissell, E. B. Joseph, Joseph F. Johnston, John B. Gaston, William A. MacCorkle, Hilary A. Herbert, Alfred M. Waddell, John Temple Graves, J.L.M. Curry, Julius D. Dreher, D. Clay Lilly, William A. Guerry, John R. Slattery, Alexander C. King, Clifton R. Breckinridge, Paul B. Barringer, C. C. Penick, John R. Straton, W. F. Willcox, and Herbert Welsh. See *Race Problems of the South,* 14–16, 141.

12. Harlan, *Booker T. Washington*, 294; Page to Murphy, April 15, 17, 1900, Page Papers; Murphy to Paul B. Barringer, April 19, 1900, Barringer Family Papers, University of Virginia; Murphy to Washington, April 19, May 3, 1900, Washington Papers. Before the conference, rumors spread throughout the northern press that Cockran would support repeal of the Fifteenth Amendment. See, for example, "Fifteenth Amendment Repeal," *Elmira* (N.Y.) *Advertiser*, May 5, 1900, Southern Education Board Papers. Following the conference, Page wrote a scathing attack against Cockran and several other speakers. See "Southern Opinion of the Race Problem," *New York Times*, May 27, 1900. On Barringer, see John David Smith, "An Old Creed for the New South: Southern Historians and the Revival of the Proslavery Argument, 1890–1920," *Southern Studies: An Interdisciplinary Journal of the South*, 18 (Spring 1979):80–81.

13. Washington to Garrison, April 30, 1900, Miscellaneous American Letters and Papers, Schomburg; Harlan, *Booker T. Washington*, 294.

14. Washington, "The Montgomery Conference," *Christian Recorder*, May 10, 1900; Washington, "Good Southern Sentiment," *Washington Colored American*, May 12, 1900; Washington, "The Montgomery Conference," *Indianapolis Freeman*, May 19, 1900.

15. Barringer, *The American Negro: His Past and Future* (Raleigh, 1900), 10–11, 15, 23, 20.

16. "The American Negro," *Richmond Times*, March 30, 1900; "The Negro in Washington," *Richmond Times*, April 3, 1900; "The Negro in the South," *Richmond Central Presbyterian*, April 11, 1900; "The Negroes and Whites," *New York Sun*, May ?, 1900, and "Dr. Barringer and the Negroes," *New York Sun*, May 3, 1900, Peabody Clipping File, Hampton University; Murphy to Barringer, April 16, 1900, Barringer Family Papers.

17. Anderson to Barringer, April 13, 1900, Barringer Family Papers.

18. Washington to Barringer, May 1, 1900; Barringer to Washington, May 5, 1900, Barringer Family Papers. Approximately 2,000 persons attended the opening session of the conference, including roughly "400 negroes in the gallery." More

than 3,000 people crowded the auditorium for the final day. See "Brilliant Inaugu-ral of the Southern Race Conference," *Montgomery Advertiser*, May 9, 1900, and "Cockran Pleads for Repeal of the Fifteenth Amendment," *Montgomery Advertiser*, May 11, 1900, Peabody Clipping File.

19. Thrasher, "The Fifteenth Amendment in Danger," *Chicago Advance*, May 24, 1900, Southern Education Board Papers; P. Butler Thompkins, "The Race Confer-ence," May 7, 1900, in *New York Times*, May 12, 1900, Peabody Clipping File.

20. *Race Problems of the South*, 21, 22, 23, 28, 29, 34–35. For an analysis of Herbert's speech, see Hugh H. Hammett, *Hilary Abner Herbert: A Southerner Re-turns to the Union* (Philadelphia, 1976), 227–31.

21. *Race Problems of the South*, 41, 42, 43, 44, 45, 46, 48; Pollard, "The Race Conference Seen by the Eye of a Negro," *Mobile Southern Watchman*, May 19, 1900.

22. "Dr. Barringer and the Negroes," *New York Sun*, May 4, 1900, Peabody Clipping File; *Race Problems of the South*, 198–99, 201, 202; Garrison, "A Reply to Bourke Cockran," *New York Evening Post*, May 17, 1900, Peabody Clipping File; "The Montgomery Conference," *Outlook*, 65 (May 19, 1900):154. Garrison added: "It is the spectre of the enlightened, and not the ignorant negro that disturbs the South and which inspired the late [Montgomery] conference." Numerous northern criticisms of Cockran appear in the Peabody Clipping File.

23. MacCorkle to H. B. Frissell, March 26, 1900, Southern Education Board Papers; *Race Problems of the South*, 63, 65, 68–69, 74, 75; Blackwell to the Editor, *Boston Transcript*, May 19, 1900, Southern Education Board Papers; MacCorkle to Washington, May 14, 1900, in Harlan, ed., *The Booker T. Washington Papers*, 5:523; *Race Problems of the South*, 71. The *Nation* praised MacCorkle for his "lofty" and "enlightened" position on the question of disfranchisement. See *Nation*, 70 (May 17, 1900):371. MacCorkle continued to advance his position on bilateral suffrage restriction after the Montgomery Conference. See William A. MacCorkle, *Some Southern Questions* (New York, 1908), 175–76.

24. *Race Problems of the South*, 50, 52–53, 55, 56. Believing that Graves's words captured the primal, reactionary tone of the conference, John E. Milholland, a wealthy supporter of Washington, said: "I would have cheerfully given a thou-sand dollars to have been present just at that time. It was an opportunity for the stupidest man that ever faced an assemblage to score a point" (Harlan, *Booker T. Washington*, 295).

25. *Race Problems of the South*, 181, 182, 183, 190–93, 194; Stone to Barringer, May 18, 1900, Barringer Family Papers. Hoffman published the highly racist *Race Traits and Tendencies of the American Negro* (New York, 1896) under the auspices of the American Economic Association.

26. *Race Problems of the South*, 196–97, 207; "The Montgomery Conference," *New York Evening Post*, May 11, 1900, Peabody Clipping File; Murphy to W. H. Baldwin, Jr., May 12, 1900, Washington Papers; Murphy to the Editor, *Boston Transcript*, May 19, 1900, Southern Education Board Papers.

27. Harlan, *Booker T. Washington*, 294; Anderson, "The Montgomery Confer-ence on Race Problems at the South," *Presbyterian Quarterly*, 14 (1900): 573; Murphy to Washington, May 30, 1900, Washington Papers; "Race Gleanings," *Mobile South-ern Watchman*, May 26, 1900.

28. Harlan, *Booker T. Washington*, 295. "Perhaps twinged by conscience," Har-lan explains, a few days after the conference Cockran sent Washington a check for

$500. Washington set the money aside for a revolving fund for black farmers who wished to purchase land.

29. *Race Problems of the South*, 216–17; *New York Evening Post*, May 9, 1900, quoted in Harlan, *Booker T. Washington*, 295.

30. Murphy to Washington, July 23, 1900, Washington Papers; Harlan, *Booker T. Washington*, 296; Washington to Howland, June 19, 1900, Miscellaneous American Letters and Papers, Schomburg. On plans for the rival black-sponsored race conference, see "National Race Congress," *Mobile Southern Watchman*, June 30, 1900.

31. Washington, "The Montgomery Race Conference," *Century Magazine*, 60 (1900):630, 631.

32. Ibid., 631.

33. Ibid., 631–32; *Race Problems of the South*, 220.

34. Washington, "The Montgomery Race Conference," 631–32; "Dr. Barringer Misquoted, Will Make no Reply," n.d., unpublished press release, Barringer Family Papers; "Talk of the Negro," *Chicago Inter-Ocean*, March 10, 1901, Southern Education Board Papers; Washington to Barringer, March 13, 1901, Barringer Family Papers. In his press release, Barringer noted correctly that his references to black industrial school graduates were based on published figures for 1889–90, while Washington's undocumented, anecdotal figures presumably referred to conditions among blacks a decade later. See *Race Problems of the South*, 193–94.

35. Jones, "Echoes From the Race Conference," *Southwestern Christian Advocate*, 35 (July 12, 1900):2. Jones was a leading black prohibitionist. See Jones, "To What Extent is the Negro Race Addicted to Strong Drink? Its Evils and Cures," in I. Garland Penn and J.W.E. Bowen, eds., *The United Negro: His Problems and His Progress* (Atlanta, 1902), 256–59.

36. Mebane, *"The Negro Problem,"* 3, 4, 5, 6.

37. Bruce, "What Herbert Didn't Say," in Mebane, *"The Negro Problem,"* 35–37.

38. "The Citadel Attacked," *Indianapolis Freeman*, May 19, 1900. On Knox's editorial policies in this period, see Willard B. Gatewood, Jr., ed., *Slave and Freeman: The Autobiography of George L. Knox* (Lexington, 1979), 34–35.

39. "Washington at Hampton," *Indianapolis Freeman*, May 5, 1900; "The Citadel Attacked," *Indianapolis Freeman*, May 19, 1900.

40. "More About Him," *Richmond Planet*, May 12, 1900; untitled editorial in *Richmond Planet*, May 26, 1900. On Virginia's 1901–2 constitutional convention that disfranchised blacks, see Charles E. Wynes, *Race Relations in Virginia, 1870–1902* (Charlottesville, 1961), 60–67.

41. "Still Against Us," *Richmond Planet*, May 5, 1900. On Mitchell's ongoing battle with Barringer and the *Richmond Times*, see Ann Field Alexander, "Black Protest in the New South: John Mitchell, Jr. (1863–1929) and the *Richmond Planet*" (Ph.D. diss., Duke University, 1972), 286.

42. "The Plea Against Us," *Richmond Planet*, May 19, 1900.

43. Ibid.

44. Ibid.

45. "The Montgomery Convention," *A.M.E. Church Review*, 17 (July 1900):88.

46. Ibid., 89, 90.

47. "Sociological Rot," *Washington Colored American*, January 5, 1901.

48. Murphy to Washington, August 7, 1900, January 11, 1901, Washington Papers. More than a year following the conference, Murphy interpreted the meeting positively because, he said, none of the speakers advocated violating the law or committing violent acts. Murphy to Washington, n.d. [August 1901], Washington Papers.

49. "Rejoinder From Mr. Murphy," *Montgomery Journal*, April 18, 1901; "Suffrage in Alabama," *New York Times*, April 20, 1901, Murphy Papers; Culley, "Muted Trumpets," 110–12; J. Morgan Kousser, *The Shaping of Southern Politics: Suffrage Restriction and the Establishment of the One-Party South, 1880–1910* (New Haven, 1974), 239; Sheldon Hackney, *Populism to Progressivism in Alabama* (Princeton, 1969), 147–79, 189, 206, 326.

50. August Meier, *Negro Thought in America: Racial Ideologies in America, 1880–1915* (1963; Ann Arbor, 1971), 77; "Southern Race Problems," *New York Evening Post*, May 17, 1900; "Restrict the Ballot," *New York Commercial Advertiser*, May 17, 1900; "A Negro on the Negro Problem," *Rochester Post Express*, June 26, 1900, Southern Education Board Papers; B. J. Ramage to the Editor, *Nation*, 70 (June 14, 1900):456–57; "The Race Problem in the South," *Chattanooga* (Tenn.) *Daily Times*, May 20, 1900. Kealing spoke on interregional trade, not on race.

51. "In Defense of His Race," *New York Times*, May 28, 1900; "Dr. Walker Defends His Race," *New York Tribune*, May 28, 1900; "Specimen Negro Leaders," *Washington Post*, June 6, 1900; "Negro Conference," *Montgomery Journal*, June 8, 1900, Southern Education Board Papers. Soon after the Montgomery Conference, Fortune singled out Barringer as the speaker most ignorant of conditions among blacks in the South. See "Is Negro Education at the South a Failure?" *New York Sun*, May 13, 1900, Southern Education Board Papers.

52. Williamson, *The Crucible of Race*, 417; Murphy to Washington, April 19, 1900, in Harlan, ed., *The Booker T. Washington Papers*, 5:488.

53. William Warren Rogers, Robert David Ward, Leah Rawls Atkins, and Wayne Flynt, *Alabama: The History of a Deep South State* (Tuscaloosa, 1994), 351–52; Hackney, *Populism to Progressivism in Alabama*, 189–90.

54. *How to Solve the Race Problem: The Proceedings of the Washington Conference on the Race Problem in the United States* (Washington, 1904), 141–44; Washington to Whitefield McKinlay, November 6, 1903, in Harlan, ed., *The Booker T. Washington Papers*, 7:336–37. In addition to Washington, black speakers at the Washington Conference included Lucius H. Holsey, Kelly Miller, John W. Cromwell, Francis J. Grimké, Lafayette M. Hershaw, P.B.S. Pinchback, and Benjamin W. Arnett.

8

The Gavel and the Sword: Experiences Shaping the Life of John Sherman Cooper

Richard C. Smoot

In Kentucky's Republican Party, the name of John Sherman Cooper (1901–1991) calls forth images of pride, success, and more than just a touch of reverence. His political career included a seat in the lower house of the Kentucky General Assembly (1928–1929) and two terms (1930–1938) as the county judge in his native Pulaski County. After losing his bid in the 1939 Republican gubernatorial primary, Cooper served in the U.S. Third Army during the Second World War and returned home to a term as a circuit court judge (1945–1946), for which he had been elected in absentia. In 1946 Cooper was elected to the first of three short terms (1946–1948, 1952–1954, 1956–1960) he would hold in the U.S. Senate. Later Cooper won election to two full terms (1960–1972) in that body. Cooper held various appointed positions, including special service to the U.S. State Department (1950) and two ambassadorships (1955–1956, 1975–1976). Finally, Cooper enjoyed several assignments to the U.S. delegation to the United Nations (1949–1951, 1968, 1981).

Though Cooper enjoyed an impressive career, it was one that nonetheless seems a paradox. Cooper was a successful liberal in a decidedly conservative state. He was a Republican in a state where Democrats dominated two to one. He was an open-minded progressive who could become, at times, quite partisan. Later, Cooper the World War II veteran emerged as a leading dove in the U.S. Senate debate surrounding the Vietnam War.

Difficulties arise in explaining Cooper's seeming inconsistencies. But certain pieces of the Cooper puzzle fit the board, helping us bring the man and his life into sharper focus. Heritage, environment, and other early influences clearly gave him a firm foundation from which to start. Often Cooper cited the influence of his parents, upbringing, family, friends, hometown, and education as significant forces shaping his world.[1] Just as frequently Cooper pointed to two other phases or periods in his life as crucial to the shaping of his thinking and political viewpoints. One period incorporated Cooper's years as Pulaski County judge; the other phase included his years of military service during the Second World War. By examining closely the judge and the soldier, with a campaign for governor set in between, we may better understand Cooper's subsequent career as U.S. senator and ambassador.

Any visions of a law degree from Harvard and perhaps some lofty legal career following graduation came to a screeching halt for Cooper in 1925, when he was compelled to return to his hometown of Somerset, Kentucky. Fortunately, his short time away had not been spent in vain. His Yale University bachelor's degree had been secured in 1923, and he had managed to complete two years of legal studies at Harvard University law school. But in 1924 Cooper's father Sherman died unexpectedly, bequeathing to him a legacy of debt and emotional trauma. John felt obliged to return home, to assume the responsibilities left behind by his father. Tradition dictated that he assume this role. The oldest son and second child of John Sherman and Helen Gertrude Tartar Cooper, young John did not expect any of his siblings to shoulder this burden. Stability had to be brought again to the house of Cooper, and John was the logical means to achieve that end.[2]

But difficulties confounded Cooper's every move. Liquidation of his father's sawmills, lumber holdings, and farmland went forward quickly since he was selling at bargain prices, but more money was needed. John took a job on a survey crew at the Southern Railway, where he had worked as a teenager. If ever he felt any embarrassment or resentment toward taking this position or toward his circumstances generally, such a view remains undiscovered in the record. What is clear is that Cooper was willing to do whatever he must to earn his own way and address the needs of the family. Other family members and friends could do little more than give their advice, and of that they gave freely, whether financial in nature or otherwise.[3]

Perhaps the most important advice Cooper received during these years came from his maternal uncle, Roscoe Conkling Tartar. An experienced politician and Republican Party operative in Kentucky, Tartar recommended that his nephew follow family tradition and his own temperament, and pursue a career in politics. Opportunity seemed to dictate just such a course for Cooper when, in 1927, the incumbent state representative for his district announced that he would not seek reelection. In predominantly Republican Pulaski County, Cooper knew that if he could win the GOP nomination it essentially meant election. Tartar saw big opportunities for both himself and his nephew. Although Pulaski County was single-party dominated, factions or interest groups existed within the Republican Party itself. Tartar headed one such faction. Interestingly, from 1918 until his death in 1924, Sherman Cooper had headed the other major GOP faction. After 1924, allegiance passed from Sherman to Napier Adams. A long-time associate of Sherman Cooper, Adams was the ultimate nemesis of Roscoe Tartar. In 1925 Adams unseated Tartar as county judge. Enmity between the two men gave no sign of abating in the following years.

But Tartar did hope to reconcile himself with the other members of the opposition faction. Joined by members of his own faction, Uncle Roscoe could invoke the name of John Cooper's popular late father to consolidate support behind his nephew's nomination. It was a strategy that worked, apparently, for Cooper was swept into the state legislature unopposed. During the 1928–1929 session, he sat in the Kentucky House of Representatives, a scarce Republican in that overwhelmingly Democratic body. Even more uncommon that year was the election of a Republican governor, Flem D. Sampson. As the decade of the 1920s came to an end, the fortunes of Cooper and his party seemed to be on the rise in Kentucky.[4]

Cooper's performance in the state legislature was respectable enough for a freshman Republican representative. But he quickly demonstrated a willingness to strike out against his own party, an independence of action that became for him a characteristic. In the Kentucky House, for example, he joined two other Republicans in voting with the Democratic majority to block the governor's attempt to wrest control of the state Board of Health away from the medical profession. Cooper considered the proposed action inappropriate and much too political. But more often he flowed with his party's view and had no difficulty in supporting such popular legislation of the day as free textbooks for public schools and uniform commercial codes. His actions did not go unnoticed. The Democratic *Somerset Journal* described Cooper as "one of the most prominent of the younger members" of the General Assembly. "No county in the state was more ably represented" than Pulaski, wrote the *Journal*'s editor, who praised Cooper for his faithful attendance at legislative sessions, his willingness to speak out and act independently, and his "sincerity and honesty of purpose." While in Frankfort, Cooper prepared for the Kentucky state bar examination, which then did not require a law degree. In July 1928 he reportedly made a "splendid grade" on the test. In December Cooper opened his first law office in Somerset.[5]

He had little time, however, to practice law, because Cooper's supporters soon launched his next political campaign. After his nephew's success in the legislature, Uncle Roscoe believed it prudent to move Cooper quickly up the ladder toward greater responsibility and more definite local power. Tartar also sought to avenge his humiliating 1925 defeat at the hands of Napier Adams. What better vengeance could Tartar hope for than to take away from incumbent Judge Adams the GOP nomination while forwarding the political career of his own nephew?[6]

County judge in Kentucky was a powerful local position. Indeed, local elected officials and their cronies constituted the "courthouse rings" that controlled the grassroots power in state politics. Usually the acknowledged leader of the courthouse crowd was the county judge. One did not have to be an attorney to hold this office; rather, it was a position perhaps more accurately termed the county's chief executive officer. Even so, the county judge did preside over the county, juvenile, quarterly, and fiscal courts. If elected, Cooper would become the "local law enforcer, political leader, friend in need of the political faithful, comptroller of patronage and state-relief funds, and father confessor to anyone with a problem."[7]

Cooper might expect other challenges along the road to becoming county judge. Petty provincialism and personality conflicts regularly prevailed in rural Kentucky politics—hardly surprising given the insularity of such settings. In deciding to run for this office, the prospective candidate customarily expected probing questions into personal character and ambition. Further, opposing candidates usually knew their competitors well, a familiarity that sometimes gave way to hard words and feelings, if not outright contempt. All sorts of accusations might issue from the mouths of candidates and their partisans, ranging from charges of bossism and corruption to cries of nepotism and favoritism. In fact, all such practices were common in Kentucky, regardless of party. Pulaski County in 1929 offered a virtual textbook model of these highly unpleasant political facts of life.[8]

Despite the obvious drawbacks, Cooper in January 1929 agreed to enter the race for judge. Interest in the primary election doubtless would be high, for both Cooper and Adams were well known throughout the county. The *Somerset Journal* praised Adams for a progressive term in office and for his leadership in supporting the funding of local improvements. A third candidate, David Jones, also entered the race. Republicans would have several months before the August primary vote to determine which of the three candidates they would choose as county judge. Candidates used that time to win loyalties, solicit support, and, of course, bedevil the opposition.[9]

Cooper had never been tested in a real campaign. But there was no time now for additional preparation; he incurred initiation by fire and called upon all he had learned and observed to stand finally on center stage. Because the radio was not yet a campaign tool in rural Kentucky, Cooper traveled across the county stump-speaking. He drove an old Chevrolet where the roads would allow; in rougher terrain he mounted a horse to reach his destination. Family reunions, church meetings, and public gatherings saw the candidate busily shaking hands, talking, eating, listening. Cooper did not know how many miles he accumulated as he walked county roads and fields to shake hands with farmers. Time, terrain, and distance kept him from home many nights, so it was not unusual for him to awaken from a night's sleep in an unfamiliar room in some isolated farmhouse.[10]

By July, John's brother Don later recalled, the campaign had turned rather "vicious." Adams charged that Cooper was nothing but a pawn, mere "pliant putty" in the hands of his political master, Roscoe Tartar. Judge Adams told voters that his was an administration of progress, a term marked by road and bridge construction that continued unhindered despite the alleged destructive efforts of Tartar and his clique. One need only listen to the misguided pronouncements of his opponent Cooper, said a patronizing Adams, to conclude that "the young man's" criticisms came from another and were without basis.[11]

Cooper turned to his record of service in Frankfort to counter Adams's strategy. Where had Adams been, asked Cooper repeatedly, when Pulaski's representative in Frankfort sat on the House Committee on Bridges? Adams had never sought Cooper's cooperation in securing county bridge construction funds. Adams responded with a critique of Cooper's work in Frankfort. He portrayed Cooper's political independence as equal to party disloyalty and added a frivolous charge of "chasing butterflies"—a contemporary euphemism for chasing women. Adams hammered away at Cooper's youth and inexperience and disparaged his Republican credentials, implying that he was interested more in social affairs than in hard work. Finally, Adams leveled his aim at Roscoe Tartar, stating outright that Tartar's interest in this race was totally self-serving, designed to secure "another office for the family" while ignoring the needs of the county and its people. County dollars might be seriously threatened by the Tartar-Cooper clan, said Adams. Cooper might use vital county road funds to help "send uncle to Congress," Adams conjectured, thereby placing the family one step higher on the political scale.[12]

Cooper never denied the influence of his family on county affairs. In fact, to do so would have been impossible. In the 1929 race alone Cooper could count five of his relatives either in local office or as candidates for office. Many other relatives before him had attained public office in Pulaski County. But was this not some indication of the prominence, the esteem, the trust placed in his family? Further, Cooper strongly denied charges that he would serve as a mere family pawn if elected. His would be an independent and liberal administration, he insisted. Then came his own caustic attacks upon Adams. Roads and bridges, the threads holding together the fabric of county life and commerce, could not be ignored by the candidates for judge. Yet here Adams had been remiss in his duty, according to Cooper, trying to cover up his shortcomings by taking credit for state-sponsored projects independent of county objectives. Pulaski County wanted the development of an east-west highway. But Adams had not approached Governor Sampson for assistance, said Cooper, any more than he had approached the state representative from Pulaski to assist in obtaining vital state funds to finance such improvements.[13]

Accusations of ingratitude and disloyalty climaxed during the last days of the primary. A large crowd turned out to hear the final volley from the political pulpit. Adams had painted Cooper as inept, incompetent, disloyal, and very possibly dishonest. Cooper replied by throwing these charges back in the face of his opponent. His late father, Sherman Cooper, had helped Napier Adams before his untimely demise, John Cooper insisted. Rather substantial sums of money had flowed from Sherman's coffers into Adams's political war fund. Now here was the fruit of such generosity, coarsely thrown down and ungratefully forgotten. Producing canceled checks proving that Adams had received thousands of dollars from his father, John Cooper asked with poignant effect whether a man could be trusted who made such terrible accusations against the son of "the best friend he ever had politically"?[14]

Meanwhile, David Jones, running a poor third behind Cooper and Adams, tried to take the high road in the campaign. Jones insisted that he was glad to be distanced from the "factional broil" in the primary. "These slanderous accusations that Judge Adams and John Cooper are making against each other are not only making them lifetime enemies," wrote Jones, "but our citizens are being divided." Jones asked the Pulaski Republican electorate to "rebuke this mud slinging and quarrels" by voting for him. Suggesting that the campaign had brought county politics to a new low, Jones promised that his election would free the people from what might prove to be a similarly unsavory administration. Considering the tone of the charges Republicans hurled at one another, one might reasonably wonder how any of them were *ever* elected.[15]

But Pulaski's Republican voters apparently saw things differently, as Cooper won the summer primary handily. He polled 4,273 ballots to Adams's 3,366 and Jones's 865. But other factors far outweighed the margin of the vote in importance. Cooper, a young and still relatively inexperienced politician, outdistanced a veteran campaigner and incumbent. In the primary, the people of Cooper's county registered a decided vote of confidence in his abilities, his character, and his promise of future leadership. Following the primary, Jones, sour over his own poor showing, alleged "conspiracy" and "bribery." But such charges were unsupported and dismissed. Unopposed in the November general election, Cooper won the seat of county judge.[16]

On January 6, 1930, at eight o'clock in the morning, Uncle Roscoe administered the oath of office to Cooper, at twenty-eight years of age Kentucky's youngest county judge. Roses arranged in a basket brightened his desk, and in his first official act he presided over the marriage of a young local couple. Now he wrapped himself up tightly in local concerns, such as improving roads and protecting commerce. Such were the duties of office; they gave him little time to notice the powerful storm brewing around national and global economic events.[17]

Difficulties existed in the economy well before the consequences of the 1929 Wall Street stock market crash. Overproduction, low wages, unregulated banking and speculative practices, overextended credit, inflated property values, and other difficulties existed nationwide. Some economic problems likewise were in evidence in Pulaski County before the Great Crash. But Cooper remained optimistic. Plans were announced to construct a new jail and to remodel the courthouse. State officials conferred with the new judge on the coveted east-west highway, and shortly before Cooper became county judge, Pulaski voters passed a $300,000 road bond issue to help construct just such a route. In September 1930 the bonds went to the largest investment house in the southern United States, Caldwell and Company of Nashville, Tennessee. It seemed a safe investment; adjudged the most favorable bid on the bonds, the Caldwell offer legally bound county officials to accept. But by the following November the mood had changed profoundly. Caldwell faced possible bankruptcy, it seemed, and already auditors busied themselves in investigating the great company's solvency.[18]

Here began what was to become a long nightmare for the fledgling judge. Cooper rushed to Nashville to salvage what he could of Pulaski County's investment. Caldwell officials assured him that the collateral on the bonds secured the investment. But such was not the case. Real estate made up most of the collateral, and property values were falling precipitously nationwide. To complicate matters, the county experienced a severe drought in 1930, causing terrible losses for farmers there and indeed throughout the country. Before the year's end, county relief rolls began to swell. Those who sought relief flocked to Judge Cooper's office, for they had nowhere else to go.[19]

Deeply moved by the plight of so many hapless folk, Cooper often dug into his own thin pocket to help an unfortunate soul. Many could not afford adequate food, shelter, clothing, or medical care. To help drought-stricken farmers, he worked with state and local Red Cross officials. Property devaluations continued, translating into lower county tax receipts and further complicating relief efforts. Even basic repairs to county property met with delay. Desperate to reduce the county's expenses, Cooper and five other county officials agreed in early 1932 to work without pay for a month.[20]

In the wake of the Great Depression, Republican elected officials throughout the United States endured for years the wrath of an unhappy electorate deeply shaken by the ugly turn in economic circumstances. Many blamed President Herbert Hoover and his party for their plight, or at least charged that the Hoover administration failed to do enough to provide the country with adequate relief. Not so in Pulaski County, Kentucky. Party loyalty ran deep there, whether voting for local, state, or national office. When, in 1932, Hoover sought reelection against Democratic candidate Franklin D. Roosevelt, the county gave a resounding 2,000-vote majority to the Republican standard-bearer.[21]

Similar results prevailed in 1933, when Judge Cooper easily defeated his Democratic opposition to win reelection. In fact, the harshest criticism he received came from the GOP primary, again from Napier Adams. Adams styled Cooper and Tartar "political parasites," masters of "waste and folly" who should be thrown out of office. Cooper replied that Adams and his faction "lied" for political gain and attempted "to prey upon the need and hardships of the people." Appropriate to such an atmosphere, the primary campaign ended in an outburst of fisticuffs among partisans at the courthouse, sending the pugilistic offenders from both sides to jail.[22]

Difficult as these times were, things would have been much worse had it not been for the federal relief programs. In the early years of his first term, Cooper saw the Reconstruction Finance Corporation (RFC) provide a limited number of jobs to local residents. But far more critical to the relief effort in Pulaski County was the assistance offered by the Works Progress Administration (WPA), sponsored by the Roosevelt administration. Cooper did not have direct control over the local WPA expenditures, but he did select specific local WPA projects and foremen. The agency repaired roads, bridges, and schools, and constructed needed sanitary outhouses. Cooper later praised the WPA's work in Pulaski County. Indeed, notwithstanding much Republican criticism to the contrary, he later acknowledged that the WPA was "a great help in our county." Exhibiting political independence, Cooper was "very proud" of its successes.[23]

Nearing the end of his second term, Cooper in April 1937 announced that he would not seek reelection to the judgeship or election to any other county post. Considerable speculation arose immediately about his political future. Some thought he would run for governor; others believed he might want to run for the U.S. Congress. But it seemed that what Cooper really wanted was rest. For over seven years he had maintained a rigorous and demanding schedule, constantly facing both financially and emotionally disturbing problems. Understanding the limitations and constraints he faced, Cooper complicated matters for himself as a person of sensitive disposition. High expectations, pressures, continuing debts, and years of stressful living now began to take their toll. His personal life offered no respite from such problems. Living a bachelor's life meant for him no close, intimate companion to whom he could turn for support and confidence. Possibly the prospect of assuming greater responsibility discouraged or even frightened him. Small wonder, then, that Cooper sank into a deep depression.[24]

In his last year as judge, Cooper began to display some outward signs of physical illness. When physicians found nothing wrong with him physically, they determined that his problems were emotional. For the next several months, he was in and out of hospitals and sanitariums in Lexington, Kentucky; Battle Creek, Michigan; and Boston, Massachusetts. Their diagnosis was a nervous breakdown. Cooper's brother Don believed that the judge's job and related problems "had damn near killed him. . . ."

Clearly, Cooper needed rest. Uncle Roscoe filled in as county judge for the remainder of his ailing nephew's term. It would take months beyond that time for Cooper to recover fully.[25]

Friends, relatives, and associates vigorously supported Cooper during this personal crisis. He welcomed letters and frequent visits. In July 1938 the Republican *Somerset Commonwealth* reported that Cooper was home, "entirely recovered from his illness and looks fit enough to go into the ring with Joe Louis and give the heavyweight champ the battle of his life." Exaggerations aside, he was visibly better. For the remainder of the year Cooper took life at a slower pace.[26]

Though he later would endure bouts of poor health and moments of mild depression, Cooper never again experienced anything comparable to this trial. Curiously, for all the abundant invective and personal vituperation that so characterized Kentucky politics, his emotional breakdown never became a major campaign issue. Some opponents may not have known of his nervous breakdown. Others may have had personal imperfections of their own they deemed important to keep hidden. Very likely, however, Cooper's reputation proved his greatest protection. Perceived as a bright, hard-working person, Cooper had endured much trouble and yet had recovered; few knew, however, just how admirably he had overcome this personal ordeal.

Cooper's respite from politics was short-lived. Kentucky Republicans in 1939 hungered for victory, especially gubernatorial success. Not since Flem Sampson was elected governor in 1927 had the GOP won a single statewide race. Cooper, for his part, had been working for some time on building up his personal network within the party. Since 1926, Cooper had attended every state and district Republican convention. Many in the party believed Cooper had compiled an impressive record in the state legislature and as Pulaski County judge. His emotional setback seemed to be regarded as an unfortunate circumstance. But it never was considered an insurmountable political liability.[27]

Republicans had hard, practical reasons for desiring Cooper's candidacy, transcending their usual hopes for seeing their party win the governor's race. Because Democrats had long dominated Kentucky politics, Republicans relied heavily on federal patronage to reward the party faithful. But since 1933 most Republicans were excluded from federal patronage by the Roosevelt administration. Democrats also held the state patronage jobs through the decade of the 1930s. Patronage served as the lifeblood of politics, and the anemic Republicans were desperate for such sustenance.[28]

As early as February 15, 1939, reports circulated that Cooper would run for governor. Pulaski natives were excited about his decision, "confident [that] the party could not offer a stronger or more deserving candidate." The Republican *Somerset Commonwealth* editorialized that their native son was "capable, progressive, honest, energetic and popular," and would have the "united support" of Pulaski County Republicans as well as many Democrats. Such a prediction was music to the ears of GOP power brokers in Louisville and eastern Kentucky. Cooper, it seemed, was just the kind of man they wanted.[29]

But the desire for a Cooper governorship was not universal within the party. Many Republicans wanted a return of their ill-starred warrior of 1935, Lexington circuit judge King Swope (1893–1961). Ruggedly built with closely cropped hair and piercing eyes, Swope was a World War I veteran and one-term congressman from 1919 to 1921. Republicans close to Judge Swope at first believed he would run for governor. In April 1939, however, Swope indicated he would not run if he had to submit to a primary. Under the Republican Party's compulsory primary rule such a race was inevitable. Swope Republicans thus adopted a strategy to persuade their favorite to seek the GOP nomination. On May 6 a so-called Draft-King Swope-for-Governor movement was initiated in Lee County. Republican State Central Committee chairman Thomas S. Yates of Grayson apparently supported the effort. Soon there were King Swope "clubs" in other counties joining in the appeal, whether motivated by rural resentment of Louisville's GOP elite or purely personal loyalty to Swope among selected party functionaries. A visible threat to Cooper's gubernatorial aspirations clearly was under way.[30]

Cooper's old Somerset friend Onie P. Hamilton was incensed by these political games played by the Swope partisans. Hamilton wrote the *Louisville Courier-Journal* charging that the attempt to draft Swope was an "artificial" campaign device designed to mislead Republicans. Claiming to be "reliably informed," probably by Cooper, Hamilton said that most Republicans in the supposedly pro-Swope counties really did not favor the Lexingtonian's candidacy. The reported "mass convention" for Swope in London, Kentucky, noted Hamilton, was "attended by three people." A draft-Swope resolution in Russell County had been "passed around on the streets and signed by a few persons." Hamilton condemned these tactics and urged Republicans not to abandon Cooper.[31]

Republicans knew the propaganda value of the draft-Swope movement. Unsurprisingly, it became apparent by early June 1939 that Swope would reverse his earlier refusal and run for governor. Thousands of letters and telegrams reportedly flooded the office of Judge Swope. Perry County Republicans for Swope attempted to file his nomination with the secretary of state's office, but this action was not legally acceptable. The *Mount Sterling Gazette and Kentucky Courier*, a staunch conservative Republican newspaper, seemed to capture the opinion of many Swope Republicans in writing that while Cooper was a "brilliant young man" and was "very popular," Swope's reputation made him the better candidate. Just one hour before the filing deadline on June 26, 1939, Swope declared his candidacy.[32]

If Cooper found Swope's candidacy discouraging, the Somerset man did not show it. In fact, Cooper stated that a vigorously contested primary would strengthen the Republican Party. With his campaign manager, Lincoln County Judge John Menifee, in early July 1939, Cooper established his headquarters at Louisville's Brown Hotel. Cooper delivered his first official campaign address in London, Kentucky, on July 11. "I will not promise anything that cannot be fulfilled," Cooper announced simply. His statewide tour of Kentucky counties, continued candidate Cooper, had made it plain that the "people are sick unto death of promises and meaningless generalities and the vulgarity and vilification of factional fighting." Cooper promised to offer Republicans and the citizens of the commonwealth something different and new.[33]

Cooper's stand on labor relations signaled his new departure. In a state where unions had never done well, in a party that had made the new unions of the 1930s an issue, it was something of a departure to sympathize with labor and promise both employer and employee "a square deal and fair treatment." Evoking the memory of Theodore Roosevelt was, very likely, not chance; for in many other ways, Cooper's program served as a direct challenge to the thinking of Progressivism. True to Republican doctrine, Cooper's platform decried waste, inefficiency, and spoilsmanship as a threat to good government. It promised further reduction of the public debt and opposed the imposition of "additional heavy taxes." Eliminate the pork of patronage, Cooper insisted, and highway construction could be accomplished for much less. The rich mineral and agricultural resources of the state could produce a greater revenue, without tax increases. So far, no conservative would have disagreed.

But Cooper's platform went beyond the nostrums of efficiency. Social progress, compassion—these, too, were the responsibilities of Republican government. There must be new laws to protect and assist labor and those unable to help themselves. More money was needed for penal and reform institutions, mental health facilities, local health resources, and relief to the aged and infirm. Most of all, Kentucky needed to bolster its educational system. Forty-fourth nationally in education, the state could not rely on federal funding to redeem matters. It must act on its own, with a heavier infusion of funding.[34]

The tone of Cooper's platform in fact offered a more marked contrast with mainstream Republicanism than did his program. Cooper and Swope were not that far apart in their embrace of efficiency and social reform. What separated them was the intensity of each candidate's response to New Deal liberalism. Both of them denounced the failures of the Democrats to bring progress to Kentucky; there was nothing gentle in Cooper's charge that the "leaders of the Democratic Party are more interested in the perpetuation in power of a faction than in service to the state." But Swope was by far the more aggressive, the more ready to take on the taxing, spending, and regulating propensities of the Democrats. "When the Nation suffered a depression," he told a Paintsville audience, "New Deal minions tied the hands of Uncle Sam while he slept, went down into all of his pockets and took everything, as they did from Gulliver in the story."[35]

It is interesting to compare the campaign voice of Swope with that of Cooper. It was not what the Democrats did but what they failed to do that Cooper stressed. Deploring a campaign built on "meaningless harangue" against the opposition, Cooper insisted on a program with specific plans to address Kentucky's problems. Distancing himself from Republicanism pure and simple, he promised to stand clear of all "party factions" and "pressure groups" as governor and to deliver "new and progressive leadership."[36]

Throughout the campaign, Cooper and Swope both adhered closely to their original platform messages. But the candidates also employed some new campaign techniques to inform voters of their positions. One modern vehicle for reaching voters was the radio, which by the 1930s had become an important election tool. Swope frequently spoke over Louisville radio station WHAS, while Cooper limited himself to only one radio appearance because of the prohibitive cost. Another recent campaign tool was the "modern sound truck" equipped with massive loudspeakers. Cooper employed this device, especially in rural districts, where the loudspeakers would announce his speaking engagements to isolated farmers. Apparently no one in the usually quiet agrarian setting found the device obnoxious or intrusive.[37]

During the campaign neither Cooper nor Swope mentioned the other by name, a common if childish practice, nor directly assaulted the other's proposals. This did not mean, however, that the campaign was devoid of specific attacks on the candidates emanating from various sources. Both major candidates received severe criticism from Dr. L. O. Smith, Harlan mayor and Republican gubernatorial hopeful. In a radio address over WHAS, Smith assailed Cooper's "poor and questionable record" as Pulaski County judge. Smith said Cooper's "absence" during his last year as judge did "not commend or qualify him as the Chief Executive of Kentucky." Smith might have received his script from Cooper's old nemesis, Napier Adams. The Harlan candidate also said that Cooper was "condemned and censored by all labor groups and many Republicans" because of Roscoe Tartar, "his master's voice." Limiting his attacks on Swope to questions of executive temperament, Smith declared that a Cooper victory would accomplish nothing but the "embarrassment" of the Somerset man and his party.[38]

And there were more pressing problems than the words of Harlan's mayor. Despite Cooper's avowal to give labor a "square deal and fair treatment," Swope received the endorsement of Kentucky unions. Edward H. Weyler, secretary of the executive board of the state chapter of the American Federation of Labor (AFL), said he had been "reliably informed" that Cooper's candidacy resulted from "solicitation of labor's greatest arch enemies in Kentucky," presumably certain members of the state Republican leadership. Undoubtedly the loss of labor's endorsement hurt the Somerset candidate, who had hoped to capitalize on union support.[39]

But Cooper was not completely abandoned by organized labor. The members of the Pulaski County local of the Federated Shop Crafts union pledged their loyalty to their former Southern Railroad coworker. Indeed, they noted that Cooper was still a member of the local machinist's union. The state Congress of Industrial Organizations (CIO) chapter apparently withheld endorsement of any Republican, reserving its support for Democratic candidate John Young Brown. There were rumors, however, that the CIO preferred Swope in the Republican race, perhaps because he was a known and once-defeated opponent more readily vanquished again by their preferred candidate from the Democratic camp.[40]

Though Cooper received the support of most of his home district's Republican newspapers, Swope fared far better in the statewide party press. The *Lexington Leader*, the state's major Republican daily, supported its hometown candidate. The *Mount Sterling Gazette and Kentucky Courier* wanted the Lexingtonian because he could "lead us to victory," or so they believed. The *Corbin Daily Tribune* thought Kentucky needed "a man of the Swope type," while the *Maysville Public Ledger* believed Swope deserved the nomination because of his "fine showing" four years earlier. The *Columbia Times* said it could support either Republican in the general election, but it recommended Swope's nomination. Swope was similarly endorsed by the *Cynthiana Log Cabin* and the *Barbourville Mountain Republican*. The Barbourville endorsement was indicative of important opposition to Cooper; it was the political mouthpiece of Congressman John M. Robsion and former governor Sampson. Newspapers for Swope therefore represented a wider geographic distribution as well as some encroachment into Cooper's vital mountain base.[41]

Cooper nevertheless sounded optimistic as the primary entered its last days. Greeted by "tremendous crowds" in northern and western Kentucky, Cooper predicted that he would win the nomination by 50,000 votes. A few days later, Cooper's campaign manager increased the margin to 57,000 and foretold of winning all but the Sixth and Eighth Congressional Districts. Arthur T. Bryson, Swope's campaign manager, made similar prognostications favoring his candidate. Bryson suggested a 51,500-vote plurality for Swope and victory in every congressional district save the Ninth, where he called for an "even break." Only the results of election day would reveal whose predictions were most accurate. Regardless of the outcome, Cooper promised to "stand by the Republican nominee in November, whoever he may be. . . ."[42]

Saturday, August 5, was primary election day. Early returns showed Swope leading in the Republican race, while Keen Johnson commanded the early Democratic majority over Brown. But the early returns did not reflect the votes of either Louisville or the Ninth Congressional District in southern

Kentucky, where Cooper expected a strong showing. By August 8, however, it was clear that Swope would win. That day Cooper conceded graciously, pledging his support for Swope in the November election. Pulaski County had given Cooper the largest plurality ever won by any local, state, or national candidate for office. Cooper received an amazing 93.8 percent of the Pulaski vote—7,054 ballots to Swope's 432. But Cooper had won only the Fourth Congressional District in the statewide race, losing his own district by several thousand votes. The final tabulation gave Swope 121,297 votes (59.5 percent) to Cooper's 73,305 (35.9 percent). Clearly in command of a superior state political network, the Lexington judge also had strong name recognition by virtue of his unsuccessful bid for governor four years earlier. It seems, too, that the message delivered by Swope was better received among the Republican faithful than was Cooper's. Republicans apparently preferred Swope's hammer blows to the Democrats to Cooper's more conciliatory language.[43]

Their favorite son defeated, the *Somerset Commonwealth* reflected on the election's final outcome. Swope had greater name recognition and a "formidable organization" of his own, observed editor George Joplin, Jr., Cooper had to build his own organization from "scratch" and was not well known among the rank and file outside of the Ninth District. The newspaper contended that the CIO "materially aided" Swope, especially in the Seventh District. In his own Ninth District, Cooper was opposed by the political "machine" headed by Congressman Robsion and former governor Sampson. Robsion and Sampson apparently were successful in "tearing down organizations" originally supporting the Somerset candidate. Joplin's assessment was essentially correct and placed in bold relief a Kentucky political reality: without a strong personal organization firmly in place, no statewide candidate could hope to win.[44]

Despite suffering his first electoral defeat, Cooper knew he had gained more than he had lost in the 1939 primary. The *Louisville Times* certainly confirmed that attitude. His "political debut" statewide had been anything but "ineffective," wrote the Louisville newspaper; Cooper had made "a good impression" everywhere. The editor commended him for avoiding "reckless" promises and predicted that the "Republican party doubtless will have him in mind for some future occasion." Cooper carried only 25 of Kentucky's 120 counties in the governor's race. Building a statewide network in Kentucky took considerable work and much time, given the commonwealth's many counties and their sundry political and social nuances. Defeat at the polls was a hard lesson for Cooper, but the young candidate made important gains that proved useful in future campaigns. From the 1939 gubernatorial race Cooper secured largely favorable statewide exposure and began construction of the rudiments of his Kentucky political network, so critical to his later races for the U.S. Senate.[45]

With the election behind him, Cooper settled back into his law practice. A quiet lifestyle ensued. Some Ninth District Republicans urged him to run for Congress against Robsion, but Cooper seemed uninterested. Here and there Cooper would give a speech locally, and in 1940 he worked for the election of GOP nominee Wendell Willkie in his luckless race to unseat President Roosevelt. Then it was back to his law practice and an even more uneventful year in 1941.[46]

But 1942 was an entirely different story. Following American entry into World War II, Cooper, a patriot in the best sense of the word, could not stand idle while his country's interests were threatened by foreign powers. No doubt Cooper realized the political importance of appropriate participation in the war effort, but his sense of duty seems more genuine than calculating. Cooper's first actions were to raise money for the troops while he served as chairman of the county Civilian Defense Committee, an agency of the U.S. Treasury promoting the sale of bonds and stamps. Meanwhile, all around him, Cooper watched as friends and family entered into the various branches of the armed forces.[47]

As the war intensified, Cooper pondered what might be his own most suitable role in the conflict. Men were being drafted up to the age of forty-five at that time, and the draft sometimes suggested an unwillingness to serve; he did not want anyone to question his resolve. As a teenager, he had witnessed the return of veterans of World War I. He was still single, and family finances were under control. Although forty-one years old, Cooper was in good physical condition from consistent jogging. After careful thought, on September 14, 1942, Cooper enlisted in the U.S. Army. From the Louisville recruiting station the new soldier was immediately sent to the induction center at Fort Benjamin Harrison, Indiana, where he would receive his initial basic training.[48]

Word soon spread of Cooper's enlistment. Cooper received a letter from Herman L. Donovan, president of the University of Kentucky, where the Somerset man was a member of the board of trustees. Donovan expressed his "profound admiration" of Cooper's decision to enlist. In reply, Cooper said he had no reason to regret his decision. "It is a strenuous life," he admitted to Donovan, "but I have enjoyed the work and am getting in good physical condition."[49]

After about three weeks at Fort Benjamin Harrison, Cooper was transferred to the Army Air Corps training camp at Clearwater, Florida. During basic training there, Cooper reported that he upheld Kentucky honor and reputation for marksmanship on the firing range. "Now, look at Cooper," declared some of his enthusiastic young comrades. "He's from Kentucky and he'll be the best." Actually, Cooper had never fired an Army rifle before, but somehow he finished second in his group. From Florida, Cooper went to Lowry Field, Denver, Colorado. There the Somerset soldier-in-the-making learned to repair airplane gun turrets and graduated with a diploma as a first-class turret operator.[50]

But Cooper would not work on airplanes during the war. The head of the turret school thought he was "a little too old for this service" and transferred him to the Military Police corps. Cooper went to Fort Custer, Michigan, on March 7, 1943, and was assigned to the 701st Military Police battalion. While at Fort Custer, Cooper also attended the school of military government. He had considered applying for Officer's Candidate School (OCS) while in Colorado, but the circumstances did not seem quite right. Now at Fort Custer, Cooper made his application.[51]

At Cooper's request, Herman Donovan submitted a strong letter of recommendation for the applicant. The University of Kentucky president then wrote Cooper to say that he thought the Pulaski lawyer should have been commissioned for the officer's corps in the first place. Donovan suggested that he could perhaps expedite the application with a letter to an acquaintance, General Allan Gullion, provost marshal general of the military police. Shortly thereafter, Cooper was admitted to OCS.[52]

Several other Kentuckians were in Fort Custer's OCS program, including Cooper's friend Robert Kipping of Carrollton. Subjected to a demanding pace, Cooper nonetheless graduated second out of 113 men. He was proud of the achievement, especially noteworthy because he was the oldest member of his OCS class. The newly minted second lieutenant was assigned to Fort Custer to teach military government and law, as well as the rules of land warfare. Donovan was delighted to hear that Cooper was now a "professor," writing that the classroom experience would help Cooper better "understand the problems of the University."[53]

For three months, Cooper taught at Fort Custer. Two men prominent in Kentucky Democratic politics, Joseph Leary of Frankfort and World War I veteran Robert Humphries of Hickman County, studied with him. He met numerous other people while at Fort Custer, including a young nurse fifteen years his junior. A native of Portland, Oregon, Evelyn Pfaff worked at the nearby Percy Jones Hospital. She was a widow with a daughter from her previous marriage. A brief courtship ensued. Cooper knew that he would soon be going overseas; perhaps he would never come back. Shortly before his first assignment abroad, he and Evelyn were married. She spent the remainder of the war with Cooper's family in Somerset.[54]

The American School Center at Shrivenham, Berkshire, England, was Cooper's first stop in Europe. Upon arrival in March 1944 he was made the legal officer of a detachment in the Headquarters, 15th U.S. Army Corps of the Third U.S. Army. At Shrivenham, teams of British, French, and American military personnel were being prepared for civil affairs assignments on the European continent. Selection was based on legal and diplomatic skills and on traits of character and personality. Significantly, although these jobs were usually reserved for colonels, Cooper, a mere lieutenant, was selected.[55]

Following D-Day, June 6, 1944, Cooper was sent to France with the 15th Corps. In September, he was assigned to the G-5 Section of Third Army headquarters, commanded by the brilliant and eccentric General George Smith Patton. Headquarters assigned him to represent its interests in liaison with various allies. His attachment to Third Army headquarters was engineered by a former student at Fort Custer, Colonel O. B. McEwan, who had been very impressed by Cooper as an instructor and legal scholar. When he realized that headquarters needed help, McEwan requested and obtained Cooper. The two men worked closely together over the next year and a half.[56]

During his service at Third Army headquarters, Cooper often described himself as a "batman," British slang for an orderly or messenger. In several ways army life imposed itself upon Cooper's usual routine. For the only time in his life, he succumbed to wearing a watch during this duty, since headquarters would not tolerate imprecision or tardiness. In addition to delivering messages, he had several unusual assignments. One involved an American supply trucking company that had commandeered a royal chateau and displayed "more than a casual interest" in the extensive wine cellar. Cooper was ordered to return the palatial residence to its owner. He was also directed to protect the interests of an international cartel that owned some French coal mines. Such assignments afforded him a broad exposure to Europe in wartime. Wherever the influence of the Third Army extended, Cooper was expected to travel.[57]

After American forces crossed into Germany, Cooper received another unique assignment. In an order passed down from the Supreme Allied Commander, General Dwight D. Eisenhower, he was instructed to locate Princess Mafalda, daughter of King Victor Emmanuel III of Italy. Schloss Kronberg, a castle near Frankfurt on the Main River, was his first stop. There he met Princess Margaret, the sister of Germany's World War I imperial leader, Kaiser Wilhelm II. Her son, Prince Philip of Hesse, had married Mafalda, but the princess was not there. Sadly, Princess Margaret informed Cooper that her daughter-in-law had been arrested by the *Schutzstaffel*, the dreaded SS, and taken to a concentration camp. "We think she may be in Buchenwald," Princess Margaret told the American.[58]

Around three o'clock in the afternoon of April 11, 1945, after driving south all day from near Frankfurt toward Weimar, Cooper arrived at Buchenwald. The Nazi concentration camp there had just been overrun by the Third Army. Nothing in Cooper's life had prepared him, or could have prepared him, for what he witnessed. O. B. McEwan was with Cooper as they viewed human bodies "still burning in the ovens," corpses "stacked up like cordwood," and hundreds of starving inmates with little more than "bones, skin . . . [and] filth" to their name. It was a traumatic experience for Cooper and the other American liberators, one they never forgot.[59]

After three days of interviewing inmates in the death camp, Cooper learned that Princess Mafalda, suffering the degradation of living in a camp brothel, had been killed in a bombing raid several months before. French journalist Christian Ozanne later reported that Mafalda's husband, an "ardent Nazi," had denounced his wife and sealed her fate. It is unclear what specific circumstances prompted Prince Philip to condemn his wife, but suspicion and questions of loyalty permeated the Nazi regime from top to bottom. Upon Mafalda's death, the daughter of the royal House of Savoy was buried in Weimar in an unmarked grave in a potter's field. Cooper carried the unhappy news back to Mafalda's waiting family, along with the haunting vision of organized genocide branded forever on his mind.[60]

Germany surrendered unconditionally on May 8, bringing to an end the war in Europe. Cooper was directed in August to the American zone of occupation in Munich, Bavaria. His first duty in Munich was to assist in the repatriation of thousands of displaced persons in the American zone. In the Yalta accords of February 11, the Allied powers had agreed to return prisoners incarcerated by the Axis powers. Soviet citizens were separated from other nationals and placed in isolated camps under Russian observation, as demanded by Soviet leader Josef Stalin. This was designed to prevent their exposure to Western influences and speed their return to the Soviet Union. Soviet citizens who objected to returning to their country were forced into compliance.[61]

Many displaced persons during the war years intermarried with citizens of different nations. In a callous interpretation of the Yalta agreements, the Russians decided to accept only Soviet citizens in the repatriation process. Numerous families were torn apart. "That's when I first realized," recalled Cooper, the "inhumanity" of the Russian communists. The cruelty of this Soviet policy led him to act. He approached Colonel McEwan and suggested they protest the Soviet practice to their commanding officer. Cooper and McEwan ultimately stood before Major General Hobart R. Gay, General Patton's executive officer. Gay promised to stop the Soviet policy at once. Although millions of Soviets were repatriated before December brought an official change in American policy, because of Cooper's protest thousands were spared extradition.[62]

One important mission of the occupation forces in Germany was the reorganization of the German government. German executive, legislative, and judicial institutions were ordered restructured and denazified. Recognized for his legal experience and knowledge, Cooper was assigned to reorganize the judicial system of the Bavarian state. Bavaria constituted approximately one-half of the American zone and contained a ministry of justice and 239 courts. Trial and appellate courts, in addition to denazification tribunals, were established. Cooper worked with appropriate German authorities to rebuild and democratize the Bavarian court system.[63]

One of the problems facing the occupation forces was finding the right replacements for Nazi officials. Cooper's superiors selected Wilhelm Hoegner, a former member of the German legislature (Reichstag) and anti-Nazi, to head Bavaria's judiciary. When the National Socialist regime took control of Germany, Hoegner and his wife fled to Zurich, Switzerland, where they remained until the end of the war. Cooper, recently promoted to captain, was acquainted with Hoegner. The latter regarded the American as a trusted friend and even insisted that Cooper escort his wife from Zurich to Munich. Later, Cooper brought Hoegner from his apartment house in Munich to be sworn in as Bavaria's minister president, a position roughly equivalent to an American governor. Before leaving Bavaria, he also met Dr. Hans Ehard, who later became the Federal Republic of Germany's minister of economics during the administration of Konrad Adenauer.[64]

Unlikely as it may seem, somewhere in the midst of all his duties and assignments in the Third Army, Cooper had managed to engage in Kentucky politics. In February 1945 he agreed to allow some of his friends in Pulaski County to file his candidacy for circuit judge of Kentucky's 28th Judicial District. (A new Kentucky statute provided that persons in the armed forces did not have to be present in order to file for office.) Unopposed in both the primary and the general elections, Cooper was elected. Kentucky law dictated that by January 1946 the new circuit judge be sworn into office and, aided by Kentucky's congressional representatives, particularly Senators Alben W. Barkley and A. B. "Happy" Chandler, Cooper made his way back to civilian life.[65]

For over seven years during America's deepest economic depression, Cooper had served his county with competence and compassion. His active participation in Republican politics did not interfere with his acceptance and praise of projects sponsored by Democrats. He never wavered in his loyalty to the GOP, and Cooper greatly enhanced his standing in the party during this period. But human needs always came first with Cooper. Judge Cooper welcomed federal and state programs to provide jobs and relief to the needy. Cooper would not oppose or support projects or legislation for purely partisan reasons. His spirit and intellect and his experiences at home, in school, and in public service would not permit such an attitude.

Cooper's candidacy for governor was an important experience that broadened him. Thousands of Kentuckians learned of Cooper during the race, and he learned of their special needs and interests. Cooper built an extensive political following and set in place the foundation of his statewide political network, so any future statewide race held after 1939 had a realistic promise of success.

Even more deeply ingrained in Cooper's thoughts were the experiences of World War II. As he left Bavaria and the U.S. Third Army, he could reflect on a wide range of feelings. War and its awful devastation was indelibly etched in his mind. Cooper always recalled Buchenwald with intense and visible emotion, as he did the tragedy of families of displaced persons separated by communist malevolence. Ever thereafter, Cooper was convinced that the United States must take an active role in the affairs of the world. Americans, Cooper believed, could not allow such government-sponsored cruelty and murder as he had witnessed at the hands of the Soviets at the end of World War II; Americans were the only people with the power and the means to stop it. This activist mentality, forged in the fires of the Great Depression and the Second World War, characterized Cooper the American internationalist in the postwar world.

Cooper also undertook important international work in the reorganization of Bavaria's judicial system, but in 1946 his legal expertise was needed back home. Before the year was out, unusual circumstances transported him from the circuit judge's bench to a seat in the U.S. Senate. As a senator, Cooper manifested his anti-Soviet biases in the viewpoints of a cold warrior. Cooper's views obviously had some basis in fact and experience. But much to his credit, Cooper remained open to dialogue with the communists throughout the cold war. Even in the throes of passion surrounding the Vietnam War, Cooper was an early voice of peace and reconciliation in the Senate. So many of his own experiences were recaptured in the sorrows and sufferings of the young American soldiers in Vietnam. Cooper's powerful capacity to empathize with the plight of those fighting to survive in Vietnam came from his own humane and sensitive nature that had itself fought to survive. Cooper's experiences as a young politician, as a county judge, as a gubernatorial candidate, and as a soldier all contributed to the views of the liberal Republican senator.

The foundation of Cooper's career was firmly in place by 1946. His youth in Somerset and his solid education prepared him for a career in public service. His years as Pulaski County judge in the Great Depression gave him perspective on the government's duty to supply human needs. As a soldier in World War II, Cooper gained exposure to human extremes, in war and peace, for good and evil. Standing on the cusp of world war and cold war, Cooper's worldview seemed intact; it would soon be tested by greater responsibilities.

NOTES

1. For additional information, see Richard C. Smoot, "John Sherman Cooper: The Early Years, 1901–27," in *Register of the Kentucky Historical Society*, 93 (1995):133–58.

2. John Sherman Cooper interview, May 13, 1979, John Sherman Cooper Oral History Project, Special Collections, University of Kentucky Library, 62 (hereafter JSC-OH Project); *Time*, July 5, 1954, 11–12.

3. Richard Cooper interview, March 18, 1985, JSC-OH Project; John Sherman Cooper interview, May 13, 1979, JSC-OH Project, 62–69; Don Cooper interview, March 18, 1985, JSC-OH Project; *Time*, July 5, 1954, 12; Clarice James Mitchiner, "Senator John Sherman Cooper: Consummate Statesman" (Ph.D. diss., Indiana University, 1976), 12, 17.

4. John Sherman Cooper interview, JSC-OH Project, 66–69; *Somerset Journal,* May 13, 1927; Don Cooper interview, JSC-OH Project; *Somerset Commonwealth-Journal,* February 13, 1968.

5. *Somerset Journal,* January 13, February 10, March 16, July 13, September 21, December 7, 1928; John Sherman Cooper interview, May 13, 1979, JSC-OH Project, 73–74; 1946 campaign flyer, Box 859, John Sherman Cooper Papers, Special Collections, University of Kentucky Library (hereafter Cooper Papers); Kentucky *Acts* (1928), 183–88, 481–518; Kentucky *House Journal* (1928), 462, 576, 805, 933, 2020; John Sherman Cooper interview, April 25, 1979, Oral History of Appalachia, Marshall University; James B. Skaggs, "The Rise and Fall of Flem D. Sampson, 1927–1931" (Master's thesis, Eastern Kentucky University, 1976), 54. See also Kentucky *House Journal* (1928), 40–46, 226, 576, 1506, and Fred Allen Engle, "The Free Textbook Controversy in Kentucky," *Filson Club History Quarterly,* 52 (1978):330–39.

6. Don Cooper interview, JSC-OH Project.

7. Thomas D. Clark, *Kentucky: Land of Contrast* (New York, 1968), 162; John Ed Pearce, "The Sage of Kentucky," *Louisville Courier-Journal Magazine,* May 18, 1986, 5–11; Bill Cooper, "John Sherman Cooper as County Judge: The Nurturing of a Social Conscience," an unpublished paper delivered at the Fourth Annual Eastern Kentucky University History Symposium, March 1, 1986, p. 5; *Time,* July 5, 1954, 12.

8. Robert M. Ireland, *The County in Kentucky History* (Lexington, KY, 1976), 15, 49; Don Cooper interview, JSC-OH Project; Don Cooper to the writer, September 18, 1985, in possession of the writer; Cooper, "John Sherman Cooper as County Judge," 3. Sherman Cooper and Roscoe Tartar split irrevocably in 1918 over the Republican nomination for congressman in their district. Cooper supported Don Edwards for the nomination while Tartar backed John M. Robsion. In the Republican primary for Pulaski County judge in 1921, Cooper encouraged the selection of Napier Adams over Tartar, but Tartar prevailed.

9. *Somerset Journal,* January 18, February 1, 8, 15, March 1, May 31, 1929.

10. John Sherman Cooper interview, JSC-OH Project, 78–79, 80–81.

11. Don Cooper interview, JSC-OH Project; *Somerset Journal,* July 5, 19, 1929; *Somerset Commonwealth,* July 10, 1929.

12. *Somerset Journal,* July 5, 19, 1929; *Somerset Commonwealth,* July 10, 1929. The standing committee on bridges in the Kentucky House was officially called the Public Bridges and Ferries Committee. Kentucky *House Journal* (1928), 44.

13. John Sherman Cooper interview, JSC-OH Project, 81–82; Cooper, "John Sherman Cooper as County Judge," 3; *Somerset Commonwealth,* July 10, 1929.

14. Don Cooper interview, JSC-OH Project.

15. *Somerset Journal,* August 2, 1929.

16. Ibid., August 9, 30, 1929; *Somerset Commonwealth,* August 14, 1929; Jasper B. Shannon, "The Political Process in Kentucky," *Kentucky Law Journal,* 45 (1957):436; *Somerset Journal,* August 23, 30, September 27, October 4, November 8, 15, 1929.

17. *Somerset Journal,* January 3, 10, 17, 24, 1930; Enos Swain interview, September 11, 1979, JSC-OH Project.

18. John Sherman Cooper interview, JSC-OH Project, 83; *Somerset Journal,* February 14, 21, March 7, May 23, June 6, 27, July 4, August 22, 1930. See also James C. Klotter and John W. Muir, "Boss Ben Johnson, the Highway Commission, and Kentucky Politics, 1927–1937," *Register of the Kentucky Historical Society,* 84

(1986):18–50, passim; *Somerset Journal*, July 19, 1934, September 12, October 3, November 14, 21, December 5, 1930, January 21, 1931; Pulaski Fiscal Court Order Book 4, April 24, September 13, 23, 24, 30, 1930, Pulaski County Courthouse, Somerset, KY. Twenty banks in Kentucky closed in 1930, forty in 1931, and over fifty in 1932. See also George T. Blakey, *Hard Times and New Deal in Kentucky, 1929–1936* (Lexington, KY, 1986), 1–2; David E. Hamilton, "The Causes of the Banking Panic of 1930: Another View," *Journal of Southern History*, 51 (1985):581–608; and Robert Fugate, "The BancoKentucky Story," *Filson Club History Quarterly*, 50 (1976):30–32, 44.

19. *Somerset Journal*, September 12, October 3, November 14, 21, December 5, 1930, January 21, 1931; Pulaski Fiscal Court Order Book 4, November 25, 1930.

20. *Somerset Journal*, January 24, March 13, April 10, 1931, January 13, 1932; *Somerset Commonwealth*, January 27, March 30, 1932; John Sherman Cooper interview, JSC-OH Project, 88. See also Blakey, *Hard Times and New Deal in Kentucky*, 36–38.

21. *Somerset Journal*, July 4, 1930, December 30, 1931, January 23, 1932; *Somerset Commonwealth*, July 27, September 28, 1932; Jasper B. Shannon and Ruth McQuown, *Presidential Politics in Kentucky, 1824–1948* (Lexington, KY, 1950), 36–38.

22. *Somerset Commonwealth*, May 17, June 14, 28, July 19, August 2, 9, 1933, September 21, 1932, February 1, April 5, 1933.

23. Harry R. Lynn, "State Supervision of County Finances in Kentucky, 1930–1940," in J. B. Shannon et al., *A Decade of Change in Kentucky Government and Politics* (Lexington, KY, 1943), 40–43; John Sherman Cooper interview, JSC-OH Project, 87. See also *The First Annual Report of the Second District, Works Progress Administration in Kentucky 1935–1936*, Box 4, Goodman-Paxton Papers, Special Collections, University of Kentucky Library; and Blakey, *Hard Times and New Deal in Kentucky*, 195. Much assistance on Pulaski County road construction was abetted by the Ninth Congressional District representative on the state Highway Commission, Ed Gatliff of Williamsburg; John Sherman Cooper interview, May 13, 1979, JSC-OH Project, 89–90.

24. *Somerset Journal*, May 23, 1935, January 9, February 13, 1936; *Somerset Commonwealth*, April 21, 1937.

25. *Somerset Commonwealth*, July 21, August 4, 11, 18, 25, September 15, 1937, July 13, 1938; Don Cooper interview, JSC-OH Project.

26. E. Wilson Reed to John S. Cooper, July 13, 1937, Box 916, Cooper Papers; Keen Johnson to John S. Cooper, Box 916, Cooper Papers; Frank L. McVey to John S. Cooper, Box 916, Cooper Papers; *Somerset Commonwealth*, July 13, 1938.

27. John Sherman Cooper interview, May 13, 1979, JSC-OH Project, 93–94.

28. The Democrats maintained "political referral files" as references for federal patronage distribution during the New Deal. See Hugh Heclo, *A Government of Strangers: Executive Politics in Washington* (Washington, DC, 1977), 70–71.

29. *Somerset Commonwealth*, February 15, 1939.

30. Blakey, *Hard Times and New Deal in Kentucky*, 176–180; *Who Was Who in America*, 4: *1961–1968* (Chicago, 1968), 923; *Lexington Sunday Herald-Leader*, May 7, 14, 1939; *Beattyville Enterprise*, May 11, 1939; *Glasgow Republican*, May 11, 1939; *Cincinnati Enquirer*, May 19, 1939; *Lexington Leader*, May 22, 26, 1939.

31. *Louisville Courier-Journal*, May 25, 1939.

32. Ibid., June 6, 11, 1939; *Lexington Leader*, June 12, 1939; *Mount Sterling Gazette and Kentucky Courier*, June 16, 1939; *Lexington Herald*, June 27, 1939; *Cincinnati Enquirer*, July 4, 1939.

33. *Louisville Courier-Journal*, July 1, 1939; *Lexington Leader*, July 12, 1939.

34. *Lexington Leader*, July 7, 1939; *Louisville Courier-Journal*, July 13, 1939.

35. *Lexington Leader*, July 15, 1939; John S. Cooper campaign letter, July 20, 1939, Volume 12, King Swope Papers, Special Collections, University of Kentucky Library (hereafter Swope Papers).

36. *Lexington Leader*, July 7, 12, 15, 1939; *Louisville Courier-Journal*, July 13, 16, 30, 1939. See also William N. Chambers, "Party Development and the American Mainstream," in *The American Party Systems: Stages of Political Development*, Chambers and Walter Dean Burnham, eds. (New York, 1967), 30; John S. Cooper campaign letter, July 20, 1939, Volume 12, Swope Papers.

37. *Corbin Daily Tribune*, July 17, 1939; John Sherman Cooper interview, May 13, 1979, JSC-OH Project, 95. Historical background on radio broadcasting in Kentucky may be found in Terry L. Birdwhistell, "WHAS Radio and the Development of Broadcasting in Kentucky, 1922–1932," *Register of the Kentucky Historical Society*, 79 (1981):333–53.

38. *Louisville Courier-Journal*, July 23, July 28, 1939.

39. *Lexington Herald*, July 3, 1939.

40. *Somerset Commonwealth*, July 26, 1939.

41. Ibid., February 22, 1939; *Jamestown Russell County News*, June 29, 1939; *Greensburg Record-Herald*, August 4, 1939; *Williamsburg Whitley Republican*, August 3, 1939; *Lexington Leader*, June 27, 1939; *Mount Sterling Gazette and Kentucky Courier*, June 30, 1939; *Corbin Daily Tribune*, July 6, 1939; *Maysville Public Ledger*, July 13, 1939; *Columbia Times*, July 21, 1939; *Cynthiana Log Cabin*, July 21, 1939; *Barbourville Mountain Advocate*, July 28, 1939.

42. *Louisville Courier-Journal*, July 18, 29, 1939; *Somerset Commonwealth*, August 2, 1939; *Lexington Leader*, August 3, 1939.

43. *Cincinnati Enquirer*, August 6, 1939; *Lexington Herald*, August 9, 1939; Malcolm E. Jewell, *Kentucky Votes*, 3 vols. (Lexington, KY, 1963), 2:22–23.

44. *Somerset Commonwealth*, August 9, 1939.

45. *Louisville Times*, August 9, 1939; John Sherman Cooper interview, May 13, 1979, JSC-OH Project, 93–98; George A. Joplin IV, "John Sherman Cooper: Kentucky Statesman" (Master's thesis, Columbia University School of Journalism, 1981), 11; Glenn Finch, "The Election of United States Senators in Kentucky: The Cooper Period," *Filson Club History Quarterly*, 46 (1972): 162.

46. *Somerset Commonwealth*, January 17, February 14, 28, March 20, April 3, May 1, 22, August 7, 14, September 18, October 23, November 13, 1940.

47. Richard Polenberg, *War and Society: The United States 1941–1945* (Philadelphia, 1972), 29, 132–36; *Somerset Commonwealth*, March 4, April 8, May 20, July 1, June 3, 1942.

48. *Somerset Commonwealth*, September 16, 1942; John Sherman Cooper interview, November 18, 1979, JSC-OH Project, 5–6.

49. H. L. Donovan to John Cooper, September 18, 1942; Pvt. John S. Cooper to H. L. Donovan, October 18, 1942; John S. Cooper to H. L. Donovan, November 23, 1942, all in Box 48, Herman L. Donovan Papers, Special Collections, University of Kentucky Library (hereafter Donovan Papers).

50. John Sherman Cooper interview, November 18, 1979, JSC-OH Project, 7–8.

51. Ibid.; John S. Cooper to H. L. Donovan, November 23, 1942, Box 48, Donovan Papers.

52. John S. Cooper to H. L. Donovan, April 18, 1943; Donovan recommendation "To Whom It May Concern," April 22, 1943; H. L. Donovan to John S. Cooper, April 22, 1943, all in Box 48, Donovan Papers; *Somerset Commonwealth*, February 28, 1945. Cooper entered OCS in May 1943 and was commissioned a second lieutenant in August.

53. John Sherman Cooper interview, November 18, 1979, JSC-OH Project, 9; Harry G. Story, "Remarks at Dedication in Honor of John Sherman Cooper," September 27, 1986, 1, from an extended version of those remarks in the possession of the writer; H. L. Donovan to Lt. (Professor) John S. Cooper, November 29, 1943, Box 48, Donovan Papers.

54. John Sherman Cooper interview, November 18, 1979, JSC-OH Project, 9–11; Richard Cooper interview, March 18, 1985, JSC-OH Project. Cooper's marriage to Evelyn simply did not work, and the couple in 1949 agreed to separate. Malcolm Holliday interview, January 28, 1981, JSC-OH Project. In 1955, just prior to his leaving the United States as the newly appointed ambassador to India and Nepal, Cooper married Lorraine Rowan McAdoo Shevlin, a Georgetown sophisticate twice divorced. They remained married until her death in 1985. Lorraine Cooper interview, April 28, 1980, JSC-OH Project; Susan Mary Alsop, "Tribute to a Gracious Manner: The John Sherman Coopers of Georgetown," *Architectural Digest*, February 1985, 102–9.

55. Story, "Remarks at Dedication," 1; *Somerset Commonwealth*, February 28, 1945.

56. Somerset Commonwealth, February 28, 1945; interview with Col. O. B. Mc-Ewan, Orlando, Florida, February 17, 1981, JSC-OH Project.

57. McEwan interview, JSC-OH Project; John Sherman Cooper interview, November 18, 1979, JSC-OH Project, 15; Story, "Remarks at Dedication," 2.

58. John Sherman Cooper interview, November 18, 1979, JSC–OH Project, 18–19; *New York Times*, September 24, 1952.

59. John Sherman Cooper interview, November 18, 1979, JSC-OH Project, 19–21; Robert S. Allen, *Lucky Forward: The History of Patton's Third United States Army* (New York, 1947), 375; McEwan interview, JSC-OH Project.

60. *New York Times*, April 20, 24, May 23, 1945. A detailed description of the scene at Buchenwald may be found in Earl F. Ziemke, *The U.S. Army in the Occupation of Germany 1944–1946* (Washington, DC, 1975), 237–38. General Patton's reaction is recorded in William Bancroft Mellor, *Patton: Fighting Man* (New York, 1946), 225.

61. John Sherman Cooper interview, November 18, 1979, JSC-OH Project, 24; *Somerset Commonwealth*, October 31, December 12, 1945; Mark R. Elliott, *Pawns of Yalta: Soviet Refugees and America's Role in Their Repatriation* (Urbana, 1982), 30, 40.

62. John Sherman Cooper interview, November 18, 1979, JSC-OH Project, 30–31; Elliott, *Pawns of Yalta*, 110–11, 125; U.S. Department of State, *Occupation of Germany: Policy and Programs 1945–46* (Washington, DC, 1947), 26, which states that "By June 1, 1946, [a total of] 2,834,242 displaced persons had been repatriated from the U.S. zone, with half a million yet on hand."

63. *Somerset Commonwealth*, December 12, 1945; U.S. Department of State, *Occupation of Germany*, 46, 178–81; John Sherman Cooper interview, November 18, 1979, JSC-OH Project, 31.

64. John Sherman Cooper interview, November 18, 1979, JSC-OH Project, 30–31; Wilhelm Hoegner, *Der Schwierige Aussenseiter: Erinnerungen einer Abgeordneten, Emigranten und Ministerpraesidenten* (Munich, 1959), 198, 200; John Sherman Cooper interview, November 18, 1979, JSC-OH Project, 32, 35–36.

65. *Somerset Commonwealth*, February 28, June 27, July 4, 1945; John Sherman Cooper interview, November 18, 1979, JSC-OH Project, 37–38.

9

Hollywood and the Mythic Land Apart, 1988–1991

Roger A. Fischer

For generations a debate over southern distinctiveness has raged among students of the region's history and culture, paralleling and often entwining the scholarly quest for a "central theme." The game has seldom been kind to its players. Supposedly immutable traits and trappings of southern distinctiveness, from climate to Cavalier culture, to agrarianism to white supremacy, with an occasional demeaning detour into pathology or benighted provincialism, have fallen victim to progress. And as they have been doomed by such agencies of change as a revolution in civil rights, initiatives in public health and education, television, jet planes and superhighways, rural electrification and mechanization, air conditioning, fast-food chains, an influx from the North, and a demographic upheaval of urban growth and suburban sprawl dubbed by C. Vann Woodward the "Bulldozer Revolution," a second group of players has taken the field to proclaim the impending demise of a distinctive Dixie. As Charles P. Roland noted in his wry 1981 Southern Historical Association presidential address "The Ever-Vanishing South," such Jeremiahs, too, have fared poorly as prophets, for the modern South has demonstrated an ability to absorb innovation without sacrificing its core identity. "Like China," Roland observed, "it has conquered its conquerors."[1]

Much more fortunate, and deservedly so, have been those who have rooted their arguments for southern distinctiveness in the intangible but more fertile ground of the southern mind or popular imagination. In his 1941 preface to *The Mind of the South*, Wilbur J. Cash noted a "fairly definite mental pattern, associated with a fairly definite social pattern—a complex of established relationships and habits of thought, sentiments, prejudices, standards and values, and associations of ideas." In his cogent 1960 essay "The Search for Southern Identity," Woodward argued persuasively that the one imperishable ingredient in the region's distinctive identity was its history, "the collective experience of the Southern people," a heritage sharply at odds with a national experience of abundance, success, innocence, individual liberty, and affinities for progress and abstraction. David M. Potter concurred in his 1961 essay "The Enigma of the South," suggesting that the South be studied through a distinctive folk culture of relationships and attitudes, much as Cash had argued two decades earlier. Three years later George B. Tindall, noting that the historian had a dual responsibility to serve simultaneously as "custodian of the past and keeper of the public memory," proclaimed mythology a "new frontier in Southern history."[2] Because Woodward had couched his rationale in terms of myth both national and regional, and both Cash and Potter had implied as much, it would appear that the quest for a central theme had become mainly a quest for a central buzzword. Mindset, collective historical remembrance, folk culture, and mythology are more often than not synonymous, all manifestations of a pervasive popular imagination. Subsequent scholarship has tended to corroborate and elaborate upon this thesis.

One of the finest recent southern studies is Jack Temple Kirby's *Media-Made Dixie: The South in the American Imagination* (1978, 1986), a perceptive analysis of successive southern images in American advertising, music, fiction, television, radio, motion pictures, and other facets of popular culture.[3] Kirby paid special attention to feature films, a prime source of mythical portrayals of southern life and culture for moviegoers North and South alike, from the 1915 debut of the D. W. Griffith epic *The Birth of a Nation*, through the grand 1939 romance of *Gone With the Wind*, to such modern-day classics as the 1962 reprise of Harper Lee's *To Kill a Mockingbird*. As Kirby and others have documented, Hollywood has played a major role in defining, popularizing, and perpetuating the mythic images of the South as a magnolia-scented antebellum Cavalier Eden, then a gothic New South notorious for its decadence, depravity, and violence. Then with the onset of a national preoccupation with civil rights the South has been portrayed as a region torn between a heritage of racial conflict and the promise of racial reconciliation, and finally in recent years as a benign, pastoral South strong on traditional down-home values of faith, family, and community, the Dixie of Earl Hamner, Jr.'s, "The Waltons" and Robert Benton's 1985 *Places in the Heart*.

In doing so, Hollywood has exploited a number of stock southern stereotypes, among them the dashing Cavalier blade, the winsome if fragile Dixie belle, the benighted and bigoted rustic redneck, the conniving wheeler-dealer exemplified by William Faulkner's Flem Snopes, and the sultry sexpots in such glandular 1958 "southerns" as *Baby Doll*, *God's Little Acre*, and *Cat on a Hot Tin Roof*. Equally pervasive as southern black Hollywood stereotypes, according to the perceptive analysis of Donald Bogle, have been the servile "Uncle Tom," the strong, nurturing "mammy" played to perfection by such actresses as Hattie McDaniel, Louise Beavers, and Ethel Waters, and the dim-witted "coon" persona exemplified in 1930s films by the roles of Willie Best and Stepin Fetchit.[4] None of these, to be sure, has been a Hollywood invention. With the exception of black stereotypes rooted in minstrel comedy and vaudeville, most of these stock caricatures evince southern pedigrees. Especially prominent in this process of invention has been the literary legacy of such native sons and daughters as Thomas Nelson Page, Thomas Dixon, Jr., William Faulkner, Erskine Caldwell, Margaret Mitchell, and Tennessee Williams. It has been Hollywood's role to bring stereotypes to life, and to define and perpetuate them, through memorable performances viewed by vast numbers of Americans more likely to visit the Bijou than the public library.

As Kirby has documented, Hollywood, like American popular culture in general, has been cyclical in its vogues, including an interest in the South. Recently the film industry experienced a special enthusiasm for Dixie, churning out dozens of movies featuring southern settings and themes. Among them are at least seven motion pictures released from 1988 to 1991 that merit commentary as artifacts of the genre of the South as a mythic land apart: *Mississippi Burning*, *Steel Magnolias*, *Driving Miss Daisy*, *The Long Walk Home*, *Paris Trout*, *Fried Green Tomatoes*, and *The Prince of Tides*.[5]

Set in mythical Jessup County, Mississippi, and filmed on location in Alabama and Mississippi, Allen Parker's 1988 Orion Pictures film *Mississippi Burning* details FBI efforts to bring to justice the killers of three young civil rights workers during the Freedom Summer, 1964. Agents Rupert Anderson (Gene Hackman), native son and former sheriff, and his naive, by-the-book supervisor (Willem Dafoe) are stymied by a white code of silence and the reticence of terrified blacks until a sadistic beating of a deputy's wife friendly to Anderson unleashes him to out-klan the Klan at violence and intimidation to bring to the bar of justice the hooded executioners. Although this final derring-do is purely fictional—the bodies were in fact found and culprits caught through the less-heroic incentive of lavish bribery—the bulk of the film seeks to serve as a quasi-documentary of historical events. The victims are clearly Michael Schwerner, James Chaney, and Andrew Goodman; the town is Philadelphia, Mississippi; and Jessup County is Neshoba; porcine Sheriff Ray Stuckey and Deputy Clinton Pell are Neshoba lawmen Lawrence Rainey and Cecil Price; and KKK kingpin Clayton Townley is the White Knights' Grand Wizard Sam Bowers. From the framework of events and an anecdotal Alabama castration, it seems likely that William Bradford Huie's cogent narrative *Three Lives for Mississippi* provided a primer for the film.

Despite such purported fealty to fact, *Mississippi Burning* is a fundamentally dishonest film reminiscent of the most tawdry exploitation movies inspired by the civil rights conflicts of the 1960s, the likes of Otto Preminger's 1963 *The Cardinal* and 1967 *Hurry Sundown*. Its examples of Klan violence and intimidation—sadistic beatings; the torching and firebombing of black shanties, churches, a cattle barn and a freedom house; an attempted lynching; the ubiquitous fiery cross—indeed represent the ugly turmoil of the 1960s. But their compression into a time span of a few weeks in a single Mississippi community constitutes manipulative sensationalism at best. Moreover, eleven episodes of Klan thuggery occur almost precisely by formula at nine-minute intervals through the first hour and a half of the movie. This suggests that the white folks of Jessup did little else but kill, maim, torch, terrorize, and ignite fiery crosses, and that their black neighbors were hopelessly retarded for remaining to endure the abuse rather than fleeing en masse to safer sanctuaries! Jessup blacks are portrayed throughout as single-dimensional studies in victimology and Jessup whites as benighted cretins incapable of conscience, an impression reinforced at regular intervals by staged sequences of television interviews.

Parker's vision of 1960s Mississippi is unremittingly bleak, little more than a Gothic backdrop for Hackman's "Dirty Harry" routine of scrotum squeezing, assault, and threats of lynching, castration, and throat-slashing. Perhaps the only manifestation of a positive southern attribute in the film is the stoic resolve of the battered Mrs. Pell to stay in Jessup: "This is my home—born here, probably die here. Things'll work out. There's enough good people here who know what I did was right, and enough ladies who like the way I fix their hair." If not exactly a ringing hosanna to a love of place, it does resonate with a southerner's stubborn refusal to embrace the open road as an easy answer to hard times. At film's end director Parker attempts to evoke another praiseworthy southern cliché, that of racial reconciliation. As black gospel singer Lannie Spann McBride soulfully performs the spiritual "Walk On by Faith" in the ruins of a firebombed church, the camera slowly pans a mixed crowd of blacks interspersed with a few white women and children. After two hours of nonstop white depravity and black victimization, the scene rings fundamentally false.

The 1989 Herbert Ross Tri-Star film *Steel Magnolias*, scripted by Alabama playwright Robert Harling from his 1987 Broadway play,[6] was filmed in Natchitoches, Louisiana, and set in the mythical Louisiana town of Chinquapin. It features the sorority of regulars at Truvy's Beauty Spot, played by Sally Field, Julia Roberts, Dolly Parton, Daryl Hannah, Olympia Dukakis, and Shirley MacLaine. The plot centers on the wedding, ill-advised pregnancy, subsequent kidney failure, organ transplant, and eventual death of young Shelby Eatenton (Roberts) and a support network of her mother (Field) and the women down at Truvy's. The film is burdened by such cloying lines as "That which does not kill us makes us stronger" and a heavy-handed symbolic structure of an Easter wedding, a Christmas disclosure of pregnancy, Independence Day birthing, death at Halloween (in much of Louisiana All Souls, a day of the dead), and at film's end an Easter baby to be christened Shelby regardless of gender. Soap opera, pure and simple, it succeeds as film only by virtue of earthy humor, tart dialogue ("If you can't say something nice about somebody, come sit next to me"), and splendid performances by Dukakis as the town matriarch, MacLaine as town curmudgeon, and Tom Skerritt as Drum Eatenton.

Steel Magnolias is confusing as a Louisiana film. References to nearby Shreveport, Monroe, and Alexandria serve to center Chinquapin in the northwestern part of the state, consistent with its filming in Natchitoches. Yet in Baptist North Louisiana, Cajun dishes and dancing are prominent and the script abounds with the surnames of Acadiana—Belcher, Dupuy, Boudreaux, Latcherie, Marmillion, and Arceneaux, the latter two mispronounced. A Latcherie wedding takes place in a Presbyterian church where Mmes. Boudreaux and Belcher worship on Sunday mornings. Accents ring false to Louisiana, upcountry or Cajun. Parton's upland Tennessee twang belies a reference to her Truvy's having lived her whole life in Chinquapin. Blacks are all but invisible in the community, even as caterers. Moreover, the film makes little effort to relate to contemporary Louisiana. As critic Julius Novick observed, *Magnolias* ignores almost altogether the oil boom and bust of such critical import to the recent Louisiana experience.[7]

Steel Magnolias is even more troublesome as a southern film. Its title heralds a frontal assault on the myth of the southern woman as a frail flower of ethereal loveliness, whose allure is her dependence on strong male protectors. This is informed by the defining scene in the cemetery, when a grieving Field relates to her friends, "We turned off the machines. Drum left. He couldn't take it. Jackson left. I find it amusin'. Men are supposed to be made out of steel or something. But I just sat there. I just held Shelby's hand." A problem with this is that unlike the play, the film has just featured a hospital scene in which Jackson signed the forms to turn off life support and neither he nor Drum left until Shelby's monitor had flat-lined. A more serious problem is that Harling's demythologizing constitutes egregious windmill tilting, for the concept of the strong southern woman, and in particular the strong southern matriarch, has long been accepted almost universally in the region. It is doubtful that even in Victorian days the romances exalting the cult of chivalry ever claimed that many true believers in feminine frailty. That it could do so in 1989 is untenable.

An even more popular 1989 movie adapted from the stage was Bruce Beresford's Warner Brothers film *Driving Miss Daisy*, adapted by Alfred Uhry from his Broadway play,[8] cast in Atlanta from 1948 to 1973, and filmed there. It stars Jessica Tandy as Jewish dowager Daisy Werthan and Morgan Freeman as her longtime chauffeur and confidant Hoke Colburn. The plot focuses on the evolving relationship between Daisy and Hoke from the day that he becomes her retainer through a final visit by Hoke to Daisy in a nursing home a quarter-century later. A resentful Daisy concedes only grudgingly to having a driver ("Only took six days," Hoke muses, "same time it took the Lord to make the world.") As decades pass, they do grow closer, but even at age seventy Hoke is forced to assert his right to "make water" by the roadside on a trip to Mobile. Their bond, a mixture of fondness for and tolerance of each other, creates a tension both racial and personal with which neither is comfortable, exemplified by her halfway invitation to come with her to hear Martin Luther King, Jr., his prideful rebuff, and her attendance alone while he stands guard over the car. As the film nears its end, she confides, "Hoke, you're my best friend—really, you are."

Miss Daisy was celebrated for its poignant portrayal of friendship and racial reconciliation. Yet this bond strikes me as a relationship perpetually in a stage of becoming. Even in the nursing home finale, as Daisy chats amiably with Hoke and for once inquires into his family, her thoughts and words betray a consuming preoccupation with herself. This becomes so tedious that the audience ages more swiftly in its seats than does Miss Daisy on the screen! Her triumph is that of survival over time, but her life seems too easy, too empty, too unexamined for her to attain heroic stature. Freeman's Hoke is played with consummate skill by a talented actor, but the role does not allow him to transcend or even really test his status as a menial, as did such memorable black portrayals as Danny Glover's Mose in *Places in the Heart* or Hattie McDaniel's legendary Mammy in *Gone With the Wind*.

Perhaps such criticism is unfair. Atlanta is a Deep South city and was even more so during the years following World War II. In such a traditional southern setting, interracial friendships would be difficult and more often than not tentative, especially those involving a white woman and a black man. For both, breaching barriers would be an uneasy proposition. For Uhry, effusive camaraderie would have been a kiss of death for contextual integrity. And yet opportunities are ignored. A case in point is the evening of the funeral of Daisy's cook Idella (Esther Rolle). Returning home, Hoke and Daisy together cook a supper of fried chicken, Idella's favorite. Hoke serves Daisy in the formal dining room and repairs to the kitchen to eat alone. Both are grieving; both really need the companionship of a friend. For Daisy to invite Hoke to join her in the dining room would have violated the folkways of a segregated South and would have made Hoke profoundly uncomfortable. But had she instead picked up her plate and joined Hoke at the kitchen table, she would have simply been conforming to an old southern tradition of the kitchen as common ground for both races, the one integrated room in a segregated household.[9] Such a gesture, surely not alien to a playwright born and reared in Atlanta, would have made a more convincing affirmation of racial reconciliation than any dialogue imaginable.

A compelling contrast in clarity on this theme is provided by the 1991 Richard Pearce New Visions movie *The Long Walk Home*, filmed in Montgomery and set there during the 1955–1956 bus boycott. Featured are Sissy Spacek as affluent Junior League housewife Miriam Thompson and

Whoopi Goldberg as Thompson maid Odessa Cotter. The plot develops around Odessa's decision to honor the boycott by walking nine miles to her job at the Thompsons' and back again, the quiet resolve of her supportive family, a growing racial animus among the Thompsons as the boycott drags on and Montgomery blacks stand firm, and Miriam's aborning social conscience and sense of ethical resolve. She begins by driving Odessa to work two market mornings a week, mainly for her own personal convenience. On Christmas Odessa walks nine miles to work; endures an earful of obnoxious racist table talk from Miriam's husband Norman, kid brother Tucker, and Mama Thompson as she serves them dinner; then plods nine miles home on bloody feet, where her own family surprises her with a new coat and comfortable walking shoes. The contrast is understated but devastating. As Norman and Tucker overcome their patrician disdain for redneck social inferiors and become involved in the White Citizens' Council, Miriam gradually awakens to larger moral issues. An ultimatum from Norman to stop driving Odessa on market mornings pushes Miriam to her moment of truth, despite Odessa's warning, "Miz Thompson, once you step over there, I don't know that you can ever step back." The next morning Miriam begins work driving for the boycott car pool.

At film's end Norman joins Tucker in a council raid on a car-pool parking lot and is startled to find his wife, young daughter, and maid among the frightened captives, but is powerless to get them to safety as the bigots surround the car-poolers and begin to chant "walk, nigger, walk." Odessa steps forward into the fury of the mob, then another maid, and then another. They join hands and begin to sing the hymn "Walking Through Jesus," at first hesitantly but steadily building in strength and volume. Then Miriam and little Mary Catherine step forward, clasp hands with Odessa, and join in the singing and the sisterhood as the suddenly cowed and confused mob parts like the waters for Moses. Melodramatic in the telling, this constitutes grand theatre in the viewing.

The Long Walk Home attracted little attention, but it may be the finest southern film since *To Kill a Mockingbird*, a triumph of discipline, economy, and historical integrity. Reenactments of 1950s black Baptist worship services resonate with authenticity and evoke the emotional context of a black community with blistered feet but unbending resolve. No part is played badly. Dylan Baker as the whining, effete snob elitist Tucker Thompson does well in a difficult role that does much to make the film revolutionary in debunking a venerable Hollywood cliché. The benighted, bigoted rural or small-town redneck has been so standard a fixture in southern films that many worthy character actors have earned steady livings playing such roles, while the country-club racism exemplified by the Thompsons and their friends has gone largely unexamined. Goldberg's performance as Odessa is understated and tautly disciplined. Spacek is convincing as Miriam, her call to conscience reminiscent of Faulkner's 1948 plea in

Intruder in the Dust that the white South must refuse to bear injustice and outrage to free itself from the prison of the past.

If *The Long Walk Home* evokes the mature Faulkner, the 1991 Steven Gyllenhaal film from 20th-Century Fox *Paris Trout* resembles a burlesque of unrestrained early Faulkner. Adapted by Pete Dexter from his 1988 National Book Award novel,[10] it stars Dennis Hopper in the title role and Barbara Hershey as his abused wife Hanna, with Ed Harris as Harry Seagraves, his lawyer and her paramour. The setting is mythical Cotton Point, Ether County, Georgia, ca. 1950. The plot centers on the manic malevolence of Paris Trout, a small-town entrepreneur who owns a general store, sells used cars, and serves as moneylender to Ether County blacks. He sells a car to a young black man and tacks on a steep insurance premium, but after an accident refuses to honor the insurance, prompting the young man to void the deal and Paris to gain vengeance by shooting and mortally wounding the lad's little sister. After Hanna visits the dying girl in the town infirmary, Paris nearly drowns his wife in the bathtub, then after she defies him and attends the funeral, he sodomizes her with a soda bottle as he taunts, "Tell *that* to the niggers!," leaving her dripping blood to tend to customers downstairs. Hanna moves into a separate bedroom and then to a hotel. She drifts into a torrid affair with Seagraves, who is defending Paris on a charge of manslaughter. He is sentenced to a token prison term, wins his freedom by bribing a judge, but returns home to Cotton Point a despised pariah. He eventually shoots his ancient mother, then Seagraves, then himself.

Despite the manic genius of Dennis Hopper, *Paris Trout* is a terrible film and unnecessarily so. Dexter's novel, perhaps somewhat excessive in its gothic southern savagery, is nevertheless a promising point of departure, a good story well told by a writer with Georgia roots, strong in character development and masterful in dialects black and white alike and in capturing the ethos of small-town Georgia life. Dexter's screenplay defies rational explanation, for he excised most of what made his novel a literary success and a perceptive commentary on southern life. Black characters are compressed and sanitized of all shortcomings and human interest, rendering them little more than politically correct studies in victimology. Seagraves, as much as Paris a protagonist in the novel, is reduced in the film to an ancillary role, transformed from an adulterer into a widower, and shorn of a complex moral ambivalence crucial as a key to that of the town. A prosecutor exemplifying community decency disappears altogether, as do vignettes of Cotton Point life unrelated to Paris. Gone is the sense of a town torn between racial imperative and Christian compassion, a place where blacks were children of a lesser god but a god nonetheless, where they not only knew their "place" but that they had one. In the film Cotton Point retains a shred of decency only because it ostracizes Paris and sentences him to a token prison term for a cold-blooded execution. In the novel Paris succeeds primarily as a catalyst for a town to come to terms with its core values, but Hopper's character lacks the depth and dimensions to carry a full-length film.

Had Paris been so foolish as to travel over to Whistle Stop, Alabama, he might have ended up barbecued and eaten, a fate which befalls evil Frank Bennett in Jon Avnet's 1991 Universal Pictures film *Fried Green Tomatoes*, adapted by Fannie Flagg and Carol Sobieski from Flagg's 1987 novel *Fried Green Tomatoes at the Whistle Stop Cafe*.[11] Set in the mythical hamlet of Whistle Stop just east of Birmingham and filmed in Juliette, Georgia, it features Kathy Bates as the dowdy forty-something Evelyn Couch, Jessica Tandy as octogenarian story-teller Ninny Threadgoode, Mary Stuart Masterson as her tomboyish sister-in-law Idgie, and Mary-Louise Parker as Idgie's "best friend" Ruth Jamison. A two-tiered plot details Evelyn's attempts to make something of her life, but mainly Ninny's flashback narratives of the Threadgoodes of Whistle Stop, the loving relationship between Idgie and Ruth, and the hamlet's main landmark, their Whistle Stop Cafe, which featured barbecue and fried green tomatoes. Ninny and Evelyn strike up an acquaintance at a Birmingham nursing home and Ninny begins a series of Sunday sagas of life in Whistle Stop, including the killing, dismemberment, and barbecuing of Ruth's abusive husband Frank. In a twist worthy of Alfred Hitchcock, the evidence is then eaten by Georgia lawman Curtis Smoote, played superbly by Raynor Schiene as a cross between Barney Fife and a ferret! Idgie later stands trial, but is exonerated by an alibi sworn by a Whistle Stop preacher on a leather-bound copy of *Moby Dick*. Ruth succumbs to cancer and the Whistle Stop Cafe never reopens, which with the end of railroad passenger travel kills the hamlet and ends Ninny's narrative.

Ninny eventually comes to live in the nursing home, where her example so inspires Evelyn that the younger woman masters aerobics and assertiveness training and acquires a new fantasy identity as "Towanda the Avenger," bane of young sex kittens who try to cheat her out of a parking space at the local Winn Dixie. Avnet's film imposes a sense of structural discipline on Flagg's novel and mutes adroitly its lesbian overlay[12] and cloying sentimentality. The result is an evening of enjoyable theater, an ingenious story well told. Outrageous but engaging in its excesses of southern gothic burlesque, blended in with pastoral evocations of sense of family and place, it mixes a Faulkner-Caldwell-Tennessee Williams tradition of eccentricity with the wholesomeness of "The Waltons." And yet it smacks somehow of insincerity, like a pair of spit-shined shoes of shoddy patent leather, with its too-slick-by-half portrayals of southern women as nurturing goddesses, blacks as objects, and most white men as reptilian slime or contemptuous cretins.

Much more ambitious as an exploration into southern myth is the 1991 Columbia film *The Prince of Tides*, produced and directed by Barbra Streisand and starring her as psychiatrist Susan Lowenstein, filmed and set in Manhattan and the South Carolina Sea Islands. Adapted from Pat Conroy's sprawling, immensely popular 1986 novel[13] by Conroy and Becky Johnston, *Prince of Tides* also stars Nick Nolte as Tom Wingo, an out-of-work football coach and English teacher recovering from a mental breakdown over the death of brother Luke and suicide attempts of twin sister Savannah. After Tom is summoned to New York to assist Savannah's psychiatrist, a mutual loathing turns slowly to respect and then romance. The plot centers on a war of cultures between Lowenstein's Big Apple and Jewishness and Tom's Colleton tidal marshes, as well as his flashback childhood narratives. In these flashbacks warm memories of an island Eden clash with those of a shrimper father more likely to express his feelings with fists than hugs, Tom's manipulative mother Lila, and one night of graphic terror when Lila and Savannah are raped and Tom sodomized by escaped convicts whom they then kill and, at Lila's behest, bury with no trace so that reputations will remain unsullied!

This is, of course, the stuff of the most dreadful Dixie melodrama—rapine lust, redneck insensitivity, a bitch-goddess southern matriarch worthy of the finest talents of a Joan Crawford or a Bette Davis, a frail flower of the poetic muse driven to self-destruction by these forces, and in dead brother Luke the last unreconstructed Confederate rebel waging a solitary, suicidal war to preserve his family's island from despoilation as site of a new power plant. And juggling all these clichés is Tom Wingo, professional southerner, at times less a protagonist than a referee between warring Dixie mythologies. In large part, *Prince of Tides* transcends melodrama because of its conscious use of stereotypes and its clever interplay between them. Perhaps the most self-consciously southern movie ever made, this film would have been even more so had it focused on the more heroic figure of Luke, Savannah's original "prince of tides," and his one-man crusade against progress and materialism, although to have done so would have sacrificed a necessary balance between mythologies and stereotypes.

Thus Streisand essentially gambled the integrity of the film on the believability of Nolte's Tom Wingo in a complex role mandating at least three distinct levels of southernness, each demanding different mindsets, body language, and degrees of accent. At home he is relaxed and speaks with a rather generic southern softness in accent. In New York he grows defensive, his herky-jerky drawl greatly exaggerated and mannerisms self-deprecating. Then in the swank West Side townhouse of Lowenstein and violinist Herbert Woodruff, at a dinner party arranged by the sadistic virtuoso to humiliate Tom as a backwoods Dixie bumpkin for the sin of coaching their son Bernard in the rudiments of football, Tom evolves into joyous self-parody. A corrosively mocking rendition of "Dixie" prompts him to drawl, "Damn it all, Herb, that Mozart sure cranked out some snappy tunes." Finally, Woodruff's bullying of his wife prompts Wingo to leave the table, bellow out from the balcony, "Yoo hoo, Herbert, southern boy's got ahold of yo' fiddle," and baton-twirl the Stradivarius over the railing as he coaxes abject apologies with such endearments as "you possum-breath cocksucker." Tom and Lowenstein then embark on a passionate love affair that ends when Tom's transcending southern love of place decrees his return to the Carolina Sea Islands and his family.

American Spectator critic James Bowman, one of the most incisive authorities alive on American film, has described Nolte's character as "a jerk" for providing a stereotype trumped by the Hollywood feminist cliché of the "sensitive man learning to get in touch with his feelings."[14] I disagree. Bowman's critique fits superbly Richard Gere's portrayal of the protagonist in the dreadful 1993 Warner Brothers film *Sommersby*, but not Nolte's Tom Wingo, a role reconciling so many mythic southern stereotypes. Unlike Savannah, Tom weighs the horrors of their childhood against the better times, discovers that "in families there are no crimes beyond forgiveness," and returns home to take up his life and be a better husband and father than his own father had been. This film may well accomplish the most ambitious reconciliation of southern mythologies and stereotypes yet attempted.

Jack Temple Kirby's task in *Media-Made Dixie* was simplified somewhat by the convenience with which decades conformed to prevailing archetypes, be they the antebellum wonderland of cavaliers and crinoline, Reconstruction travails of demonic forces unleashed upon a prostrate South, the gothic excesses of a degenerate New South, the clashing metaphors of southern savagery and promises of an interracial Eden during the civil rights era, or the benign, pastoral South of "The Waltons" and *Places in the Heart*. But recently, American media culture, Hollywood in particular, has rebelled against such niceties of category and has presented a veritable Tower of Babel in southern mythologies. Moviegoers have encountered the visceral excesses of *Paris Trout*, the neoabolitionist Dixie-bashing of *Mississippi Burning*, the mythological sleight-of-hand of *The Prince of Tides*, and the nurturing feminism of *Steel Magnolias* and *Fried Green Tomatoes*. In the tradition of *In the Heat of the Night* (1967) and *To Kill a Mockingbird*, arguably the best of the civil-rights era southern films, *Driving Miss Daisy* and *The Long Walk Home* carried on the theme of a reconciliation of the races. Only *Fried Green Tomatoes* and *The Prince of Tides* paid even marginal obeisance to the image of the pastoral South so prominent in media culture during the 1970s and early 1980s.

Out of this confusion of categories two salient themes emerge as worthy of analysis. The first is the prevalence of feminist ideology and strong, sympathetic female characters—Mrs. Pell, the sisterhood of *Steel Magnolias*, Miss Daisy, Miriam Thompson, Odessa Cotter, Hanna Trout, Evelyn Couch, Idgie, Ruth Jamison, Miss Ninny. In all of these films, only Kate Nelligan's manipulative Lila Wingo in *Prince of Tides* suggests negative qualities in a substantive southern female character, while a great majority of white male roles exemplify at best "good ole boy" irresponsibility and insensitivity and at worst the demonic evil of a Mississippi klansman, Paris Trout, or Frank Bennett. This gender exploitation is especially prevalent in *Fried Green Tomatoes* and *Paris Trout*, both made in 1991, concurrent with the dreadful but immensely popular Susan Sarandon-Geena Davis feminist classic *Thelma and Louise*. Even in recent southerns that rise above such shrill man-bashing, the most decent, likable male protagonists—Nolte's Tom Wingo in *Prince of Tides* and Tom Skerritt's Drum Eatenton in *Steel Magnolias*—fall woefully short of the heroic stature of Clark Gable's Rhett Butler or Gregory Peck's Atticus Finch. Indeed, a review of recent Hollywood southerns entitled "Thelma and Louise do Dixie" would not be wholly inappropriate.

A second theme, perhaps more troublesome in light of recent American social history, is Hollywood's continuing preoccupation with a bygone era of southern racial conflict. If the South was for most of its troubled past the land of racial exploitation, Jim Crow, and Judge Lynch, it was also the one region where the two races could claim an element of symbiosis and where, once the dust had settled, a federal mandate has evolved into uneasy but essentially honest cultural accommodation.[15] For a generation most southerners, black and white alike, have experienced racial turmoil primarily via television news reports from such troublespots as South Boston and south-central Los Angeles. But still, with few exceptions, when American movie-goers partake vicariously of such conflict, the background remains long on live oaks and magnolias. One cannot complain of such a theme in *The Long Walk Home*, for its context was the historical reality of a racially polarizing boycott. This might be said of *Mississippi Burning* as well, but excesses of compression and a complete absence of countervailing white decency smack of exploitative sensationalism, as does the Pete Dexter adaptation of *Paris Trout* from novel to screenplay. A Klan episode in *Driving Miss Daisy* appears ancillary at best, and in *Fried Green Tomatoes* it is difficult to attribute honest motivation to the need to portray Frank Bennett fomenting evil in Whistle Stop in the Klan attire of his Valdosta klavern 250 miles distant.

Five of these seven films represent the handiwork of playwrights and novelists with southern roots, wholly or partially—Fannie Flagg and Robert Harling of Alabama, Alfred Uhry and Pete Dexter of Georgia, Pat Conroy of South Carolina. So this confusion of mythic categories cannot be sloughed off on the flawed perception of outsiders. And it must be noted that the least exploitative film of the group, *The Long Walk Home*, was one of two with no apparent southern roots, as was *Mississippi Burning*, surely the most exploitative and most condescending to the South. Perhaps worthy of note is that the two most racially exploitative of the films with southern pedigrees, *Paris Trout* and *Fried Green Tomatoes*, have flowed from the imaginations of novelists or screenwriters who have not lived in the South during the years of reconciliation since the 1960s. Even so, this vision of a troubled region divided along lines of race and gender cannot be dismissed as pure invention from the minds of unsympathetic outsiders.

Two possible explanations spring to mind, not mutually exclusive. We are all to some extent prisoners of our pasts, and as Vann Woodward and others have argued, the peculiarities of southern history have gone far to perpetuate an ongoing distinctive southern identity. Like the scriptural admonition on the sins of the fathers, collective remembrance cannot be cleansed in a single generation, especially if the primary cleansing agent is the relative misfortune of distant communities. It is likely that the Banquo's ghost of the southern past will continue to haunt the creative talents of its future for years to come. Nonetheless, it is equally probable that the troubled tenor of recent southern films owes much to a temptation among these myth makers to seek national acclaim and the almighty dollar by pandering to widespread perceptions of the South, however outmoded by reality. Motion pictures often succeed through innovation, but these break-throughs are usually technological—sound, color, animation, special effects—challenges to the senses rather than to the intellect. From such recent box-office successes as *Mississippi Burning* and *Fried Green Tomatoes*, it seems clear that Hollywood remains receptive to excess and eccentricity in its southerns, that in theaters if not in reality the South is destined for years to come to live on as a mythic land apart.

NOTES

1. Charles P. Roland, "The Ever-Vanishing South," *Journal of Southern History*, 48 (1982):3–20. For a more detailed exploration of this phenomenon, see Carl N. Degler, *Place over Time: The Continuity of Southern Distinctiveness* (Baton Rouge, 1977).

2. Wilbur J. Cash, *The Mind of the South* (New York, 1941), vii–viii; C. Vann Woodward, *The Burden of Southern History* (Baton Rouge, 1960), 3–25; David M. Potter, "The Enigma of the South," *Yale Review*, 51 (Autumn 1961):142–51; George B. Tindall, "Mythology: A New Frontier in Southern History," in *The Idea of the South: Pursuit of a Central Theme*, Frank E. Vandiver, ed. (Chicago, 1964), 1–15. A useful anthology of explorations of this theme is Patrick Gerster and Nicholas Cords, ed., *Myth and Southern History*, 2d ed. (Urbana, 1989).

3. Jack Temple Kirby, *Media-Made Dixie: The South in the American Imagination* (Baton Rouge, 1978).

4. Donald Bogle, *Toms, Coons, Mulattoes, Mammies, and Bucks: An Interpretive History of Blacks in American Film*, rev. ed. (New York, 1989). Excellent in detailing the origins of such stereotypes is Joseph Boskin, *Sambo: The Rise and Demise of an American Jester* (New York, 1986).

5. My process of selection is purely arbitrary. I have excluded such local genre films as *The Big Easy* (1987) and *Texasville* (1990) because their focus was New Orleans or Texas and not comprehensively southern, the romances *Mississippi Masala* (1991) and *Sommersby* (1993) because they are dreadful films seen by few moviegoers, the 1990 science-fiction fantasy *Edward Scissorhands* and 1991 Martin Scorcese remake of the 1962 suspense classic *Cape Fear* because they attempt no real exploitation of southern myth or analysis of southern culture, and such comedies

as *Fletch Lives* (1989) and *My Cousin Vinny* (1992) because it is difficult to regard seriously as cultural commentary slapstick comedies intended purely for laughs. For a contrary viewpoint on the latter, see Ethelyn G. Orso's impassioned critique of the Chevy Chase film *Fletch Lives* as a distortion of Cajun life and culture in "Paradise Lost: Louisiana as a Microcosm of the South in Fictional and Documentary Films," in Karl G. Heider, ed., *Images of the South: Constructing a Regional Culture on Film and Video* (Athens, 1993), 9–23.

6. Robert Harling, *Steel Magnolias* (New York, 1988). The play opened at the WPA Theater in New York on March 22, 1987, and on June 19, 1987, continued its run of more than two years at the nearby Lucille Lortel Theatre.

7. Julius Novick, "Southern Comfort," *The Village Voice*, April 7, 1987.

8. Alfred Uhry, *Driving Miss Daisy* (New York, 1987). The play featured Dana Ivey as Daisy and Morgan Freeman as Hoke and opened at Playwrights' Horizons in New York on April 15, 1987.

9. An informed contrast is provided in Stanley Kramer's 1953 film adaptation of Carson McCullers' *The Member of the Wedding*.

10. Pete Dexter, *Paris Trout* (New York, 1988).

11. Fannie Flagg, *Fried Green Tomatoes at the Whistle Stop Cafe* (New York, 1987).

12. Critic Jack Butler had written of Flagg's novel, "The core of the story is the unusual love affair between Idgie and Ruth, rendered with exactitude and delicacy, and with just the balance of clarity and reticence that would have made it acceptable in that time and place." *New York Times Book Review*, October 18, 1987, 14.

13. Pat Conroy, *The Prince of Tides* (Boston, 1986).

14. James Bowman to author, September 16, 1993.

15. An outstanding exploration of this theme is David R. Goldfield, *Black, White, and Southern: Race Relations and Southern Culture, 1940 to the Present* (Baton Rouge, 1990). Even more imaginative is the intriguing novel of Mississippian John Grisham, *A Time to Kill* (New York, 1989).

Selected Bibliography of Charles Pierce Roland

THESES

"Louisiana Sugar Plantations During the Civil War." M.A. thesis, Louisiana State University, 1948.
"Louisiana Sugar Plantations During the Civil War." Ph.D. diss., Louisiana State University, 1951.

BOOKS

Louisiana Sugar Plantations During the American Civil War. Leiden, The Netherlands: E. J. Brill, 1957.
The Confederacy. Chicago: University of Chicago Press, 1960.
Albert Sidney Johnston: Soldier of Three Republics. Austin: University of Texas Press, 1964 (paperback reprint, 1987).
Editor. Richard Taylor, *Destruction and Reconstruction: Personal Experiences of the Late War*. Waltham, MA: Blaisdell Publishing Company, 1968.
A History of the South (with Francis Butler Simkins). New York: Alfred A. Knopf, 1972.
The Improbable Era: The South Since World War II. Lexington: University Press of Kentucky, 1975.
An American Iliad: The Story of the Civil War. Lexington: University Press of Kentucky, 1991 (also published by McGraw-Hill, 1991).
Reflections on Lee: A Historian's Assessment. Mechanicsburg, PA: Stackpole, 1995.

ARTICLES

"Difficulties of Civil War Sugar Planting in Louisiana." *Louisiana Historical Quarterly*, 38 (October 1955):40–62.

"Albert Sidney Johnston and the Loss of Forts Henry and Donelson." *Journal of Southern History*, 23 (February 1957): 45–69.

"Albert Sidney Johnston and the Shiloh Campaign." *Civil War History*, 4 (December 1958):355–82.

Foreword to Francis Butler Simkins, *The Everlasting South*. Baton Rouge: Louisiana State University Press, 1963, pp. vii–x.

"The Generalship of Robert E. Lee." In *Grant, Lee, Lincoln, and the Radicals*, Grady McWhiney, ed. Evanston: Northwestern University Press, 1964, pp. 31–71 (paper reprint, Harper and Row, 1966).

"The South, America's Will-o'-the-Wisp Eden." *Louisiana History*, 11 (Spring 1970):101–19. Reprinted in *Myth and Southern History, Volume Two: The New South*, Patrick Gerster and Nicholas Cords, eds. Chicago: Rand McNally, 1974, pp. 183–97.

"Louisiana and Secession." *Louisiana History*, 19 (Fall 1978): 389–99.

"Historiography of Confederacy on the Home Front" and "Fts. Henry and Donelson Campaign." In *The Encyclopedia of Southern History*, David C. Roller and Robert W. Twyman, eds. Baton Rouge: Louisiana State University Press, 1979, pp. 266, 479–80.

"The Ever-Vanishing South." *Journal of Southern History*, 48 (February 1982):3–20.

"The South of the Agrarians." In *A Band of Prophets: The Vanderbilt Agrarians After Fifty Years*, William C. Havard and Walter Sullivan, eds. Baton Rouge: Louisiana State University Press, 1982, pp. 19–40.

"Sun Belt Prosperity and Urban Growth." In *Interpreting Southern History: Historiographical Essays in Honor of Sanford W. Higginbotham*, John B. Boles and Evelyn Thomas Nolen, eds. Baton Rouge: Louisiana State University Press, 1987, pp. 434–53.

"Gang System." In *Dictionary of Afro-American Slavery*, Randall M. Miller and John David Smith, eds. Westport, CT: Greenwood Press, 1988, pp. 283–84.

"Albert Sidney Johnston" and "Otis Arnold Singletary, Jr." In *The Kentucky Encyclopedia*, John E. Kleber, ed. Lexington: University Press of Kentucky, 1992, pp. 476–77, 823–24.

"Albert Sidney Johnston." In *Encyclopedia of the Confederacy*, 4 vols., Richard N. Current, ed. New York: Simon & Schuster, 1993, 2:858.

BOOK REVIEWS

Creole City: Its Past and Its People, by Edward Larocque Tinker. *Mississippi Valley Historical Review*, 41 (June 1954):163–64.

A Southern Reader, by Willard Thorpe. *Journal of Southern History*, 22 (February 1956):99–100.

Gray Ghosts and Rebel Raiders, by Virgil Carrington Jones. *Journal of Southern History*, 23 (May 1957):245–46.

Huey Long's Louisiana: State Politics, 1920–1952, by Allan P. Sinder. *Mississippi Valley Historical Review*, 44 (June 1957):167–68.

Confederate Engineers, by James L. Nichols. *Journal of Southern History*, 24 (May 1958):381–82.

Generals in Gray: Lives of the Confederate Commanders, by Ezra J. Warner, and *South of Appomattox*, by Nash K. Burger and John K. Bettersworth. *Mississippi Valley Historical Review*, 47 (June 1960):137–38.

Reluctant Rebel: The Secret Diary of Robert Patrick, edited by F. Jay Taylor. *Louisiana History*, 1 (Winter 1960):92.

The Compact History of the Civil War, by R. Ernest Dupuy and Trevor N. Dupuy; *Our Incredible Civil War*, by Burke Davis; *The Civil War at Sea, Vol. 1: The Blockaders, January 1861–March 1862*, by Virgil Carrington Jones; and *The Civil War in the Northwest: Nebraska, Wisconsin, Iowa, Minnesota, and the Dakotas*, by Robert Huhn Jones. *Journal of Southern History*, 27 (May 1961):261–63.

Romance and Realism in Southern Politics, by T. Harry Williams. *Louisiana History*, 4 (Fall 1963):330–31.

The Civil War in Louisiana, by John D. Winters. *American Historical Review*, 69 (January 1964):550.

The Lost Cause, The Confederate Exodus to Mexico, by Andrew F. Rolle. *Louisiana History*, 6 (Winter 1965):423–24.

General William J. Hardee: Old Reliable, by Nathaniel Cheairs Hughes, Jr. *Civil War History*, 12 (March 1966):76–77.

The Overseer: Plantation Management in the Old South, by William Kauffman Scarborough. *Civil War History*, 13 (June 1967):187–88.

The World the Slaveholders Made: Two Essays in Interpretation, by Eugene D. Genovese. *Journal of Southern History*, 36 (May 1970):278–80.

Dearest Susie: A Civil War Infantryman's Letters to His Sweetheart, edited by Carl E. Hatch. *Register of the Kentucky Historical Society*, 69 (October 1971):387–88.

My Beloved Zebulon: The Correspondence of Zebulon Baird Vance and Harriett Newell Espy, edited by Elizabeth Roberts Cannon. *Journal of American History*, 58 (December 1971):752–53.

The Image of Lincoln in the South, by Michael Davis. *Journal of Southern History*, 38 (August 1972):489–90.

The Papers of Jefferson Davis, Vol. 1: 1808–1840, edited by Haskell M. Monroe, Jr., and James T. McIntosh. *Journal of American History*, 59 (September 1972):422–24.

Kirby Smith's Confederacy: The Trans-Mississippi South, 1863–1865, by Robert L. Kerby. *Journal of Southern History*, 39 (May 1973):298–300.

Disrupted Decades: The Civil War and Reconstruction, by Robert H. Jones; *The War That Never Ended: The American Civil War*, by Robert Cruden; and *The American War and Peace, 1860–1877*, by Emory M. Thomas. *Civil War History*, 20 (June 1974):157–59.

The Unwritten War: American Writers and the Civil War, by Daniel Aaron. *American Historical Review*, 80 (June 1975):723–24.

Louisiana Reconstructed, 1863–1877, by Joe Gray Taylor. *Journal of American History*, 62 (December 1975):704–5.

The Papers of Jefferson Davis, Vol. 2: June 1841–July 1846, edited by James T. McIntosh. *Journal of American History*, 62 (March 1976):950–52.

The Enduring South: Subcultural Persistence in Mass Society, by John Shelton Reed. *American Historical Review*, 81 (October 1976):953–54.

A History of the Old South: The Emergence of a Reluctant Nation, by Clement Eaton. *Register of the Kentucky Historical Society*, 74 (October 1976):320–21.

Stand Up For America, by George C. Wallace. *Register of the Kentucky Historical Society*, 76 (January 1978):81–82.

Joseph E. Brown of Georgia, by Joseph H. Parks. *Journal of Southern History*, 44 (February 1978):129–31.

Slaves and Freedmen in Civil War Louisiana, by C. Peter Ripley. *Louisiana History*, 19 (Summer 1978):372–73.

Biographical Dictionary of the Confederacy, edited by Frank E. Vandiver. *North Carolina Historical Review*, 55 (Autumn 1978):448–49.

Shiloh: In Hell before Night, by James Lee McDonough. *Register of the Kentucky Historical Society*, 76 (October 1978):328–31.

The Poet President of Texas: The Life of Mirabeau B. Lamar, President of the Republic of Texas, by Stanley Siegel. *American Historical Review*, 83 (December 1978):1345.

Media-Made Dixie: The South in the American Imagination, by Jack Temple Kirby. *Tennessee Historical Quarterly*, 37 (Winter 1978):464–66.

The Confederate Nation, 1861–1865, by Emory M. Thomas. *Journal of American History*, 66 (December 1979):654–55.

Intellectual Life in the Colonial South, 1585–1763, by Richard Beale Davis. *Register of the Kentucky Historical Society*, 78 (Winter 1980):72–73.

Southern Writers and the New South Movement, 1865–1913, by Wayne Mixon. *Louisiana History*, 22 (Fall 1981):439–41.

Eisenhower's Lieutenants: The Campaigns of France and Germany, 1944–1945, by Russell F. Weigley. *Register of the Kentucky Historical Society*, 80 (Summer 1982):354–56.

Goodmen: The Character of Civil War Soldiers, by Michael Barton. *Journal of Southern History*, 48 (August 1982):435–36.

Perspectives on the American South and An Annual Review of Society, Politics, and Culture, edited by Merle Black and John Shelton Reed. *South Atlantic Quarterly*, 82 (Spring 1983):223–24.

Attack and Die: Civil War Military Tactics and the Southern Heritage, by Grady McWhiney and Perry D. Jamieson. *American Historical Review*, 88 (April 1983):475–76.

Southern Honor: Ethics and Behavior in the Old South, by Bertram Wyatt-Brown. *Georgia Historical Quarterly*, 67 (Winter 1983):546–48.

The Papers of Jefferson Davis, Vol. 3: July 1846–December 1848, edited by James T. McIntosh, Lynda L. Crist, and Mary S. Dix, and *The Papers of Jefferson Davis, Vol. 4: 1849–1852*, edited by Lynda Lasswell Crist, Mary Seaton Dix, and Richard E. Beringer. *Journal of American History*, 71 (June 1984):125–26.

Northernizing the South, by Richard N. Current. *Register of the Kentucky Historical Society*, 82 (Summer 1984):296–98.

Growth in the American South: Changing Regional Employment and Wage Patterns in the 1960s and 1970s, by Robert J. Newman. *Journal of Southern History*, 51 (August 1985):469.

Thinking Back: The Perils of Writing History, by C. Vann Woodward. *Register of the Kentucky Historical Society*, 84 (Autumn 1986):424–25.

Those Terrible Carpetbaggers, by Richard Nelson Current. *Civil War Times Illustrated,* 27 (November 1988):14–16.

The Evolution of Southern Culture, edited by Numan V. Bartley. *Georgia Historical Quarterly,* 73 (Fall 1989):621–23.

Jefferson Davis and His Generals: The Failure of Confederate Command in the West, by Steven E. Woodworth. *Journal of Southern History,* 58 (May 1992):355–56.

Not in Vain: A Rifleman Remembers World War II, Leon C. Standifer. *Register of the Kentucky Historical Society,* 91 (Spring 1993):239–40.

William Howard Russell's Civil War: Private Diary and Letters, 1861–1862, edited by Martin Crawford. *Journal of Southern History,* 60 (February 1994):147–48.

The D-Day Encyclopedia, edited by David G. Chandler and James Lawton Collins, Jr. *Register of the Kentucky Historical Society,* 92 (Summer 1994):338–39.

What They Fought For, by James M. McPherson. *Journal of Southern History,* 61 (November 1995):812–13.

Index

About the Editors and Contributors

THOMAS H. APPLETON, JR., is editor of publications at the Kentucky Historical Society. His doctoral dissertation, completed at the University of Kentucky in 1981, examined the temperance and prohibition movements in Kentucky. He is currently collaborating with Charles P. Roland on a biography of A. B. "Happy" Chandler.

DWAYNE COX is university archivist at Auburn University. He directs Auburn's project to collect archival and manuscript material related to agriculture and rural life in Alabama. Previously, Dr. Cox served as associate archivist at the University of Louisville.

ROGER A. FISCHER is professor of history at the University of Minnesota, Duluth. He is the author of *The Segregation Struggle in Louisiana* (1974), *Tippecanoe and Trinkets Too: The Material Culture of American Presidential Campaigns* (1988), and *Them Damned Pictures: Explorations in American Political Cartoon Art* (1996).

MELBA PORTER HAY is manager of the Research and Publications Division of the Kentucky Historical Society. Dr. Hay previously served as editor of the *Papers of Henry Clay* documentary editing project at the University of Kentucky.

CAROL REARDON is associate professor of history at Pennsylvania State University. A specialist in American military history, she is author of *Soldiers and Scholars: The U.S. Army and the Uses of Military History, 1865–1920* (1990) and a forthcoming study on Pickett's charge in American history and memory. Dr. Reardon is currently studying the ongoing military legacy of the American Civil War.

DONALD E. REYNOLDS is professor of history at Texas A&M University, Commerce. He holds B.A. and M.A. degrees from the University of North Texas and a Ph.D. from Tulane University, where he studied with Charles P. Roland. Dr. Reynolds has published *Editors Make War: Southern Newspapers in the Secession Crisis* (1966).

JASON H. SILVERMAN is professor of history at Winthrop University. A former South Carolina Governor's Professor of the Year and a Winthrop Distinguished Professor, he is the author or editor of five books and over fifty articles. Dr. Silverman is author of the forthcoming *Beyond the Melting Pot in Dixie: Immigration and Ethnicity in Southern History* and has begun a study of Jews and slavery in the antebellum South.

JOHN DAVID SMITH is Graduate Alumni Distinguished Professor of History at North Carolina State University. In 1977 he received the first Ph.D. supervised by Charles P. Roland at the University of Kentucky. Dr. Smith has written or edited seven books, including *An Old Creed for the New South: Proslavery Ideology and Historiography, 1865–1918* (1985) and *Black Voices from Reconstruction* (1996).

RICHARD C. SMOOT works for Appalachian Regional Healthcare, Inc., Lexington, Kentucky, and is writing a history of that organization. He received his doctorate in 1988 from the University of Kentucky, where he studied under Charles P. Roland.

ISBN 0-313-29304-X

HARDCOVER BAR CODE